THE DWELLERS
ON THE NILE

1. Gold plaque, inlaid with coloured pastes, representing Usertsen III, in the form of hawk-headed lions,. trampling on his foes. XIIth Dynasty. In the Egyptian Museum, Cairo.
2. Gold plaque, inlaid with coloured pastes, representing Amenemhat III slaughtering his enemies. XIIth Dynasty. In the Egyptian Museum, Cairo.

THE DWELLERS ON THE NILE

The Life, History, Religion and Literature of the Ancient Egyptians

E.A. WALLIS BUDGE

DOVER PUBLICATIONS, INC.
NEW YORK

This Dover edition, first published in 1977, is an unabridged republication of the work originally published by The Religious Tract Society, London, in 1926, under the title *The Dwellers on the Nile: Chapter on the Life, History, Religion and Literature of the Ancient-Egyptians.*

International Standard Book Number: 0-486-23501-7
Library of Congress Catalog Card Number: 77-72195

Manufactured in the United States of America
Dover Publications, Inc.
180 Varick Street
New York, N.Y. 10014

PREFACE

EARLY in the year 1925 the Rev. Dr. C. H. Irwin, General Editor of the Religious Tract Society, informed me that the Committee wished to keep on their List of Publications a little book entitled *The Dwellers on the Nile,* which I wrote for them so far back as 1885. The book, he said, had been well received by the public, and had been reprinted from stereotype plates several times. It would have been reprinted again had the plates been available, but unfortunately during the Great War the Government, being in need of lead, requisitioned them for military purposes and they were, together with those of the books of many other writers, melted down. The first idea of the officers of the Society was that the book might be revised before reprinting, and they brought with them the last available copy of the book, viz., the file copy, to discuss the matter with me. A glance at the Chapters in the book showed that no revision, however drastic, would be satisfactory either to the Society or their readers, for the book was written when the long series of important excavations, which only became possible after an occupation of Egypt by the British in 1882–83, was about to begin.

During the forty and more years that have elapsed since I wrote the little book excavations have been carried on in many parts of both Upper and Lower Egypt, Nubia, the Egyptian Sūdān, and the Sinaitic Peninsula, by the accredited Agents of the Governments of Great Britain, America, Egypt, France, Germany, Italy and Russia, and by numerous Societies and private individuals. Besides these, the natives in many parts of Egypt who possessed local knowledge embarked on excavations of sites and tombs known to them, either clandestinely, or with the permission of the various Directors of the Service of Antiquities in Egypt. All these excavations have brought to light an enormous number of historical monuments and funerary antiquities, and the information derived from them through the exertions of scholars both in and out of Egypt has completely revolutionized the science of Egyptology in all its branches. The objects recovered from the cemeteries at Abydos and the sites in its neighbourhood, and from Nakādah and Gebelēn (Jabalēn), the date and historical value of which were first recognized by the late, alas! J. de Morgan, have revealed to us much of the civilization of the Egyptians towards the close of the Neolithic Period in Egypt, and supplied

much information about the kings of the earliest
Dynasties. The results obtained from excavations in the Delta, in the pyramid-fields at
Sakkārah, in the Fayyūm, in the Thebaïd, in
Nubia and in the Egyptian Sudan, have made
it possible to construct a nearly complete list
of the kings of Egypt, to write with very considerable accuracy the history of Egypt, and to
describe the foreign influences, both Asiatic and
European, that transformed the rude and semi-
savage aboriginal peoples of the Nile Valley
into one of the greatest and most civilized
nations of antiquity. The discovery, made by
a peasant woman at Tall al-'Amārnah in 1888,
of a hoard of clay and mud tablets inscribed
in a Semitic language (two are written in the
language of Mitani, at present unknown), has
placed in our hands some hundreds of letters
and dispatches which were sent by the kings of
Babylonia, Mitani and Assyria and by the
governors of cities and towns in the land of the
Hittites, Syria and Palestine, to Amenhetep III
and his son Amenhetep IV in the XVth
century B.C. These illustrate the foreign relations of Egypt during the period when she might
be correctly described as a military power and
the mistress of the world, and from the historian's
point of view their value and importance cannot
be overestimated. The excavation of the tombs
of all periods has also increased to a most
remarkable degree our knowledge of the daily
life, manners and customs, trade and commerce, and the religious beliefs of the Egyptians.
The publication of the newly discovered texts,

both historical and funerary, with translations and commentaries, proceeded rapidly in England, France and Germany, and the information which became available as the result compelled the older Egyptologists to revise drastically their opinions on many important points of Egyptian chronology and history. The great pioneer of Egyptology, Samuel Birch, on reading Maspero's edition of the texts from the pyramids of Unas and Teta in the *Recueil de Travaux*, remarked sadly, " Ah ! The new Egyptology can only be dealt with by strong young men."

Now all these facts were as well known to Dr. Irwin as to myself, and when I told him that *The Dwellers on the Nile* must be re-written and enlarged he cordially agreed, and the present volume is the result. It was impossible to deal even briefly with the difficult subjects of origin, race, language, chronology, etc., of the Ancient Egyptians in a small work of this kind, and it was therefore decided to concentrate on the daily life of the people, and to add only such fundamental facts as would enable the reader to understand the general character of their History, Religion and Literature. An attempt has been made in this book to describe the life of the Ancient Egyptians from, so to speak, their cradles to their graves. The Introduction contains a brief summary of the growth and development of the rule of the Dynastic kings over a unified Egypt, and a list of their names derived from the monuments. To assign exact dates to the kings who reigned before the XVIIIth Dynasty (about 1580–1350 B.C.) is at

present impossible, for the necessary facts are
wanting ; accurate dating is not possible until
the end of the VIIIth century B.C.   It is known
now that scores of kings reigned independently
in Lower Egypt, and presumably in Upper
Egypt also, before the unification of the two
Egypts under Nārmer or Āha, but the total
length of their reigns cannot be even guessed
at, and the predynastic monuments are silent
on this point.

According to Manetho, who wrote a History
of Egypt for Ptolemy II Philadelphus in the
IIIrd century B.C., the first rulers of Egypt were
Gods, who were followed by the Demi-gods
and the Nekues or Spirits, and the total length
of their reigns was 24,836 years.   These figures
(like those which state that ten kings reigned
in Babylonia for 456,000 years) are of course
fabulous, but they are useful as showing that
Egyptian civilization was believed to be very,
very old.   From the time of Lepsius, who
published his great work on Egyptian Chronology
in 1848, Egyptologists have devoted much time
and energy in trying to find out when the first
dynastic king of Egypt ascended the throne.
One after the other has formulated chronological
systems, but no two of them agree, and the
difference between the dates assigned to the
beginning of dynastic rule in Egypt is sometimes
as much as 2,500 years, for Champollion-Figeac
gives 5869 B.C. and Meyer 3315 B.C.   Some
scholars have tried to fix dates in Egyptian
history by calculations based on astronomical
data, and have assumed that the Egyptians were

acquainted with and used the Sothic Cycle, but these are not to be depended upon, for the Egyptians were as ignorant of the Sothic Cycle of 1,461 years as they were of the Phoenix Period. This has been well shown by Nicklin (*Classical Review*, vol. xiv, 1900, pp. 146–148), Legge (*Recueil de Travaux*, vol. xxxi, 1909, p. 106) and Torr (*Memphis and Mycenae*, 1896). The native Egyptian King Lists, as exemplified by the series of names found at Abydos, Karnak and Sakkārah, have been shown by the evidence of the monuments to be incomplete, and the fragmentary List found in the Turin Papyrus is only helpful in the case of certain Dynasties. Valuable information about the order of succession and acts of several of the kings of the Dynasties of the Old Kingdom has been supplied by the fragment of the stele now known as the "Palermo Stele," the chronological importance of which was first recognized by H. Schaefer, but it does not enable a complete scheme of Egyptian chronology to be formulated. Within the last few years various scholars have suggested restorations of the portions of the text that are lacking on the Stele, but none is satisfactory or convincing. For a discussion on the subject *see* Meyer, *Die ältere Chronologie Babyloniens, Assyriens und Ägyptens*, Stuttgart, 1925, pp. 40 ff. The cuneiform inscriptions have helped greatly in fixing approximate dates for the kings of the XVIIIth Dynasty (about 1580–1350 B.C.), but for no earlier period.

The Egyptians of the earliest dynasties dated their years by events, as did the Sumerians, and dating by regnal years was not adopted until a much later period. If we had a complete list of kings and knew the length of the reign of each the construction of a correct chronological table would be comparatively easy; but such material does not exist, and the difficulties of Egyptian chronology are due chiefly to this fact. The earlier Egyptologists made lists of kings and then assigned to each an average length of reign, and in this way Lepsius found that the first dynastic King of Egypt began to reign about 3892 B.C., while Brugsch gave his date as 4400 B.C. It has been shown that the latter date is too early, and that the lengths, according to him, of the periods between the VIth and the XIIth and the XIIth and the XVIIIth Dynasties were too long. Taking the evidence available as a whole there seems to be no doubt that the first dynastic king of Egypt began to reign about the middle of the fourth millennium before Christ, or a little earlier. It is unnecessary to consider the period of the introduction of the Calendar, if there ever was one, for the agriculturists of Egypt never had any doubt when the seasons of the year began, and the annual Inundation of the Nile regulated the affairs of the whole country. It is probable that originally the Egyptians only recognized two seasons—Winter and Summer — though the copies of the Calendar extant mention three—Winter, Summer, and the period of Inundation—each containing four thirty-day months. The five additional days at the end of the year provided for irregularity in the coming of the Nile Flood.

The Calendar, which according to Brugsch and other Egyptologists began on July 19, was, it seems, an invention of the priestly class for the benefit of the business and commercial sections of the community, but was useless to the agriculturist.

The reader who is specially interested in Egyptology because of the light which it has thrown on many portions of the Bible narrative will probably think that some paragraphs dealing with the sojourn of the Israelites in Egypt, and particularly with the **Exodus,** ought to have been found in this book. But these subjects cannot be treated adequately in a few paragraphs. The explanation of the Exodus is exceptionally difficult, and it must be said at once that in the present state of Egyptological knowledge no solution of the problem which it presents is possible. That an Exodus of Israelites from Egypt, whether they were traders or nomad shepherds, or both, took place is beyond doubt, though some regard the account of it given in the Bible narrative as a legend pure and simple which is full of many hopelessly irreconcilable statements. But even so there must be a definite historical fact underlying the legend, for no mere legend could affect so deeply the thoughts and belief and life of the Hebrew people for so many centuries. Josephus connected the Exodus with the expulsion of the Hyksos from Egypt, and very probably he is right, but it is doubtful if the writer of the Book of Exodus knew anything about the triumph of Amasis I **and the flight** of the Hyksos from Egypt into

Palestine and Syria. The Exodus has been supposed to have taken place in the reigns of Thothmes III, of Amenhetep III and of Merenptah, and it has been stated definitely that the last-named was the Pharaoh who pursued the Israelites and was drowned in the Red Sea. Viewed as an ordinary event the Exodus would have been impossible under Thothmes III, who held Western Asia in the palm of his hand, or under Amenhetep III, but an exodus of Semites from Egypt in the early years of the reign of Merenptah was possible. It is true that this king boasts in his Triumph Inscription (dated in the fifth year of his reign) on the stele in Cairo that he had left Israel without seed and Syria a widow. But this remark can only apply to the Israelites who had been settled in Palestine for some time, and not to their kinsmen who for some reason or other were domiciled in or near the fertile district now called the Wādī Tūmīlāt in the Eastern Delta. The Book of Exodus tells us (i. 11) that the Israelites built for Pharaoh treasure cities, Pithom and Raamses, and were compelled to make bricks under the supervision of cruel taskmasters (i. 7–19). It is quite clear then that the Israelites had to serve in the *corvée* somewhere in the Delta, and there is no evidence whatever to show that they were condemned to forced labour in the copper mines at Wādī Maghārah or Sarābīt al-Khādim in the Peninsula of Sinai, as has been recently suggested. If the Israelites referred to were shepherds or men engaged in commerce in the towns of the Delta, they, being wholly unaccustomed to perform manual labour, would find the work of the *corvée* unbearable. Whether Rameses II or another king was the " Pharaoh of the oppression " matters little, but it is manifest that the Israelites of any king's *corvée* would take the first opportunity of escaping from Egypt. Whether they did so in the reign of Merenptah or not cannot be said, but I cannot see that this king's boast of his destruction of the Israelites in Palestine makes an exodus of Israelites from the Delta on the death of Rameses II impossible. It does not follow that there was only one exodus of Semites from Egypt, in fact it is reasonable to suppose that during every period of anarchy, when neither life nor property was safe, such as could escape to a place of refuge would do so. There is no good reason for doubting that Israelites were dwelling in the Wādī Tūmīlāt, or Goshen, in the XIIIth or XIVth century B.C., or even earlier, and that owing to some conflict with the Government of the day, either about taxes or forced labour, they decided to flee into the desert, and did so. The remains of Pithom, one of the two עָרֵי־מִסְכְּנוֹת or " treasure cities," built by the Israelites for a Pharaoh, have been discovered by Naville, who has identified them with **Pa-Tem,** or **Pa-Atem,** the modern Tall al-Maskhūtah at the eastern end of the Wādī Tūmīlāt (*see* his *Store-city of Pithom*, London, 1885). Where the other was situated is unknown, unless it may be identified with the great city of Tanis (the Zoan of Psalm lxxviii, 12, 43, and

Isaiah xix, 11), which was rebuilt and beautified by Rameses II.

An interesting theory as to the date of the Exodus has been put forward by Prof. T. E. Peet in his *Egypt and the Old Testament*, London, 1922, who rejects utterly the theory of an Exodus under Merenptah, Rameses IInd's successor, who reigned about 1220 B.C., and thinks it not worth the trouble of defending. He bases his theory upon the statement in 1 Kings vi. 1 to the effect that Solomon began to build his Temple in the fourth year of his reign, 480 years after the children of Israel were come out of the land of Egypt. He thinks that Solomon ascended the throne 970 B.C., and that the building of the Temple was begun 966 B.C. Adding 480 years to 966 years we get 1446 B.C. as the date of the Exodus. According to the now generally accepted chronology of the XVIIIth Dynasty, the year 1446 B.C. would fall within the reign of Amenhetep II, who began to reign about 1448 B.C. and reigned some 20 years. Thus Amenhetep II becomes the " Pharaoh of the Exodus." Prof. Peet is inclined to believe that the Israelites who went up out of Egypt were the people called " Khabiru " in the Tall al-ʿAmārnah Tablets, and that they formed a section of the invaders who were led into Palestine by Joshua. He thinks that " Khabiru " means " Hebrew," but others would translate it by " confederates " (*see* Knudtzon, *Die El-Amarna Tafeln*, Leipzig, 1915, vol. i, p. 47). All the theories described above are interesting, but it will be noted that no

Egyptologist is able to say exactly when the Exodus took place.

A substantial contribution to the literature of the Exodus has been made by the Rev. J. W. Jack in his *Date of the Exodus*, Edinburgh, 1925. In a series of fourteen chapters the author has discussed the question from almost every point of view, and he supports his statements for and against the theories advocated by various scholars with a large number of references to books and articles that illustrate the subject. The evidence of the Tall al-'Amārnah Tablets, Atenism, the Ḥabiru, the SA GAZ, and other highly controversial subjects are deftly handled, but only in very few cases is a definite conclusion arrived at which will be generally accepted as final by archaeologists. This is not Mr. Jack's fault ; it is due to the lack of sufficient evidence for settling the question under discussion once and for all. The arguments in the book, for and against, are set forth with rigid fairness, and the writer's impartiality is so strict that the lay reader will find it difficult to decide for himself which opinion is the more probable, and which authority is the most likely to be right. Many of the statements made by older writers about the Date and Route of the Exodus were palpably absurd, even before the archaeological evidence that we now possess was available ; most of these have been capably dealt with and consigned to the limbo of dead conjectures, but it is not possible to disprove all the old speculations. As a result of the " corroborations, correspondences and coincidences not found in other theories,"

Mr. Jack concludes that his own theory is the most likely one to be correct, and he agrees with Prof. Peet that the Exodus took place in the reign of Amenhetep II, and that the oppressor of the Israelites was not Rameses II, but Thothmes III. And he finds it difficult not to "compare" Queen Hatshepsut with the "Pharaoh's daughter" who took Moses from the little papyrus chest on the river in which his mother had laid him. Mr. Jack has rendered Biblical archaeology real service by showing that the date of the Exodus still remains unknown.

The question of the date of the Exodus is difficult enough, but that of the route taken by the Israelites from Goshen to Palestine is more difficult still. The earlier Egyptologists assumed that the Israelites made their way eastwards along the Wādī Tūmīlāt and, crossing some northern extension of the Red Sea, passed into the Peninsula of Sinai, and received the Law from Mount Sinai, which was thought to be situated in the Peninsula, where they wandered about for 40 years. It is, of course, possible that the Red Sea extended far northwards into the Isthmus in those days, perhaps as far as the northern end of Lake Timsāh, but the Hebrew text says nothing at all about the Red Sea. The Israelites crossed the **Yam Sūph** יַם־סוּף, *i.e.* the "sea of reeds" (rushes), and the identification of this swamp as the Red Sea is due entirely to the compilers of the Septuagint, who have thereby misled many commentators. Some modern Egyptologists reject the old conservative opinions of their predecessors absolutely and take the view that the Israelites, who were anxious to get into Palestine as fast as possible, marched northwards from Goshen and on leaving the town of Rameses (Pelusium) followed the road, of immemorial antiquity, which ran from the north-east of the Delta and along the south side of Lake Serbonis, direct into Palestine and Syria. They discredit all the identifications of the holy places made by Antoninus Martyr and other Christian pilgrims of the IIIrd and IVth centuries, and would place the mountain from which God gave the Law to Moses somewhere near Mount Seir. They further point out that most of the places mentioned in the Old Testament narrative cannot be identified, and that such identifications of sites on the supposed route of the Exodus as have been made by Naville cannot be accepted. The arguments in favour of the view that the Israelites left Egypt by way of the Wādī Tūmīlāt and crossed one end of Lake Timsāh or the Bitter Lakes and proceeded to the Peninsula of Sinai are well set forth by Naville in his *Store-city of Pithom and the Route of the Exodus*, London, 1903 ; *The Shrine of Saft el-Henneh and the Land of Goshen*, London, 1888 ; and *Archaeology of the Old Testament*, London, 1913. The arguments which are adduced to show that the Israelites followed the old highway from Egypt to Palestine are set forth by Gardiner in the *Jnl. of Eg. Archaeology*, London, 1918, vol. vi, pp. 99 ff., and are summarized by Peet (*op. cit.* pp. 105 ff.). But so long as we do not know what the original form

of the Story of the Exodus was, and cannot
eliminate from the version that we have the
obvious interpolations and omissions and mis-
takes of the editors and scribes, who lived many
centuries after the events recorded in it, and
so long as we know nothing of the physical
condition of the Isthmus of Suez at the time
when the Exodus took place, and of its geography, we are powerless to say which theory
is right or wrong. No Pharaoh would instruct
his court scribes to set down in writing an
account of the manner in which the Israelites
who had succeeded in escaping from one or
other of his *corvées* left his country. Therefore
it is futile to look to the Egyptologist for
an " explanation " of the Exodus for, like the
critic of the Hebrew text, he lacks the necessary
information and evidence. And it must never
be forgotten that the account of the Exodus
given in the Bible is the story of a **miracle,** or
rather a succession of **miracles,** which are beyond
the experience of every-day life, and cannot be
dealt with by the ordinary canons of criticism.

Whilst writing the last chapter in this book,
that on the Egyptian Dead, it was suggested to
me by a scholar of eminence that I should
devote a section of it to a full description of the
Egyptian tombs, and discuss in it the Pyramids
of Gîzah, and especially the Great Pyramid,
one of the most remarkable tombs in the world.
He was anxious that the discoveries made by
Messrs. D. Davidson and H. Aldersmith, and
described in their joint work, *The Great Pyramid :
its Divine Message,* London, 1924, should be

made known to all who are interested in the
history of Egypt, and thought that a popular
work like *The Dwellers on the Nile* would help
to bring this about. Now the three pyramids of
Gîzah have always appealed to the imagination
of visitors to Egypt, many of whom have refused
to believe that they were funerary buildings
intended to cover the graves of the three great
kings of the IVth Dynasty—Khufu, Khāfrā
and Menkaurā—and thought and maintained
that they had some other, but unknown, purpose.
What this purpose was many thinkers have tried
to find out. In the second half of the XVIIIth
century of our Era, John Taylor published a
book in which he stated that the Great Pyramid
was built to convey to man a Divine Revelation,
and that its unit of measure was the Polar
Diameter inch. In 1864–65 Piazzi Smyth confirmed this view and said that the base circuit
was a representation of the solar year. In 1865
Robert Menzies started the theory that the
Passage System of the Great Pyramid was
a chronological representation of prophecy, that
the scale was one Polar Diameter to a solar year,
and that the Great Gallery symbolized the
Christian Dispensation. This Dispensation Col.
J. Garnier, R.E., said (in 1905) started with the
Crucifixion, placed by him in A.D. 31. Messrs.
Davidson and Aldersmith have taken the matter
up, and they think that :—

(1) The Great Pyramid is a geometrical representation of the mathematical basis of the science
of a former civilization.

(2) This civilization, which was the source

of all subsequent civilizations, reduced its
knowledge of natural law into a single general
formula, the application of which was anal-
ogous to the modern application of Einstein's
Theory of Relativity.   This application left
its impress on every form of constructional
expression.

(3) The Passage System is a graphical representation of a system of prophetical chronology,
intimately related to Biblical prophecy.

To the explanation of these and other conclusions the learned authors devote about 556
pages of text, illustrated by a series of plans,
diagrams, tables, calculations, etc., of a highly
technical character.   The subjects discussed by
them in their marvellously erudite work, *e.g.*
prophetical chronology, datings for events of the
Christian Dispensation, such as the Great War
of 1914–18, are not usually studied by Egyptologists, and I doubt if any one of them, however sympathetically inclined he may be to
such matters, is capable of criticizing effectively
the results of the researches of Messrs. Davidson
and Aldersmith.   But whether this be so or
not there is no doubt that such highly controversial subjects ought not to be introduced into
an elementary work on Egyptian Archaeology
such as mine.

In connection with the chapter on the Egyptian Dead another point must be mentioned.
The excavation of the dynastic tombs of all
kinds in Egypt has shown that the Egyptians
took endless trouble in the burying of their dead,
and that they tried to hide their bodies in places

where they hoped or believed they would **never** be disturbed. We know that the bodies of kings, nobles, officials and men of rank and position were mummified and swathed in bandages, and laid in triple coffins, each of which had its cover fastened on it by means of dowels driven through flat pieces of wood fixed in slots cut in both coffin and cover. The coffins were placed in sarcophagi of stone or wood with massive covers fastened to them, and these were lowered down shafts from 20 to 90 feet deep, and laid in chambers which were entered from the bottom of the shafts. The chambers were walled up and the shafts filled up with stones, sand and earth, and it is only the excavator who really knows how difficult it is to obtain access to the bodies of the dead in well-constructed Egyptian tombs. It has always been assumed that the Egyptians expended such time and thought on the burial of their dead because they loved and revered them, and many English writers have denounced the excavator for disturbing the dead in their last sleep and destroying the " houses of eternity " in which loving hands had placed them. But it is possible that the Egyptians did not take all this trouble in hiding their dead in what they deemed to be inaccessible places through love, but through **fear,** and there is good reason for believing that they did not want the dead to return to this earth. After the death of the body the various spiritual and mental parts of a man continued to live, and, as Osiris had given them immortality, it was feared that they might put on once again

their old material body, or take some other
form, and come back to prey upon the living.
The beings capable of doing this were called
Aakhu, 𓇋𓄿𓄿𓅱 , a word that may be
rendered by " spirit souls " or " ghosts," and
some were benevolent and some malevolent.
They lived upon the offerings made in their
tombs or at their graves by the living, sharing
them with their Kau, or " doubles," but it was
believed that some of them came to earth and
fed upon the lives of the living. The pre-
dynastic Egyptians, with the view of preventing
any return on the part of " ghosts " to earth,
dismembered their dead or burnt them (in places
where fuel was to be had).   Neither dismember-
ment nor burning destroyed the Aakhu, but it
deprived it of its power to injure the living and
of returning to its body and of assuming the
form of a bird or reptile by which it might deceive
men and do them harm.   At a later period the
head of the deceased was cut off and placed
between his legs, and later still the hands and
the feet were also cut off ; it was thought that
such mutilations would render the body unsuit-
able for the purpose of the Aakhu.   Even so it
was thought that the Aakhu might make use of
magic to effect his purpose, and it is said in the
Pyramid Texts (lines 181 and 629) that King
Unas did so and was able to company with
as many women as he pleased. The whole
question of the Egyptian belief in the existence
of **vampires** has been discussed with characteristic learning and abundant references to

original sources by Prof. A. Wiedemann in *Der Lebende "Leichnam" im Glauben der alten Ägypter*, Elberfeld, 1917. According to him mummification of the body (after the removal of the heart and viscera), the bandaging of the same, the nailed anthropoid coffin and sarcophagus, the well-constructed tomb with its walled-up doorways, and shafts filled with stones and concealed entrance, were all intended to keep the deceased in his tomb and to prevent him from coming back among the living and working his will upon them. And Wiedemann has shown that the belief in immortality went hand in hand with the belief in the existence of the " living corpse " in the tomb.

I am indebted to the Trustees of the British Museum for permission to photograph the objects which are reproduced on some of the plates in this book. And my thanks are due to the Rev. Dr. C. H. Irwin for his unfailing courtesy and assistance, to Mr. H. R. Brabrook for the care which he has taken in the production of this book, and to the staff of Harrison and Sons, the printers. The Bibliography will, I hope, be found useful to the beginner in Egyptology, and perhaps also to the reader who has made some progress in the study. For further information about monographs and papers on special branches of Egyptology the reader is referred to Miss Ida A. Pratt's invaluable work *Ancient Egypt: Sources of information in the New York Public Library*, New York, 1925. I have added a full Index to all the important names of persons, places and things mentioned herein. In the transliteration of Egyptian and Arabic names and words I have not attempted to use diacritical marks over and under letters, *e.g.* ȧ, ḥ, ḫ, ḳ, ṣ, ś, š, ṭ, ṭ; but wherever possible the long vowels are marked.

E. A. Wallis Budge.

48, Bloomsbury Street,
    Bedford Square, W.C. 1.
      December 30th, 1925.

CONTENTS

LIST OF PLATES AND ILLUSTRATIONS IN THE TEXT

PLATES

ILLUSTRATIONS IN THE TEXT

INTRODUCTION

HISTORICAL OUTLINE

Palaeolithic Age ends, 10,000 (?) B.C.
Late Neolithic Kingdom, 5000–4500 B.C.
Independent Kings in Upper and Lower Egypt, 4500–3860 or 3500 (?) B.C.

OLD KINGDOM

Ist Dynasty. Union of Upper and Lower Egypt under Nārmer and Āha Mena (Mēnes ?). Art of writing introduced, native pictographs being employed. Religious texts composed and chronological tablets compiled. Capitals, Tarkhan and Memphis. Raids in Peninsula of Sinai and in Libya. 3500 (?)–3350 (?) B.C.

The high state of Egyptian civilization under the early kings of the Ist Dynasty is well illustrated by the monuments which have been recovered from the tombs of Nārmer and Āha, either of whom may have been the **Mēnes of Manetho,** for each adopted " Men " or " Mena "

as one of his strong names. The sculptured
green stone palette (?) of Nārmer in Cairo (there
is a cast of it in the British Museum) proves
that the workers in stone had brought their
craft to a high pitch of perfection. The king's

Horus name, Nārmer, 〈image〉, is given on each

side of the palette (?) between two heads of
Hathor, the Cow-goddess, who even in that
early period was represented as a woman.
On the **obverse** we see the king, wearing the

crown of the South, 〈image〉, and a short tunic

with belt and an animal's tail, about to smash
in the head of a captive with a stone-headed

mace 〈image〉. Behind him stands an attendant

carrying the royal sandals, 〈image〉, in his left

hand and a vase or pot in his right. In front
of him is a hawk, *i.e.* Horus, holding a short
chain or cord with a hook which is fixed in the
nose of a bearded captive. From the body of
the captive project six flower-like objects which
have been considered to represent the number

, 6,000, and to indicate the number

of prisoners taken in a certain campaign.
Under the king's feet are two dead enemies.
On the **reverse** we see the king wearing the

crown of the North, 〈image〉, and accompanied by

his sandal-bearer. Before him is the officer
Thet, 〈image〉, who is directing the carrying of
four standards, two with hawks, one with a

Obverse. Memorial Tablet of Nármer. 1st Dynasty. Reverse.

1. Nármer slaying a captive with a stone-headed mace; beneath his feet are slain enemies. He took 6,000 prisoners in Ua.

2. Nármer, with his officers bearing sacred emblems, inspecting decapitated enemies. The king, in the form of a bull, destroying a fortress.

jackal and one with an object which has not yet been identified with certainty. These men are conducting the king to inspect the bodies of decapitated captives, whose heads are placed between their legs. Below these are two fabulous long-necked lions (?) each with its attendant, who wears a loin-cloth, and below these is a bull, symbolic of the king, breaking into a strongly fortified building, either round, ☼, or oval, ⬭, and trampling upon the body of one of its defenders. The scene of the king smashing the skull of a captive enemy was repeated on the monuments from this period, say 3500 B.C., to the time of the rule of the native kings and queens of Meroë, say about A.D. 200 The bull was the symbol of the king as well as the hawk, and the greatest kings of the XVIIIth Dynasty delighted to call themselves " Mighty Bull," 🐂 ⚊, *Ka Nekht*. And it was the bellowings, 𓅓𓂝𓅓𓂝, *hemhemt*, of the royal bull that were supposed to make the whole world quake.

The scene on p. 5 is taken from the great stone mace-head of Nārmer, which Mr. J. E. Quibell discovered at Hierakonpolis (see *Hierakonpolis*, London, 1900–02, two Parts). Here we see Nārmer seated like a god in a shrine, with sloping roof and pillars, one on each side of the open front ; the king wears the crown of the North, and holds the whip, ⚸. The shrine rests on a platform with nine steps, which became the recognized support for the throne of the

" god who is on the top of the stairway," *i.e.*
Osiris. By the side of the platform are two
bearers of long-handled fans made of ostrich
feathers. Above the shrine hovers the hawk
of Horus. In the top register are a cow and a
calf and the four standards already noticed.
In the middle register, under a canopy resting

Scene from the great mace-head of Nārmer. The king seated in state, with his queen (?)
facing him.

on a stretcher with short legs, is the " king's
woman," or queen, and behind her are three
men dancing a special dance, probably the
" dance of the god," which was so greatly beloved
by the kings of the Vth and VIth Dynasties.
Below these is a summary of the spoil taken by
Nārmer during his wars, namely " cows, 400,000,

goats, one million, four hundred

and twenty-two thousand, 🦌 𓀮𓆓𓆓𓆓𓆓𓏥𓏥,
and captives, one hundred and twenty thousand,
𓆉 𓆓𓏥." The figures of men, birds and animals,
are well shaped, and the workmanship leaves nothing to be desired. Everything about this m o n u m e n t shows that the craftsmen who made it were not only skilled, b u t e x p e r i - enced.

IInd Dynas- ty. C u l t o f A p i s a n d Mnevis Bulls e s t a b l i s h e d. Rā and Set worshipped. 3350 (?)–3190 (?) B.C.

Wooden tablet recording the celebrating of a festival by King Semti, when he danced before his god. Ist Dynasty. The great events of each year were noted on a tablet of this kind, and the history of the king's reign was compiled from such tablets.

IIIrd Dynasty. Wars in Libya. Memphis the capital. Step Pyramid of Sakkārah built. Iemhetep, architect and physician, and Kagemna the Wazīr flourish. 3190 (?)–3100 (?) B.C.

IVth Dynasty. Seneferu conquers Sinai, builds the Step Pyramid at Mēdūm and a true pyramid at Dahshūr, raids the Sūdān for slaves and gold, and establishes a fleet in the Mediterranean Sea. Pyramids of Gīzah built. 3100 (?)–2965 (?) B.C.

Vth Dynasty. Cult of Rā of Heliopolis established, and three of his high priests succeed each other as kings of Egypt ; kings styled themselves " Son of Rā." Sun-temples built. Pyramids built at Abusīr and Sakkārah. Expeditions to Punt, quarries in the Wādī Hammāmāt worked. Tomb of Unas inscribed with religious hieroglyphic texts. 2965 (?)–2825 (?) B.C.

VIth Dynasty. Raids in the Peninsula of Sinai. Canal made in the First Cataract, and negotiations for trading purposes opened with the feudal lords of Elephantine (Syene, Aswān). Expeditions made to Punt, *i.e.* the south-east Sūdān. Raids in Northern Nubia ; " Blacks " serve in the Army. Generals Una and Herkhuf flourish. Pyramid tombs, with religious inscriptions, built at Sakkārah. Pepi II reigns more than 90 years. Feudal chiefs assert their independence and the **Old Kingdom** ends. 2825 (?)–2631 (?) B.C.

The Old Kingdom practically ended with the downfall of the VIth Dynasty.

VIIth and VIIIth Dynasties. Period of anarchy. Descendants of the Memphite kings and upstarts claim the throne.

IXth and Xth Dynasties. Feudal lords of Henesu (Herakleopolis) attack the Memphites and proclaim themselves, with the help of the lords of Lykopolis (Asyūt), kings of Egypt. One of them, Khati, writes a book of Precepts for his son. Wars of the lords of Herakleopolis and Lykopolis against the lords of Thebes ; the Thebans are victorious.

XIth Dynasty. Two kings called Antef are succeeded by four or five called Menthuhetep; one of the last-named builds a pyramid tomb and a funerary temple at Thebes.

MIDDLE KINGDOM

XIIth Dynasty. Many raids in Nubia ; that country conquered so far south as the head of the Third Cataract. Raid in Syria. Canal re-made in the First Cataract, and one made to join the Nile and the Red Sea. Gold mines in the Eastern Desert worked, commerce with Punt, Syria and Mediterranean peoples developed, and Egypt becomes very rich. Systematic irrigation introduced and great reservoirs made in the Fayyūm. Pyramid tombs built at Lisht, Dahshūr, Allahūn and Hawārah. Labyrinth built. Great development of literature, the first Recension of the Theban **Book of the Dead** compiled. End of the **Middle Kingdom.** 2200 (?)–2000 (?) B.C.

XIIIth and XIVth Dynasties. Period of anarchy. Struggle between descendants of kings and usurpers in Upper and Lower Egypt; length of period uncertain.

THE HEQU SHASU, 𓏠𓏠𓏠𓈖𓏤 𓇾𓇾𓇾 𓅓𓃀𓏤𓈖𓏥,
OR HYKSOS

XVth and XVIth Dynasties. The Hyksos, or Shepherd Kings, *i.e.* the nomad tribes of Palestine and Syria, supported by Hittites and others, invade Egypt with chariots and horses, and conquer the country and oppress the people.

They suffered defeat by the Thebans **(XVIIth Dynasty)** under Seqenenrā III, who was slain in battle. Length of the rule of the Hyksos unknown.

NEW KINGDOM

XVIIIth Dynasty, ruling from Thebes. **Hyksos expelled** by Aāhmes I, and Palestine and Syria become provinces of Egypt ; under Aāhmes, a truly military dictator, Egypt becomes a warlike power with horses and chariots and a large army. Wars in Libya and Syria ; Nubia conquered as far as the foot of the Fourth Cataract. Wars in Western Asia, the country conquered as far north as the Upper Euphrates, Egyptian colonies made, and governors of all important towns and cities appointed by Pharaoh. Western Asia and the Sūdān pour tribute into Egypt, which becomes the richest country in the world. All trade routes seized by the Egyptians ; trade with Punt, Arabia, Syria, Palestine and many islands in the Mediterranean quickly developed. Thothmes IV marries a princess of Mitani, and Amenhetep III marries several Mesopotamian princesses. Treaties made with kings of Babylon and Assyria. Great temples built at Abydos, Thebes, Sulb, and other places. Granite obelisks and the Colossi erected. Amenhetep IV confiscates the revenues of Amen, founds a capital at Tall al-'Amārnah, builds temples to Aten, the Solar Disk, alienates his people, fails to support Egyptian authority in Western Asia, which throws off the yoke of Egypt. Art and sculpture, and the handicrafts, greatly developed, magnificent buildings and tombs constructed, display of vast wealth, and luxury universal. Egypt loses her Asiatic Empire. 1600–1350 (?) B.C.

XIXth Dynasty. Worship of Amen restored and his priests reinstated. Code of Laws compiled. Wars with Libyans and Nubians and the Hittites and their allies ; Egyptians finally compelled to make a treaty with the Hittites. Gold mines of the Eastern Sūdān worked, the rock-hewn temples of Kalābshah and Abu Simbel made, the Hall of Columns at Karnak and other great buildings constructed. Splendid tombs on the plan of those of the XVIIIth Dynasty hewn in the hills in Western Thebes. **Israel,** Syrians and others reduced to captivity. Period of anarchy. 1321–1205 B.C.

XXth Dynasty. Wars with the Libyans and the " peoples of the sea," who were defeated on sea and land. Egypt ceases to be a military power and employs foreign mercenaries. Commerce greatly developed ; the country prosperous and wealthy. Decay of Thebes. The priests of Amen usurp the royal power, and Herher, one of them, seizes the throne. 1205–1100 B.C.

XXIst Dynasty. Priests of Amen ruling at Thebes, and Nesbanebtet and his descendants at Tanis in the Delta. The Libyans acquire great power in Egypt. 1100–947 B.C.

XXIInd and XXIIIrd Dynasties, from Bubastis. Shashanq (Shishak) the Libyan seizes the throne. Raid in Palestine and Jerusalem captured. The history of this period is not clear. 947–720 (?) B.C.

. . . . Conquest of Egypt by Piānkhi the Nubian.   721–715 B.C.

XXIVth Dynasty, from Saïs. Bakenrenef slain by Shabaka the Nubian. 718–712 B.C.

XXVth Dynasty, from Napata in Nubia. The Nubians rule all Egypt. Esarhaddon invades Egypt, defeats Tirhākāh, takes Memphis, and appoints governors over the cities of the Delta. Rebellion in the Delta, which is quelled by Ashurbanipal, king of Assyria, who retakes Memphis, advances to Thebes, and plunders and destroys the city, appoints a new set of governors and returns to Nineveh ; Tirhākāh and Tanutamen escape his vengeance.   715–650 B.C.

XXVIth Dynasty, from Saïs. Egypt prosperous. Necho invades Palestine, defeats Josiah and is defeated by Nebuchadnezzar II. Raids in Nubia and on the Syrian coast. Alliance with the Greeks, who enter Egypt in large numbers. Naucratis founded in the Western Delta. Increased prosperity and great development of trade. Egyptians make an alliance with the Greeks against the Persians. 663–525 B.C.

XXVIIth Dynasty, from Persia. The **Persians** under Cambyses conquer Egypt, 525 B.C. Temple of Amen in the Oasis of Khārgah built, a school for priests established at Saïs, and stamped coinage introduced. Revolt of Khabash.

XXVIIIth Dynasty, from Saïs. Of the acts of its one king, Amyrteos, nothing is known.

XXIXth Dynasty. Three kings, who reigned in all about 20 years.

XXXth Dynasty, from Sebennytus. Renewed prosperity in Egypt. Temple to Horus built at Behbīt al-Hajārah, and many temples repaired, *e.g.* Abydos, Edfū and Karnak. Constant fighting between the Egyptians and Persians, but at length the latter were victorious. Large temple built at Philae.

XXXIst Dynasty, from Persia. Second period of Persian rule lasted from 359–331 B.C.

332 B.C.   Alexander the Great becomes king of Egypt.

323 B.C.   Death of Alexander the Great. Ptolemy Lagus administers the kingdom on behalf of Arrhidaeus, son of Philip II of Macedon, and Alexander II (died 311 B.C.), son of Alexander the Great.

305 B.C.   Ptolemy Lagus.

305–30 B.C.   Ptolemies I–XVI rule Egypt.

30 B.C.   Egypt becomes a province of the Roman Empire.

PLATE I.

Cleopatra, the last Ptolemaïc Queen of Egypt, wearing the Vulture headdress of Mut, the horns of Hathor, and the lunar disk surmounted by the symbol of Isis. The cartouche contains her name—

The signs ⊖ are feminine determinatives.

LIST OF THE PRINCIPAL KINGS OF EGYPT WHOSE NAMES HAVE BEEN RECOVERED FROM THE MONUMENTS

PREDYNASTIC KINGS OF

UPPER EGYPT

Seka ⎫
Tau ⎪
Thesh ⎬ From the Stele
Uatchnar ⎪ of Palermo
Mekha ⎭

LOWER EGYPT

Ro or Ru
Ap, the " Scorpion "

DYNASTIC KINGS

Ist Dynasty

Nārmer Men ⎫
Nārmerza (?) ⎭
Āha Mena. Nārmer or
  Āha was the Mênes of
  Manetho
Tcher (or Khent)
Tche (or Atche), the " Serpent "
Ten (or Den) Semti (or Khasti)
Merpeba Āntch-ab
Smerkhat Nekhti
Sen (or Qebh)

IInd Dynasty

Hetep or ⎫
Hetep-Sekhemui ⎭
Rāneb or ⎫
Kakau ⎭
Baenneter or ⎫
Banetru ⎭

IInd Dynasty—contd.

Sekhemab ⎧ the first two
Perenmaāt ⎪ names are
Perabsen ⎨ the King's
 ⎪ Horus-names;
 ⎪ the third is
 ⎩ his Set-name

Senti
Neferkarā
Neferkaseker
Hutchefa (?)

IIIrd Dynasty

Khāsekhem ⎧ Horus-
Khāsekhemui ⎨ names
 ⎩ of Besh
Besh
Tcheser
Sanekht
Tcheserteta
Neferka[rā]
Huni (?)
Seneferu (perhaps first
  king of the IVth Dynasty)

IVth Dynasty

Sharu
Khufu (Cheops)
Tetefrā
Khāfrā (Chephren)
Menkaurā (Mycerinus)
Shepseskaf

Vth Dynasty

Userkaf
Sahurā
Neferarikarā Kakau
Neferefrā Shepseskarā
Khāneferrā
Enuserrā An
Menkauher
Tetkarā Assa
Unas

VIth Dynasty

Teta
Userkarā Ati
Merirā Pepi I
Merenrā Mehtiemsaf I
Neferkarā Pepi II
Merenrā Mehtiemsaf II
Neterkarā
Menkarā (Nitôcris)

VIIth and VIIIth Dynasties
[From King Lists and the
Turin Papyrus]

Neferka
Neferseh . . .
Ab
Neferkaurā
Khatti
Neferkarā
Neferkarā Nebi
Tetkarā Maatua (?)

VIIth and VIIIth Dynasties
—*contd.*

Neferkarā Khentu
Merenher
Seneferkarā
Enkarā
Neferkarā Terrl
Neferkaher
Neferkarā Pepi-senb
Seneferkarā Ānnu
Menkaurā
Neferkaurā
Neferkauher

IXth and Xth Dynasties

Abmerirā Khati I
Uahkarā Khati II
Kamerirā

XIth Dynasty

Antef or ⎱
Antefā ⎰
Uahānkh Antefā I
Nekhtnebtepnefer Antefā II
Sānkhabtaui Menthuhetep I
Nebheprā Menthuhetep II
Nebtauirā Menthu-
    hetep III (?)
Sānkhkarā Menthu-
    hetep IV (?)

XIIth Dynasty, 2500 B.C. or
2200 B.C.

Sehetepabrā Amenemhat I
Kheperkarā Usertsen (or
    Sen-Usrit) I
Nubkaurā Amenemhat II
Khākheperrā Usertsen (or
    Sen-Usrit) II

XIIth Dynasty—*contd.*

Khākaurā Usertsen (or Sen-Usrit) III
Enmaātrā Amenemhat III
Maātkherurā AmenemhatIV
Auabrā Her
Sebekneferurā
Seneferabrā Sen-Usrit IV

XIIIth and XIVth Dynasties (reigned simultaneously)

Khutauirā Ugafa (?)
Sānkhtaui Sekhemkarā (?)
Aufni
Sānkhabrā Ameni Antef Amenemhat
Sekhemkhutauirā Sebekhetep I
Semenkhkarā Mermashāu
Sekhemsuatchtauirā Sebekhetep II
Khāseshēshrā Neferhetep
Khāneferrā Sebekhetep III
Khāheteprā Sebekhetep IV
Khāānkhrā Sebekhetep V
Uahabrā Āaab
Merneferrā Ana
Merneferrā Ai
Nebmaātrā Aba
Nehsirā
Menkhāurā Ānab
Sekhemuatchkhāurā Sebekemsaf
Sekhemseshettauirā Sebekemsauf
Enmaātrāenkhā Khentcher
Sekhemneferkhāu Upuatemsaf
Seshesh(?)rāherherimaāt Antefā III

XIIIth and XIVth Dynasties —*contd.*

Sesheshrāupmaāt Antefā IV
Nubkheperrā Antefā V
Sekhemuahkhāurā Heteprā
[and about 60 others; order of succession very doubtful]

XVth and XVIth Dynasties

Semqen
Ānther or Ānthel
Meruserrā Igebārh
Khāmurā
Khāuserrā
Aaheteprā
Maāabrā
Āasehrā
Āapehtirā Nubti
Seuserenrā Khian
Nebtkhepeshrā Apepa I
Āauserrā Apepa II
Āaqenenrā Apepa III
[order of succession doubtful]

XVIIth Dynasty

Seqenenrā I Tauā
Seqenenrā II Tauāā
Seqenenrā III Tauāqen
Uatchkheperrā Kames
Scnekhtenrā

XVIIIth Dynasty

Nebpehtirā Aāhmes I
Tcheserkarā Amenhetep I
Āakheperkarā Tehutimes, or Tchehutimes (Thothmes) I
Āakheperenrā Tehutimes II
[Queen] Maātkarā Hatshepsut

XVIIIth Dynasty—*contd.*

Menkheperrā Tehutimes III
Āakheperurā Amenhetep II
Menkheperurā Tehutimes IV
Nebmaātrā Amenhetep III
Neferkheperurāuāenrā ⎫
  Aten meri Amen- ⎬
  hetep IV or ⎭
Aakhuenaten
Sākarā
Kheperunebrā ⎫
  Tutānkhaten ⎬
Tutānkhamen ⎭
Kheperkheperurāarimaāt Ai
Tcheserkheperurā Heremheb

XIXth Dynasty

Menpehtirā Rāmeses I
Menmaātrā Seti I
Usermaātrāsetepenrā Rameses II
(Khāmuast, co-regent)
Merenptah I Hetephermaāt
Menmarāsetepenrā Amenmeses
Merenptah II Saptah
Seti II Merenptah III

XXth Dynasty

Arsu (?) a Syrian
Userkhāurāsetepenrā Setnekht
Usermaātrā Rameses III
Heqmaātrā Rameses IV
Sekheperenrā Rameses V
Nebmaātrā Rameses VI
Usermaātrā Rameses VII
Usermaātrāaakhuenamen
  Rameses VIII
Sekhāenrā Rameses IX

XXth Dynasty—*contd.*

Neferkarā Rameses X
Khepermaātrā Rameses XI
Menmaātrā Rameses XII (?)

XXIst Dynasty

Kings ruling in the Delta :—
  Nesbanebtet
  Pisebkhānu I
  Amenemapt
  Saamen
  Her Pisebkhānu
Priest-kings ruling at Thebes :—
  Herher, high priest of Amen
  Piānkhi
  Pinetchem I
  Menkheperrā
  Pinetchem II
  Pisebkhānu II

XXIInd and XXIIIrd Dynasties

At Bubastis

Shashanq (Shishak) I
Usarken I
Teklet I
Usarken II
Shashanq II
Auput
Shashanq III
Pimai
Shashanq IV

At Thebes (?)

Hersaast
Petabast
Teklet II
Usarken III

XXIInd and XXIIIrd
Dynasties—*contd.*
Teklet III
Rutamen
Usarken IV
[The order of succession is
doubtful]

XXIVth Dynasty
Tafnekht
Bakenrenef

XXVth Dynasty
Piānkhi meri Amen
Neferkarā Shabaka
Tetkhāurā Shabataka
Aakhu Nefer-Tem-Rā Ta-
harqa (Tirhākāh)
Bakarā Tanutamen

XXVIth Dynasty
Uahabrā Psemthek I
Uhemabrā Nekau (Necho)
Neferabrā Psemthek II
Hāāabrā Uahabrā (Hophra)
Khnemabrā Aāhmes II
(Amasis)
Ānkhkaenrā Psemthek III

XXVIIth Dynasty
Mesutrā Kembathet (Cam-
byses)

XXVIIth Dynasty—*contd.*
Setutrā Anthriush (Darius)
Senenenptah Setepentanen
Khabbasha
Artakhshashs (Artaxerxes)
Userkhepeshmeri Anthriu-
sha (Darius)

XXVIIIth Dynasty
[Wanting]

XXIXth Dynasty
Baenrā Naifāaurut
Khnemmaātrā Hagr
Userptah Setepenrā Psamut

XXXth Dynasty
Senetchemabrā Nekhther-
hebit
Arimaātenrā Tcheher
Kheperkarā Nekhtnebef

XXXIst Dynasty
Ochus
Arses
Darius III

Macedonians
Alexander the Great
Philip Arrhidaeus
Alexander II

THE CRY OF THE OPPRESSED IN EGYPT

Work, my brother, rest is nigh—
　　Pharaoh lives for ever !
Beast and bird of earth and sky,
Things that creep and things that fly—
All must labour, all must die ;
　　But Pharaoh lives for ever !

Work, my brother, while 'tis day—
　　Pharaoh lives for ever !
Rivers waste and wane away,
Marble crumbles down like clay,
Nations dwindle to decay ;
　　But Pharaoh lives for ever !

Work—it is thy mortal doom—
　　Pharaoh lives for ever !
Shadows passing through the gloom,
Age to age gives place and room,
Kings go down into the tomb ;
　　But Pharaoh lives for ever !

Whyte-Melville, *Sarchedon*, London, 1871, p. 175.

CHAPTER I

THE MOTHER, THE FAMILY, THE HOME AND THE SCHOOL

THE Egyptian was in all periods of his history a lover of his home and family, and the relations between parents and their children were usually of the most affectionate character. His world was the village where his home was, and his kinsfolk were the only inhabitants of it that counted in his sight. He regarded sojourning in a strange village or town as exile and, if it had for any reason to be prolonged, as banishment. The same feeling existed in Egypt until a very few years ago, and when young men were drafted into Cairo from Upper Egypt and the Delta to serve in the army it was no uncommon thing to see a recruit weeping bitterly and cursing the fate that had torn him from his *balad*, or village, and his father's " house," *i.e.* his mother and his near

relations.   Naturally these strong, hefty young
men hated the duties and restraints of military
service, but the sting that brought the tears to
their eyes was the enforced separation from their
homes and families, and the absence of daily
intercourse with them which it entailed.   The
Egyptian loved his home more than his country,
and service in any part of it outside his village
or town was, and still is, an abomination to him.

The master of the house, *i.e.* the father and
bread-winner, was the most important person in
it from one point of view, but his wife, whether
she was his " sister," or his " woman," or " the
lady of the house," , who bore him
children and brought them up was almost more
important, for she provided for the continuance
of his family and preserved his name among
the living, and safeguarded his property.   In
Egypt and in many other parts of Africa the
mother was regarded as the predominant partner
in the house, and though a man might honour
his father's name, it was the name of his mother
that he was proud to mention.   And after that
the name of his mother's father, rather than that
of his father's father, was the name to be
commemorated.   On a large number of the
funerary stelae preserved in the Egyptian
Museum in Cairo and in the British Museum the
name of the mother of the deceased person is
given, but no mention is made of the name of
his father.   The wise and prudent mother in
ancient Egypt ruled from inside her house, and
her influence was very great, and the more

attention she gave to the well-being of her husband and the management of his property and his children, the greater was her power. It has often been said that the Egyptians, like other Orientals, regarded women as their inferiors and as playthings, but everyone who has read Oriental history, or who knows the East even as it is to-day, is well aware that whenever the wise mothers of families in a village or town have decided collectively that an order of the local council in respect of their homes and families is or is not to be carried out, they usually have their way. Egyptian women, however well educated, never went about in public as Western women do, or made public speeches on any subject, for such a course of action was contrary to the public opinion, not only of the men but of the women. There is no reason to doubt that women in Egypt held property in their own names and had money invested in businesses, especially under the New Kingdom, and we know that some learned to read and write the Egyptian language correctly, and some became expert scribes. Princess Nesitanebtashru (about 1000 B.C.) wrote her own copy of the Book of the Dead, and about A.D. 1000 a woman copied the fine Zouche manuscript containing the Encomiums on Saint Michael the Archangel, which is now in the British Museum.

To found a family and establish a house was held to be the duty of every right-minded man, and the first step towards its fulfilment was **marriage.** The scribe Ani wrote : " Marry a

wife whilst thou art a young man " (or, perhaps,
" marry a wife who is a young woman ") " and
she will give thee thy son.   If thou begettest a
son whilst thou art young, thou wilt be able to
train him to become a proper man.   It is good
for a man to have a numerous progeny, for he
will be applauded by reason of his children."
How a marriage was " arranged " or brought
about in the early period is not known, but we
are justified in assuming that the method
employed was the same then as it is now.   The
father, or rather mother, who had a son about
15 years of age looked about among the neighbours for a maiden about 12 years old, and when
one suitable for a daughter-in-law had been
found, an intermediary probably was employed
to carry on negotiations.   After the maiden's
beauty had been described in glowing terms to
the father of the youth, and the youth's manly
attributes and physical attractions had been
enumerated to the maiden's father, the intermediary, who knew the circumstances of both
fathers, brought them together and assisted
them to settle what and how much the maiden's
father was to receive in exchange for his
daughter.   In early times the price of the maiden
was arranged by word of mouth, and when an
understanding had been arrived at the marriage
took place without delay ; but at a later period
it seems that the marriage contract was drawn
up by a scribe, or notary, as we should say,
who took good care to safeguard the maiden's
interests.   In due course an evening was fixed
for the **wedding,** and the **bride** was brought to

the bridegroom's house and handed over to the
bridegroom.   At the marriage festival and during
the rejoicings that took place on the days following
the marriage-night the friends and kinsfolk of
the bride and bridegroom were entertained on
a scale commensurate with the social position
of the parents ; animals were slaughtered and
the poor were fed, and acrobatic performances
and singing and dancing amused the guests.
Whether any religious ceremony was performed
to consecrate the marriage is not known, but it
is not likely ; nothing has yet been found that
can be regarded as a Marriage Office.

Among well-to-do Egyptians young men often
married their sisters, and the **sister-wife** is
often mentioned on the inscriptions.   In some
cases such marriages were the result of affection
pure and simple, but generally they came about
through the desire, which was deep-seated in
the mind of the Egyptians, to keep property in
the family.   The gods Osiris and Set married
their sisters Isis and Nephthys respectively,
and Osiris begat Horus by Isis and Set begat
Anubis by Nephthys ; therefore the marriages of
brothers and sisters were sanctioned by the
gods, and there is no doubt that they existed
in the earliest times in Egypt.   It is not certain
that the sister-wife was in every case a real wife
to her husband, but even if she was it did not
prevent the man from marrying another woman
if his sister-wife for any reason failed to give
him a son.   And it does not follow that the wife
whom the Egyptian called " his sister,"

sent-f, was really his sister, for the love-songs of the Egyptians prove that the lover often called the loved one " sister," using the word as the equivalent of the words " beloved," " dearest," and " darling " of modern Western peoples. The word used for the woman who was a real wife to a man and gave him children was ☖, *hemt*, and there is no doubt that she was regarded as joint owner of her husband's property, and that she shared the control and disposal of it with him. As to the woman who is called the " lady of the house," we may assume that she held a position somewhat resembling that of the " housekeeper " in the establishment of a well-to-do man, and it is possible that she was also one of her master's wives. Many funerary stelae of women who held the position of " lady of the house " are known to us, and it is quite clear that these women were held to be as worthy of honourable burial as the women who had given their husbands many children. Kings and nobles undoubtedly kept large *harīms* and married many of the women who were kept secluded in them, but the inscriptions show that theoretically, at least, the king was a monogamist, and that he only bestowed the title of " King's chief woman " on one woman at a time. And certainly **monogamy** was the rule in Egypt ; **polyandry** seems to have been unknown.

As among all African peoples, the love of children among the Egyptians was very great, and it was generally held that every man who could afford to keep a wife should marry, and that every woman should give her husband offspring. **Virginity** and **celibacy** were not approved of by the Egyptians in their pagan state, though in some religious ceremonies the women performers were obliged to be virgins. Convents and nunneries were unknown in Egypt until after her people embraced Christianity. It is a remarkable fact that the founder of Christian asceticism, Anthony the Great, was a pure Egyptian. So convinced were the primitive Egyptians that every man, living or dead, should possess a wife and concubines that, on the death of a man of wealth and importance, several women were killed in order that their spirits might go to the Other World and minister to his wants there as their bodies had served him in this world. The bodies of some of the women who were murdered for this purpose at the death or burial of Amenhetep II, about 1448 B.C., may be seen lying on the ground near his sarcophagus, in his tomb at Thebes, to this day. When in the course of centuries funerary murders became too expensive or unpopular, the figure of a naked woman, made of wood or terra-cotta, or painted on wood or papyrus, was buried with the deceased, so that the spirit of the woman that would be evoked from it by the *heka*, or "word of power," might comfort him in the world beyond the grave. Sometimes the figure or model of the naked woman is represented as lying on a bed with a child by her side, the child symbolizing the offspring that the woman would bear to her husband in the Land of the Dead. Examples of such figures may be seen in the British Museum.

Now although **polygamy** existed in Egypt in
all periods, the Egyptians well understood the
moral and material advantages that accrued to
the man who loved and honoured his wife and
was faithful to her. Ptah-hetep the Sage said :
" If thou wouldst be wise (or prosperous)
stablish a house for thyself (*i.e.* get married).
Love thou thy wife in the house wholly and
rightly. Fill her belly and clothe her back ; oil
for anointing is the medicine for her limbs.
Make her heart to rejoice as long as thou livest ;
she is a field profitable to her lord. Enter not
into disputes with her. She will withdraw
herself before violence. Make her to prosper
permanently in thy house. If thou art hostile
to her she will become like a ditch. . . ." And
about 1,500 years later the scribe Ani said :
" Attempt not to direct a married woman in her
house, when thou knowest that she is an excellent
housewife. Say not to her, ' Where is that
thing ? Bring it to me,' when she has set it in
its proper place. Watch her with thine eye,
and hold thy peace, and then thou wilt be able
to appreciate her wise and prudent management.
Happy wilt thou be if thou goest hand in hand
with her ! Many are the men who do not
understand this. The man who interferes in his
house only stirs up confusion in it, and never
finds that he is the real master thereof in all
matters."
And the sages were never tired of impressing
upon men, both married and single, the folly
and the danger incurred in running after the
strange woman and the women in the houses of

neighbours. Ptah-hetep says : " If thou wishest to maintain a permanent friendship in the house to which thou art in the habit of going, whether as master, or whether as brother, or whether as friend, or in fact in any place to which thou hast the entry, strive against associating with the women there. The place which they frequent is not good [for thee] ; but the imprudent man follows them. A thousand men have been destroyed by them in their quest of what is beautiful. A man is made a fool of by their dazzling limbs, which turn into things that are harder than quartzite sandstone. The pleasure lasts only for a brief moment, and it is even as a dream, and when it is ended a man finds death through having experienced it." And Ani the scribe says : " Guard thyself well against the strange woman who is not known in her quarter of the town. Cast not longing glances after her, as do those who are like unto her, and have no intercourse with her of any sort or kind whatsoever. She is a deep ditch, and where her currents will lead no man knows. When a woman whose husband is absent from her [reveals her] charms, and beckons thee to her every day, and says that there is none present to bear witness, and arranges her net to snare thee therein, it is a most abominable deed which merits the penalty of death for a man to hearken to her, even if she does not succeed in her object. . . Nevertheless men commit abominable deeds in order to gratify a passion of this kind." For the unfaithful husband Egyptian law had no penalty, and the wronged wife presumably had no redress ; but for the unfaithful wife the case was entirely different, and two instances are known in which she suffered the penalty of death. Under the Old Kingdom the guilty wife was burnt alive and her ashes were scattered, and under the New Kingdom Anpu killed his wife, cut up her body, and fed the dogs, or jackals, with the pieces.[1]　In the first instance the paramour was thrown into the Nile and a crocodile devoured him.

A father claimed implicit obedience from his son, but the Egyptians thought a boy owed more to his mother than to his father, and it was, therefore, his duty not only to obey her but to love her and to give her constant proof of his devotion to her.　The scribe Ani especially

---

[1] "His elder brother went to his house with his hand clasping the top of his head, and he smeared himself with mud.　Then he went into his house and slew his wife and cast her forth to the jackals" :— *Tale of the Two Brothers*, p. 8.

exhorts his son, Khensuhetep, to cherish his mother, and though his Book of Precepts belongs to a comparatively late period, his admonition on the subject of a son's duty to his mother so well illustrates the general feeling about it in ancient Egypt that the paragraph may be quoted in full. Ani says : " Multiply the bread-cakes which thou givest to thy mother, and carry her as she carried thee. When thou wast a heavy load she carried thee often, leaving me nothing to do for thee. When she had brought thee forth after thy months [were fulfilled], she set thee like a veritable yoke upon her neck, and her breasts were in thy mouth for three years. Though whilst thou wast a babe her task as nurse was loathsome she felt no disgust at thee, saying ['Consider] what I have to do.' And afterwards, when she had placed thee in the house of instruction (i.e. school), and whilst thou wast being taught [thy] letters, she [came] to thee there day by day, regularly and unfailingly, with bread-cakes and beer from her house. When thou art a young man, and dost marry a wife, and art the master and possessor of a house, I pray thee to consider thine own childhood, and how thou wast reared, and to do for the child that shall be born to thee everything that thy mother did for thee. Let it not happen that she (i.e. his mother) shall have cause to blame thee, and give her not occasion to lift up her hands to God [in complaint], and let it not be necessary for Him to hear her supplications." Ani thought that God would hear a mother's complaint against an unkind or undutiful son, and would punish the offender.

The wife, whilst awaiting the birth of her child,
wore amulets of various kinds to protect her
and her unborn babe from the attacks of the
evil spirits that were held to be hostile to
expectant mothers, and recited incantations in
order to obtain the help of the benevolent
goddesses who presided over child-birth. Two of
these goddesses were believed to dwell in a
special kind of stone, and two tablets made of
this stone were laid down on the spot where it
was arranged that the birth of the child should
take place. The Hebrew women also used such
tablets, as we see from the passage in Exod. i. 16,
where they are called הָאָבְנָיִם *hâobhnayim*,
literally, "the two stone tablets." When the
son of a king was born several of the old
gods and goddesses were believed to come
into the birth-chamber to protect the child,
and among these were Heqt or Heqit, the Frog-
goddess, Taurit, the Hippopotamus-goddess, and
the very ancient god, Bes. Both Heqit and
Taurit were goddesses of fertility and birth, and
Bes was supposed to disarm by his jests and
drolleries and laughter the less harmful of the
evil spirits, and to attack with his sword and
put to flight the demons who would injure the
mother or her child.

Women who belonged to the industrial classes
and peasant women relied for protection upon
the pictures or figures of these deities that were
kept in their houses. The birth of a son was
followed by great rejoicings in the house, and
warm congratulations on the part of the neighbours ; births of daughters, then as now, were

not specially welcomed. Usually the mother suckled her child and devoted herself to him, or her, for about three years; in rich men's houses nurses were often employed, and these frequently obtained great influence and power. Whether any ceremonial washing of the child took place after its birth, as was customary among many African tribes, is not known, and no religious ceremony seems to have accompanied the naming of the child. The evidence of the inscriptions shows that the Egyptians in general did not cultivate pride of family and the perpetuation of family names, and the prominent man of each generation seems to have been content to proclaim his own exploits and merits, and to allow those of his ancestors to fall into oblivion. Only here and there is an instance found in the texts in which a man refers with pride to the generations of his ancestors, and the few genealogies of great officials and others known to us were compiled during the later period of Egyptian history.

In the use of formal names the Egyptians were somewhat careless, for some names were common to men and women, and a man might have two wives each having the same name, or two or three sons with the same name, or two or three daughters with the same name. In very early times names were short and simple, and **nicknames** and **diminutives** of them and pet names were common. The formal name of a man was called his " great name," and the name by which he was known in everyday life his " beautiful name," and besides these he might have a nickname; on the other hand it is doubtful if people in the lower classes had formal names at all. A boy might be given the name of his grandfather or uncle because he was supposed to resemble him, and a girl was often called " Nefert " because she was pretty or good, or " Mausherau," " little cat," *i.e.* " Pussy," because of her wheedling and coaxing ways. A child who was supposed to be sent as a special favour to its parents by Rā or Ptah or Horus would be called Petarā, or Petaptah, or Petaher, *i.e.* " gift of Rā," " gift of Ptah," or " gift of Horus." Or he might be called the son of a god or goddess, *e.g.* Sa-Menthu, " son of Menthu," or Sa-Ast, " son of Isis," and so on. Some names indicated that their possessors were begotten by gods, *e.g.* Rāmessu, " Rā begot him." In many cases the names of gods and goddesses were given to children, and we find men called Horus, Khensu, Thoth, etc., and women called Isis, Hathor, Sekhmit, etc. The names bestowed upon children often had a definitely religious meaning, and signified the adherence of their possessors to the cults of the gods whose names they bore. Sometimes the great name of a man formed a complete sentence, *e.g.* Tchet-Ptah-auf-ānkh, " Ptah spake, he (*i.e.* the child) lived." Many names of this class somewhat resemble the names borne by some of Cromwell's soldiers. Religious Egyptians often made the name of some deity a part of their names, and loyal officials and others made the name of the reigning king a part of their names.

Among the names of Egyptian kings and persons referred to in the Bible may be mentioned :—1. **Rameses.** The original Egyptian forms of this name are RĀ-MESES, ⊙𝍢𝌆𝌆 or 𝍦𝍢𝌆𝌆 (variants, ⊙𝍢𝌆— and 𝍦𝍢 ═), and RĀ-MESSU, 𝍦𝍢𝌆 or ⊙𝍢𝌆𝍦. This was the personal name of twelve kings of Egypt, and it indicated that the king was the " son of Rā," 𝍦⊙, and that it was Rā who had produced him. In Hebrew it appears as the name of a city in the Eastern Delta, רַעְמְסֵס, RA'AMSÊS (Exod. i. 11), built by Rameses II ; this city was near Pithom = Egyptian PER TEM, ⌐▭ ◠ ⊗, the site of which is marked by the ruins of Tall al-Maskhūtah in the Wādī Tumīlāt. **2. Shishak** (1 Kings xi. 40). In Egyptian (𝍯𝍯 𝍯𝍯 ᰁ), SHASHANQ (XXIInd Dynasty). **3. So,** king of Egypt (2 Kings xvii. 4). In Egyptian (𝍯𝍯 𝍣 ⊔), SHABAKA, the first king of the XXVth Dynasty. **4. Tirhāqāh** (2 Kings xix. 9 ; Isaiah xxxvii. 9). In Egyptian (⚊▭🐊 ᰁ), T-H-R-Q (variant (▭ ᰁ) or (▭ 𓃀 ◠ 𓃀), T-H-A-R-Q-A) **5. Necho** (2 Chron. xxxv. 20 ; 2 Kings xxiii. 29). In Egyptian (∿ 🐂 𓃀) or (∿ ⊔ 𓃀), NEKAU

(XXVIth Dynasty). **6. Hophra** (Jer. xliv. 30). In Egyptian ⟨ ☉ 🎐 ⟩, Uahabrā (XXVIth Dynasty). **7. Pharaoh.** In Egyptian ▭, Per-ā, *i.e.* the "Great House" [in which all Egyptians took asylum]. **8. Potipherah** (Gen. xli. 45). In Hebrew פּוֹטִי פֶרַע, Pôti-phĕra'. In Egyptian 𓏏𓇗𓏤𓅆, Pa-ti-pa-Rā, "The gift [of] the Rā" (*i.e.* of the Sun-god), or "He whom the Rā gave." Potipherah was the priest of On (Egyptian 𓉻𓊖, Anu), whose daughter Joseph married. A shortened form of the name occurs in Gen. xxxvii. 36, where we have פּוֹטִיפַר, Pôtîphar. **9. Âsnath,** daughter of Potipherah, priest of On, who married Joseph. This name seems to be undoubtedly Egyptian, and it is possible that it represents some name like 𓈖𓏏𓅆, Nesi-Net, "belonging to the goddess Neith." Others would make it = 𓊨𓏏𓅆, Isis-Neith. **10. Zaphnath-paaneah** (Gen. xli. 45). This name, which was given to Joseph by the Egyptians, appears in Hebrew as צָפְנַת פַּעְנֵחַ, Ṣophnath-pa'nêakh, and probably represents the Egyptian

Tchet -	pa -	neter -	af -	ānkh
"Speaks	the	God	he	lives,"

or "the God spake [and] he came to life." If we omit the vowels from the Hebrew form of the name it will be seen that the consonants represent remarkably well the Egyptian words, thus :—

In rapid pronunciation the  ṭ of  would not be heard ; the sign  is the determinative which would be placed after a man's name and would not be pronounced. Under the New Kingdom many Egyptian names had this form, *e.g.* 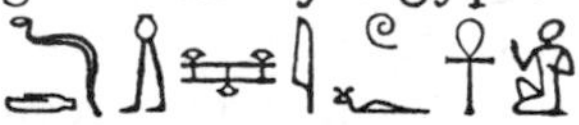, Tchet-Anher-auf-ānkh, , Tchet-Khensu-auf-ānkh, , Tchet-Her-auf-ānkh, etc.

From a religious point of view a man's name formed a very important part of his spiritual economy, and his very existence, certainly in the Other World, depended upon its preservation. To destroy the name was equivalent to destroying the person who bore it, and to mutilate and obliterate the name of the deceased from his tomb was to doom him to oblivion, both in this world and in the Kingdom of Osiris. In the inscriptions found in the tombs of the Middle Kingdom the visitor who "hates death and loves life" is entreated by the deceased to pray

that offerings " beautiful, sweet and pure " of
all kinds may be given to the *ka* of the deceased,
whose name is given at full length, for by so
doing he would make the name of the deceased
to live.   Many statues from the tombs bear
inscriptions which state that they have been
placed there by the sons or wives of the deceased
persons in order " to make their names to live."
Pious sons not only repaired or restored the
masonry of their fathers' tombs, but took care
to recut the damaged inscriptions, both inside
and outside.   It was thought that a man might
lose his memory in the Other World, and so forget
his name, and a spell was included in the Book
of the Dead (Chap. xxv) to prevent this hap-
pening to the deceased.   In the Chapter of the
Heart (xxx*b*) in the same work the deceased
prays that " his name may not be made to
stink " before the Tchatchau, or judges, in the
Judgment Hall of Osiris ;   the nameless spirit
could not be judged, and therefore could not
enjoy everlasting life and its happiness in the
Kingdom of Osiris.   The early kings of Egypt
thought more of preserving their names than
of recording their exploits.   The pyramids of
the VIth Dynasty contain long prayers for
the preservation of the names of the kings who
built them, and in the Saïte and later periods
of Egyptian history the scribes composed a
special work (the recital of which on behalf
of the deceased would ensure the preservation
of his name), entitled " May my name
flourish."   Thothmes III cut out the name of
Hatshepsut from her monuments with the view

of destroying her existence, and Amenhetep IV
cut out the name of Amen and the word
for " the gods " from the monuments, thinking
that by so doing he would cause them to cease
to be.

In Egypt the children of rich and poor alike
went about naked during the earliest years of
their existence. The children of the rich and
well-to-do folk played with **balls** made of rags,
dolls made of wood and rags, and figures of
animals, birds, etc., with movable legs and
heads ; peasants' children played with each other
and lay and rolled about in the dust near their
fathers' houses, and threw balls of mud at each
other, and made friends with the cows, and
goats, and pigeons. Even when quite young
they helped their elders to tend the cattle
and drive them to the canals or water channels
to drink, and to keep the goats from straying.
The children of slaves were made to work
at a very early age, and large numbers of them
must have died when quite young. When we
consider the conditions under which the children
of the peasant farmers and field labourers
must have been born and reared, especially
in the Delta, it is impossible not to assume that
infant mortality was very great. Those who
survived their childhood were made to help
their fathers and uncles in the labours of
the field and to do as their forbears had done
—that is, to collect the droppings of the animals
for fuel, to tend cattle, dig irrigation channels
and water the fields, clear out the canals, build
up dykes, and serve in the *corvée* whenever

ordered to do so, under penalty of a beating. The life of people of this class was hard and laborious, their food was coarse and scanty, and their amusements few; magic and witch-craft flourished among them, and they passed their lives in constant dread of the attacks that the fiends and devils whom they believed to exist might make upon them. The above remarks really describe the conditions under which slaves of the field-labourer class lived in the days of Muhammad 'Alî and his immediate successors, but there is reason to think that they are equally applicable to the slaves of the kings and nobles in all periods of Egyptian history.

The children of the king were educated in the palace, and school-fellows and playmates were chosen for them from among the families of the official classes. There they learnt to read and to write and to copy and understand the meaning of the texts that were selected for them to study. Those among the people generally who wished their children to be educated sent them to one of the schools that were maintained out of the temple revenues and were directed by the priests. The king and nobles who possessed arge estates were obliged to employ a number of educated youths and men to keep their accounts and manage their farms, and these studied arithmetic and land surveying and any and every subject of which a knowledge was necessary for the performance of their duties in a satisfactory manner. Such men were compelled to be expert scribes and to have

a good knowledge of practical farming and
the market values of farming products. The
prosperity of Egypt depended upon successful
agriculture. The various priesthoods of Egypt
also were large landowners and possessed much
property, and they educated scribes in considerable numbers, not only to keep the accounts of
their temples, but also to copy religious texts
and keep registers of the offerings made to
the gods, and to draft the inscriptions that
were to be cut on the temples and painted in
the tombs.

Boys were sent to school when they were about
four years of age, and the period of their education lasted for ten or twelve years ; there is no
evidence that schools for girls existed, and it is
not probable that they did. Whilst at school it
seems that a boy was taught the subjects that
would be most useful to him in the career that
his father had decided he should follow, for
the Egyptian father was eminently practical,
and had little desire that his son should receive
what may be described as a " general education."
The value of the arts of reading and writing, and
the knowledge of books, was generally recognized
by all classes in Egypt, and especially by the
merchant and artisan classes, who believed that
there was no position to which the " learned
scribe " might not attain in the country. The
art of the scribe had a pecuniary value ; it
opened the way to lucrative employment in the
service of the Government, it gave to the man who
possessed it social standing, and raised him above
the greater number of his fellow-countrymen

who earned their living by performing manual labours. Men in general never considered it as a key that would unlock the treasures of learning laid up in the papyrus rolls in the temples, and would enable them to acquire the wisdom and knowledge that the sages of Egypt had stored up. Though among the nations round about them the Egyptians were famed for their learning, there is no evidence that, as a nation, they loved learning for its own sake, or sought after knowledge because they loved it. A proof of this fact is supplied to us by the " Teaching " of one Tuauf as it is given in two papyri in the British Museum (Nos. 10182, 10222). Tuauf set out one day to take his son Pepi to school, and as they were sailing up the Nile to the place where the school was, he talked to his son and tried to show him the merits of the scribe's profession. Some of his remarks may be summarized thus :

I have considered hard work, and have concluded that books are the best things to study ; I say, then, Give thy mind to books. In an ancient work it is written : " The scribe may attain to every position at Court ; he need not go begging for employment there." The man who works for another never gains an independent position for himself. I have considered other trades and professions, and the same remark applies to them also. I would have thee love books as thou lovest thy mother, and I will set their beauties before thee. The profession of the scribe is the greatest of all professions ; it has no equal upon earth. Even when the scribe is a beginner in his career his opinion is consulted. He is sent on missions of state and does not come back to place himself under the direction of another. Now take the worker in metals. Was a **smith** ever sent on a mission of state ? The **coppersmith** has to work in front of his blazing furnace, his fingers are like the crocodile's legs, and he stinks more than the insides of fish. The **metal engraver** works like a ploughman. The **mason** is always over-hauling blocks of stone, and in the evening he is tired out, his arms are weary, and the bones of his thighs and back feel as if they were coming asunder. The **barber** scours the town in search of customers ; at the end of the day he is worn out, and he tortures his hands and arms to fill his belly. The **waterman** is stung to death by the gnats and mosquitoes (?), and the stench of the canals chokes him. The **ditcher** in the fields works among the cattle and the pigs, and must cook his food in the open ; his garments are stiff with mud. The **builder of walls** is obliged to hang to them like a creeper ; his garments are filled with mortar and dust, and are in rags. The **gardener** must work every day, and all he does is exhausting. His shoulders are bowed by the heavy loads he carries, and his neck and arms are distorted. He watches onions all the morning, and tends vines all the afternoon. The **farm labourer** never changes his garments, and his voice is like that of a corncrake. His hands, arms, and fingers are shrivelled and cracked, and he smells like a corpse. The **weaver** is worse off than a woman. His thighs

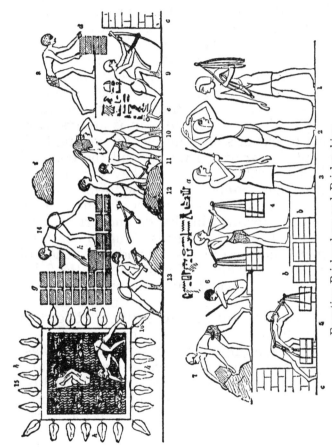

Egyptian Brickmakers and Brickmaking.

1. Man waiting to be laden. 4, 5. Men carrying bricks. 8, 14. Stacking the moulded bricks. 3, 6. Taskmasters. 9. Digging the clay. 10. Man laden with prepared clay. 11. Mixing the clay. 15. Tank for water.

are drawn up to his body, and he cannot breathe.
The day he fails to do his work he is dragged
from the hut, like a lotus from the pool, and
cast aside. To be allowed to see the daylight
he must give the overseer his dinner. The
armourer is ruined by his expenses. The
caravan man goes in terror of lions and nomads
whilst on his journey, and he returns to Egypt
exhausted. The **reed-cutter's** fingers stink
like a fishmonger ; his eyes are dull and lifeless,
and he works naked all the day long at cutting
reeds. The **sandal-maker** spends his life in
begging for work; his health is like that of a
fish with a hook in its mouth. He gnaws strips
of leather. The **washerman** spends his whole
day in beating clothes. He is a neighbour of
the crocodile, his whole body is filthy, and his
food is mixed up with his garments. If he
delays in finishing his work he is beaten. The
lot of the **fowler** is hard, for though he wishes
for a net God does not give him one. The
fisherman has the worst trade of all, for he has to
work in the river among the crocodiles, and there
is nothing to warn him of the vicinity of a crocodile.
His eyes are blinded by fear. There is no occupation than which a better cannot be found except
the profession of the scribe, which is the best of
all. Every toiler curses his trade or occupation,
except the scribe, to whom no one says : " Go and
work in the fields for So-and-so." I am sailing up
the river to the Court, and I do it because of the
love which I bear to thee. One day only spent in
school is profitable for thee, and the work thou
doest there will endure as long as the mountains.

Tuauf continues : I will now say a few other words to thee for thy instruction. Decide carefully what thou wilt do ; he who acts hastily knows not what the result will be. Use

Osiris, the judge of the words and deeds of men. His throne is set above the water whence comes the Nile. The walls of his shrine are fire and the " living uraei " are above its cornice. Isis and Nephthys are behind him, and the four sons of Horus on a lotus before him.

not words of doubtful meaning, for they will react against thee. Utter not words of pride and arrogance, even to thyself. When thou art dismissed from school at midday, go not about singing and shouting, and trespass not in the houses round about. Deliver accurately the message given thee to carry; add nothing thereto, omit nothing therefrom. And for the sake of the Great Chief (Osiris), speak not lies against thy mother; do nothing contrary to her wishes, even when thou art alone. If thou wilt control thy appetite thou wilt be listened to ; if having eaten three loaves and drunk two pitchers of beer thy belly is not full, thou must fight against it. The scribe who hears is noted ; he who hears (*i.e.* obeys) becomes a man of power. Dawdle not on thy way, spare not thyself. Keep on friendly terms with thy young schoolfellows. The goddesses Renenit and Meskhenit are with the scribe from his birth until he becomes chief of the Town Council, and they make him to prosper and flourish. His father and mother give praise to Rā; they have set him on the path of life. These are the things that I would set before thee and thy children's children.

Tuauf is thought to have composed his " Teaching " near the end of the Old Kingdom, but, as his work was made a text-book for schools under the New Kingdom two thousand years after, it is pretty clear that his views about the profession of the scribe were endorsed by the fathers of sons in the later period of its popularity. Tuauf cared nothing for the training of the mind which the study of books should give the student; all he wanted for his son was freedom from manual labour, a good social position, and remuneration for his work on a generous scale.

The **schoolmaster** probably received his pupils in his own house, and provided the materials on which they learned to write hieroglyphs, and the rolls of papyrus from which they copied the passages selected by him for study. Whether he wrote out these passages in black ink upon thin slices of limestone, or upon whitened boards, as did the Copts, cannot be said. The pupils learned to draw hieroglyphs from lists prepared by him, and day by day they probably committed to memory, by frequent repetition, groups of words copied by him from a vocabulary in which the words were classified, as in a Coptic *Scala*. The *Scala*, or vocabulary, consists of a series of lists of objects, animate and inanimate, arranged in classes. Thus we have lists of names of countries and cities, lists of animals, birds, reptiles, trees, plants, minerals, parts of the body, etc., and it is probable that the early compilers of the *Scala* borrowed their system from their ancestors, the Egyptians. The school-master's authority over his pupils was absolute. They came to his house in the early morning and worked until noon, when they were dismissed for the day. They sat literally at his feet, and it is quite clear from statements made in the papyri that their master frequently supplemented his oral instruction with corporal punishment. Sleepy and lazy boys often felt his rod on their backs, for he had no fear of being summoned for assault on their persons before the local magistrate. In one of the Anastasi papyri in the British Museum we read : " A boy has a back, and he listens (or obeys) when he is beaten." Schoolmasters argue that if horses and

lions and hawks can be made to learn and be
trained to obey man, why not the boy and the
youth ? In addition to the education derived
from books, boys were taught to be active and
industrious, and the letters which great scribes
wrote to their pupils contain many rebukes for
laziness and many exhortations to work with
all their might.   The lazy were always threatened
with a beating, and one sage pertinently
remarks : " The ears of a boy are set on his back,
and if you beat him he will listen."   At some
time during school hours the boys ate their three
bread-cakes and drank their two jugs of beer ;
the boy who was not satisfied with these was
held to be a gluttonous creature. Unfortunately
the inscriptions give no details of the system of
instruction followed by a schoolmaster, and it
is not known how he was paid or by whom
the school was supported.   The apparatus
used by him in teaching was of a very simple
character, and scarcely any school furniture
was necessary.   There may have been secondary
schools attached to the temple, wherein clever
youths were trained for special work, but this is
uncertain.

The scribe's equipment consisted of **writing
reeds**, a **palette**, a **water-pot**, and a **wrist-
rest,** all of which are represented in the hieroglyph for scribe, 𓏞. The palette was a long
narrow strip of wood or piece of stone in which
there were two shallow round hollows, one to
hold black ink and the other red, and a
groove in which the writing reeds were placed.
These varied in length from 4' to 12 inches,

and were about $\frac{1}{16}$ inch thick. The water-pot
was attached to the palette by a short cord,
and both were fastened to the wrist-rest. The
principal material used for writing upon was
papyrus, but **leather** was also used, and
drafts of important documents were written
upon slices of fine white limestone and upon
pieces of broken pots **(ostraka).** Papyrus was
made by gumming together layers of strips cut
from the stalk of the papyrus plant, which grew
in abundance in the swamps and marshes of
Egypt. The heads of the large variety of the
plant which is found in the Sūdān were cooked
and eaten by the natives. The strips were peeled
off from the stalk and laid in a row, and their
edges were fastened together by gum. Another
layer of strips was laid horizontally across the
first layer and fastened to it by gum ; when
pressed and trimmed the sheet of papyrus thus
made was ready for use. The sheet could be
made almost any length by attaching new strips
from a plant at one end. The width of the
largest sheet of papyrus known is about 20 inches,
and the length of the longest roll about 133 feet.

The papyrus roll was called *tchamā,*

The colour of papyrus varied in different periods
from dark to light brown, but in the Ptolemaïc
and later periods many papyri are light yellow
or cream colour, and some are nearly white.
Papyrus, as a writing material, plays a very
important part in the history of Egyptian scripts.
The pre-dynastic Egyptians used **pictographs**
in their writing, just as did the Anzanites and

Sumerians. But whilst these people, who had nothing but clay to use as a writing material, finding that they could not easily draw figures of animals, circles, etc., on it, developed the cuneiform system of writing, in which the original forms of the pictographs disappeared, the Egyptians were able to draw their pictographs in ink easily on papyrus, and so preserved the use of hieroglyphs in writing until the Roman Period.

Papyri were preserved in the form of rolls, and the hieroglyph for " book," ⫯ or ⇌, shows that the papyrus roll was kept in shape by a papyrus cord, later a strip of linen, which was tied in a knot and sometimes fastened by a clay seal. Important rolls were usually preserved in wooden boxes ; the Papyrus of Nu and the Harris Papyrus No. 1 (both in the British Museum) were found in boxes, and both papyri and their boxes were sealed with clay seals bearing impressions made by inscribed scarabs. Business documents, letters, etc., were stored in earthenware pots, especially in the Graeco-Roman and Coptic Periods. The **black ink** used was in early times made of charcoal, water and a little gum, but in later days a mineral preparation, which made the ink " bite " into the papyrus, was added. It was found that characters written in the ink with gum in it often flaked off. The **red ink** and the various coloured paints that were used in the decoration of papyri were made of mineral substances ; red ink was used chiefly in writing the titles and

" catch words " in literary compositions, and in making the red dots that mark the ends of the members of sentences. In the Book of the Dead the titles of the Chapters and many Rubrics and names of devils are written in red ink. Full descriptions of all the implements used by the Egyptian scribe will be found in the *Guide to the First, Second and Third Egyptian Rooms in the British Museum*, London, 1924.

CHAPTER II

THE earliest inhabitants of Egypt, long before the course of the Nile was fixed, and whilst the valley was full of swamps and marshes, sheltered themselves behind straight **screens** made of reeds tied together with vegetable fibre. Later it occurred to some of them that they would obtain more shelter if they bent the screen round so as to form a circle, leaving a space to serve as a door, and very soon they began to plaster the screen with mud, which served as a protection against wind and sun. A roof was formed by laying reeds and palm branches on the top of the circular screen, and little by little the **circular hut** was evolved. Long before the Dynastic Period of Egyptian history the Egyptians began to make their **huts** or **houses** of the mud deposited by the Nile. At first the walls were made by piling up the mud in lumps, one on top of the other, but experience showed that such walls often fell in or fell out, because the lumps of mud contained nothing that would bind them together. Gradually the circular form of hut or house was abandoned, and men began to build houses rectangular in form. One of the oldest examples of this kind of mud house is preserved in the British Museum (No. 35505), and from this we see that in the Late Neolithic Period the Egyptians built houses with both **windows** and **doorways,** and with " battered " sides. The inclination of the walls inwards gave them greater stability. The doorposts, etc., were made of wood, and it seems that wooden doors were known. When the Egyptians began to make **bricks** is unknown. Some authorities think that the art of brick-making was introduced into Egypt from Mesopotamia, but there is no good reason why the Egyptians should not have found it out for themselves. The early Sumerian bricks (say 3000 B.C.) are plano-convex, but the oldest Egyptian bricks have not this form, and all of them are unbaked. In building the primitive house of unbaked bricks no mortar was used. The circular or square hut made of reeds and palm branches and mud contained only one room ; the later mud-brick houses in which wood was used for doors and their frames, etc., probably contained two rooms or more. But from first to last the Egyptians generally lived in mud-brick houses, and everyone who has lived for any length of time in their country will admit that, provided the walls are thick enough, mud-brick houses are preferable to those built according to European models. Gods as well as men lived in plaster-and-reed houses, even in the early Dynastic Period, and the form of the circular hut which served as a shrine for the god Menu is represented on stelae of the XVIIIth Dynasty. But the shrines of several of the gods were rectangular, and their shape and some of their characteristics are preserved in the granite shrines down to the Ptolemaïc Period. The early kings also dwelt in houses, or "palaces," made of mud bricks and decorated with stonework. The fact that Tcheser, a king of the IIIrd Dynasty, built a "house of stone" for himself was considered to be such a remarkable event by Manetho (a priest of Sebennytus in the IIIrd century B.C.) that he specially mentions it when speaking of Tcheser in his List of the Kings of Egypt. It may be noted in passing that Mr. C. J. Firth, of the Government Service of Antiquities of Egypt, found the remains of this house and its fluted stone columns in 1924. It is impossible to give details of the early Egyptian houses, for, being built of mud or mud bricks, they soon, owing to the annual Inundation of the Nile, cracked or fell down, and others were promptly built on their ruins. Under the New Kingdom stone and metal were freely used in the construction of the houses of well-to-do persons. The doors, which were sometimes single and sometimes double, were often set in stone frames, on which were cut the name of the owner and magical symbols, as at the present day, and sometimes to these was added an inscription containing phrases of laudation of the god under whose protection the master of the house placed himself and his house. Rich men framed their doors in copper, and the frame-plates were often inscribed. A good example of **an inscribed house door** (belonging to Khensuhetep) is exhibited in the British Museum (No. 566). Doors were secured by **bolts,** made of wood or metal, and simple contrivances which served as **locks ;** modernized forms of such contrivances can be seen in many outlying districts of Egypt and in Nubia and the Northern Sūdān at the present day.

Up to a comparatively late period, when a man of wealth was going to build a house, an animal (originally a man ?) was sacrificed by him in order to obtain the good-will of the spirits of the earth, and, as figures of gods and amulets of various kinds have been dug up from the floors and out of the walls, we may assume that they were placed there to protect the fabric of the house from the attacks of evil spirits. From the large Vignette in the Papyrus of Nekht in the British Museum (No. 10471) we learn that the houses of well-to-do folk were provided with what are commonly called " windcatchers," *i.e.* triangular wooden erections which were placed on the roof and were open to receive the cool wind from the north. These caught the wind and made it to blow down into the house ; every purely Arab house has its **Malkaf,** which has the same form as its old Egyptian

PLATE II.

Vignette from the Papyrus of Nekht, a military scribe who flourished about 1250 B.C. The deceased and his wife are standing in their garden, between their house and the ornamental lake, and adoring Osiris, behind whom stands the goddess Maât. The house is provided with "wind-catchers" on the roof. The text above is a Hymn to Râ.

equivalent. In some parts of Upper Egypt large houses may have been provided with **sardābs,** or underground chambers, to which the inmates withdrew for coolness during the heats of summer, but in Lower Egypt such chambers would be made uninhabitable through the infiltration of Nile water. In the Vignette mentioned above, the house is built on a platform in the form of the hieroglyph ⌐, *maāt,* which means "truth," and it has four rectangular windows placed high up in the wall, to prevent surface dust from blowing through them. Many large houses stood in a courtyard planted with vines and palms and other fruit-trees, and close by it was a small ornamental lake containing fish, and lotus and other water-plants. Such a garden formed a paradise for birds. Near by were the quarters of the servants or slaves, which consisted of a series of low mud huts, and the storehouses for grain and other articles of food.

The **granary** was strongly built and was usually rectangular in form ; it was provided with a stout wooden door and massive bolts and other fastenings. Along one side of it was a series of bins, with shutters through which the grain was poured in or taken out ; the name of the grain in each bin was sometimes written above the shutter. A stairway led up to the roof of the bins, which was perforated in several places, probably for the purpose of pouring in grain or for ventilating the grain below. In some houses a stairway led from the ground floor to an upper storey, and in almost every house a stairway gave access to the roof, where at one corner there stood a small shed to which the master of the house might retire for rest and meditation in the cool of the evening. At a little distance from the house of the rich man were the **byres** for the cattle and the buildings in which the servants of the estate did their work and kept their tools and implements. Here, too, was the **threshing floor,** which was circular and resembled a shallow bowl. Every drop of water used in the house had to be brought from the river, and was stored in large porous jars either set in a row in the ground or on a wooden stand, and all sanitary arrangements were of a primitive character.

The mud on which the house stood formed the floor, and usually it was left in its natural state. The dust which worked up from it through the traffic over it was swept up and carried away, and water was sprinkled over the floor to prevent for a short time more dust from rising. Sometimes, as we see at Tall al-'Amārnah, the floor was decorated with **frescoes** representing aquatic landscapes with birds, animals, flowers, etc., but if they were trodden on by many feet the dust soon rose up as before. The walls of the rooms, and sometimes the roof, or as we should say, ceiling, were either washed over with a neutral-coloured wash or decorated with frescoes.

From time immemorial the Egyptians built along the walls outside their houses long low " **benches** " of mud bricks, the tops of which

were carefully plastered with mud, from 3 to
4 feet wide, and about 2 feet high ; " benches "
of this kind may be seen to-day in many parts of
Egypt and the Sūdān, and the Arabs use them,
as did the Egyptians, as beds or couches. Boys,
youths, and some of the watchmen, slept on
them, a bundle of their own garments serving for
a pillow, and a reed mat as a mattress. Those
who slept on them probably had no other
covering than the cloaks which they wore by day,
and, if we may judge by the habits of the modern
Egyptians, their chief anxiety was to keep their
heads covered. The master of the house and
some of his family slept upon **bedsteads,**
which closely resembled the *ankarīb* used by the
modern Egyptians. The rectangular framework
and the four legs, which were carved in the form
of the legs of a lion, were made of stout pieces
of wood and, when the wood used was ebony,
were often inlaid with ivory. The framework
was decorated with a lion's head at one end and
a lion's tail at the other, but occasionally the
head of a hippopotamus took the place of the
lion's head. The bed of the early period, as
well as the bier, was represented by the hieroglyph 𓈔. The space between the framework
was filled in either with wood or cordwork, as at
the present day, and on this were laid simple
reed mats or cushions. Men and women alike
used a **pillow** or head-rest, 𓊽 , which was often
buried with them in their tombs. It " lifted up
the head " of a man when living and the head
of his mummy when dead. The pillow was
sometimes made of limestone and was inscribed

with the name of its possessor in hieroglyphs inlaid with blue or green paste. Pillows of wood were frequently ornamented with ivory inlay, and on the rounded portions beautifully carved figures of the head of Bes are often found. The single upright support is often replaced by folding legs, the ends of which are carved to resemble the heads of geese. These brought to the sleeper the protection of the **goose,** which the Egyptians believed to be a good, ever-wakeful watcher that would warn the sleeper of danger. The Egyptians made amulets in the form of the pillow and buried them with their dead; on these was generally cut a version of Chap. clxvi of the Book of the Dead.

The mats or cushions that served as **mattresses** varied in thickness, and it seems that they were sometimes supplemented by what may be termed a padded quilt, like the *lihaf* which is found in Egypt to-day. The sleeper lay on one part of this and drew the other part over him to serve as bed-clothes. Good bed-steads stood high, and footstools were often needed to get on them. The well-to-do provided themselves, as Herodotus says (ii. 95), with network coverings under which to sleep, and these were the equivalents of the modern **mosquito nets.** These were, of course, un-necessary in hilly districts, but in places near the river and in the Delta at certain seasons of the year sleep would be impossible without them. Palladius tells the story of a certain ascetic who went to a marshy district in the Delta in order to mortify the flesh through the bites of the gnats, *i.e.* mosquitoes, and when he had been there but a short time his skin became covered with lumps and was like the hide of the hippopotamus. The **chairs** had high, straight backs, decorated with inlaid work, and must have formed very uncomfortable resting-places ; the seats of some were so high that **footstools** or cushions were necessary for comfort. The seats were often made of wood, and for these cushions were provided ; the seat made of papyrus cords or leather was the most comfortable to sit upon. The **arm-chair** with a low back was well known and much used by people of good position. Chairs of State were elaborately carved, inlaid with ivory and ebony, and otherwise decorated, and those that served as thrones for kings were regarded with the same awe and reverence as is the king's stool among modern African peoples. Favourite chairs, stools, cushions, pillows, etc., were often buried in the tombs of their owners, as the collections of furniture from the tombs that are exhibited in the great museums in Europe and America testify.

The various kinds of tables used by modern nations were unknown to the Egyptians, and their one **table** was that from which they ate their food. It consisted of two parts : a round stand, about 12 inches high, with projecting ends, and a thick flat circular slab, which formed the table proper, on which the food was placed. The slab was often covered with a layer of pieces of palm branches, but sometimes the branches were stuck into holes in the slab and stood upright, and so kept away flies. The dish or tray with the food was placed on the slab, and the family and the guests seated themselves round it on stools and took the food with their fingers. The **clothes** of the family were kept in wooden **chests** or in small crates made of thin strips of wood or the stems of palm branches; the former were divided into sections by wooden partitions, and some of them contained small wooden receptacles in which objects of special value could be placed. **Jewellery** was kept in little square or rectangular coffers, made generally of wood, and their sides and covers were inlaid with ivory, glass paste, plaques of blue and green Egyptian porcelain, etc. Under the Middle Kingdom, and probably earlier, an official, when travelling about on his duties, carried the necessary changes of apparel in small wicker-work cases like the modern suit-case. These were divided into sections, like those of a dressing-case, in which articles for the toilet, etc., were kept.

How the Egyptians warmed their houses is not known exactly; fireplaces in the modern sense of the word were unknown to them. In making **fire** they used a fire-drill, ⌡, which was similar in form to that which has been employed in Africa from time immemorial. The drill itself was a piece of very hard wood, around one end of which several ridges were cut; this was inserted in a hole made in a piece of soft dry wood, and made to revolve rapidly by the two hands between which it was placed being rubbed quickly each over the other, or by means of a cord. A little inflammable material was placed in the hole in which the borer worked, and this soon burst into flame. There is reason to believe that the Egyptians knew how to strike fire from flints. For **fuel,** straw of various kinds and dried cow-dung were used, and rarely wood; nothing in the nature of coal was known to the Egyptians. The houses were lighted by **lamps** from the earliest times. It is probable that the ordinary lamp was made of stone or earthenware, and was round or shell-shaped and very shallow, with a projecting lip. Into this a small quantity of castor oil, or some other vegetable oil, was poured, and a few linen threads, laid in the oil, served as a wick. These threads were drawn out over the lip and lighted, and trimmed from time to time. Forty years ago many such lamps were to be seen in many parts of Egypt and in the Sūdān ; they gave very little light, it is true, but they made no smoke. The Egyptians must have used artificial light of some kind in painting the walls and ceilings of the tombs, but nowhere do we find any trace of blackening by lamp smoke, and the only light they can have had was that given by lamps. We may dismiss from consideration the statements that have been made to the effect that the Egyptians used electricity for lighting purposes, for they are wholly unsupported by any evidence. But it is possible, as Herodotus suggests (ii. 62), that the wicks of their lamps were placed in some earthy substance which was saturated with oil and served as a feeder of them. Judging by the appearance of the objects that have been found in graves of the Old Kingdom, and have been identified as lamps, early lamps had no projecting lip, and the wicks were placed in the centre. If this be so the shape of the lamp was that of a small bowl, and the oil-saturated material and the wick resembled the modern night-light. A **lamp-stand** that would accommodate several lamps was found in a Theban tomb, and we know from the inscription on a stele found at Jabal Barkal that a lamp-stand, ☥, was dedicated to the temple of Amen-Rā there. The lighted or burning lamp played an important part in some of the religious and magical ceremonies of the Egyptians, as may be seen from the Vignette of Chap. cxxxvii of the Book of the Dead. The Egyptian Christians, *i.e.* the Copts, made their lamps of bronze and earthenware, and some of them had as many as seven burners.

Egyptian Dress. A mere summary of the different kinds of articles of apparel worn by the Egyptians during the long period of their history would fill a good-sized volume, and in a little book like the present only a few of the most important of them can be mentioned. The primitive **waist-cord,** with its knot of magical significance, became a **belt** or girdle made of costly material, the **loin-cloth** made of linen became a tunic of elaborate form, and under the influence of the wealth, derived from conquered or raided nations, the Egyptians attained to a height of luxury in dress which it is hard to understand, and harder still to describe. It was not modesty or shamefacedness that drove them to multiply the size and number of their garments, but love of display and of personal adornment. The naked human body at no time troubled them. Boys and girls went about naked, the former even whilst they were at school. Men and women worked in the fields naked, servants of both sexes went about their work in the house and around naked, and women of the upper classes were not ashamed to leave their necks and breasts uncovered before the public gaze. The bas-reliefs and paintings of the New Kingdom show that about 1400 B.C. women loved to have their longest garments made of diaphanous materials, through which every part of their bodies could be seen. And noblemen sat at meat and took part in religious festivals with the upper half of their bodies and their legs bare. The **dress of the god** and the king had much in common. The god had on his head a sort of helmet-cap, above which was his characteristic symbol. He wore a tunic which reached from his breast to his knees, and was held in position by two bands or straps, one over each shoulder. Round his waist was a girdle, and from its centre at the back hung a long **tail** made to resemble that of an animal. His legs, from the knees downwards, and feet were bare. In one hand he held a sceptre, $\mathcal{l}$, and in the other $\frac{Q}{T}$, the symbol of " life." The **goddess** wore on her head her characteristic symbol, and usually a collar round her neck. Her body was covered by a garment woven in one piece, reaching from her breasts to a little above her ankles ; it was held in position by a band or strap over each shoulder. The top of this long garment was covered by a band, which was put on after the garment, and its position was immediately below her breasts. Her ankles and feet were bare. In some pictures the goddess wears bracelets or bangles and anklets.

The **king,** like the god, wore a loin-cloth, which was kept in its place by means of a band or belt and a strip of linen that passed between the legs ; sometimes this was supplemented by a kind of short tunic, the fold of which projected in front. From the back of the waistband or belt hung, in the earliest times, a jackal's tail, but at a later period an artificial tail took its place. Round his neck the king wore a collar, which was sometimes deep enough to cover the upper part of the breast, and on his head a helmet-cap (usually made of leather or linen), with two side flaps which fell one over each shoulder on to the breast. Under the New Kingdom shoulder-cloths and long garments like the cloaks worn by the Egyptians at the present time came into use. The **artisan classes** also wore loin-cloths and short tunics over them, and their forms and styles varied very little in the course of centuries. The peasant class wore very little clothing, and their dress, both for men and women, consisted of a single garment, even as it does in Egypt and the Sūdān to-day. The slave usually wore nothing. **Women,** including the queen, wore a single garment, which was held in position by a band tied under the breasts and which reached to the ankles. Both the upper and lower hems were ornamented with designs in needlework which were more or less elaborate. Originally women of all classes were content to wear garments made of homespun linen, which closely resembled the *damūr* linen seen in the Sūdān at the present day ; but as time went on weavers learned how to make the fine, diaphanous fabrics which are now generally called **byssus,** and these were commonly used in making the apparel of the queen and the princesses and the wives and daughters of rich men and high officials. The head-dress of the queen was usually made in the form of the Vulture-goddess Mut, *i.e.* the " Mother," because the queen was held to be the mother of the nation.

The linen garments of the rich were washed in the River Nile by professional **washermen,** and those of the poorer classes by the women of the household. The clothes were laid upon flat stones and well beaten with palm sticks, or even stones, and it seems that fine sand or earth was used in the process of cleansing instead of **soap.** In the Ptolemaïc Period, and probably earlier, the Egyptians used cakes of a kind of soap which was called ANTCHIR, This word is preserved in Coptic, and in the Homily of John, Archbishop of Constantinople, on Susanna, it is said that when she went into the garden to rest she sent her servants away to bring her ⲟⲩϩⲟⲥⲙⲙ ⲙⲛ̄ ⲟⲩⲁⲛⲭⲓⲣ, *i.e.* " soda and soap." (*See* Budge, *Coptic Homilies*, page 49 (text).) **Socks, stockings, handkerchiefs and boots** seem to have been unknown in Ancient Egypt, but many **sandals** have been found in the tombs. Their shape is shown by the hieroglyph for sandal, 𓋴. They were made chiefly of plaited papyrus, but examples in wood and leather are known. Most people, and certainly the lower classes, went about barefoot, and many must have suffered from the stings of scorpions in consequence. The sandal latchet was frequently made of leather. Kings and men of high rank numbered a sandal-bearer among their servants, and noblemen were proud to be royal sandal-bearers. Then, as now, the sandals were put off on entering a house or royal or sacred precincts. Closed sandals, *i.e.* shoes, became common in the Graeco-Roman Period, and were adopted by all who could afford to protect their feet. The Christian monks made sandals as well as mats and baskets, and added to the revenues of their monasteries by their sale. The fingers and toes of statues of gods and kings, when " dressed " for days of festival, were covered with finger-stalls, similar to the fingers of the modern **gloves.** Those that were placed on the fingers and toes of Thothmes III were made of massive gold, and the royal finger-nails and toe-nails were represented by thin nail-shaped plaques of lapis-lazuli. They reached to the second joints of the fingers, and were held in position by straps of gold, which were fastened to gold bands round the wrists and ankles.

The articles of **jewellery** and other decorative objects used as personal adornments were originally **amulets**.[1]   Among these may be mentioned **collars, necklaces** and **pectorals** formed of rows of **beads** made of semi-precious stones, gold, crystal, etc.   The earliest known beads were unpierced.   Under the XIIth Dynasty necklaces were made entirely of **scarabs** in amethyst, sard, carnelian, agate and lapis-lazuli ; at a later time the amulets 𓏤, 𓂭, 𓋹, 𓏲, and figures of the gods and flies and heads of Hathor, all in gold, were interspersed with the beads. **Armlets** and **bracelets** were worn by large numbers of women ;   the former were usually made of copper, and the latter of gold.   A few examples of bracelets or bangles made of flint and glazed Egyptian porcelain are known. **Anklets** closely resembled armlets in shape, and were made of copper or gold.   Small earrings made of gold inlaid with semi-precious stones were common in early days ; in the later periods of Egyptian history they were made very long. The most elaborate examples of them are found in graves of the first five centuries of the Christian Era.   The varieties of the **finger ring** are many. The greater number of them were made of gold wire of varying thickness, and the bezel was formed by an inscribed scarab or a plaque,

---

[1] The word " amulet " is derived from the Arabic ﺔَﻠَﻤْﺣ which means something that is worn or carried to protect a person against the attacks of evil spirits.   Compare " phylactery."

rectangular or oval, on which were carved figures of gods and goddesses or magical inscriptions. Some of the massive gold rings have bezels of cylindrical form, and some have elongated projections in the form of a cartouche with royal names written in it. The finger ring had a special importance in the Other World, and when a man was too poor to afford one in metal he provided himself with one made of plaited grass or straw.

The Egyptians of the upper classes paid great attention to their **personal appearance** and to the physical well-being of the body. In early times women, and sometimes men, cut or punctured designs of various kinds on certain parts of their body, with the idea that they would protect them against the attacks of evil spirits. In later times loyal officials had the name of the reigning king **tattooed** on their shoulders or breasts, and royal cartouches were often cut on the shoulders and breasts of the statues of officials, perhaps with the idea of placing them under the magical protection of the king. As a rule men shaved off their beards and side-whiskers, but not the **hair** of their head. Their **razors** were made of flint in early times, and in later of copper. The models of the elaborately plaited beard which we see attached to coffins represent the traditional form of the beard of the natives of Punt in the Northern Sūdān, to whom the primitive Egyptians were related. The purely native form of the beard is represented by the short, almost square, tuft of hair which is seen on the point of the chin in paintings of all classes of people of all periods. Figures of Osiris generally have the Puntite beard, a fact that suggests that it had a special ceremonial or religious character. Men wore **wigs** made of sheep's wool, and several paintings in the tombs show that they wore **false beards.** Some paintings suggest that the hair of some Egyptians curled naturally, but whether curly or straight the hair was cut comparatively short. Women dressed their hair in many different ways. Sometimes it fell naturally over the neck and shoulders, sometimes it was arranged in plaits of different lengths, and sometimes it was done up in a mass which was fastened by a band or fillet at the back of the head. In many cases the hair was divided into two parts, each of which fell down in front ; an ornamental fillet placed immediately above the forehead prevented it from falling over the face. At festivals and entertainments women wore lotus flowers in their hair, the blossoms projecting over their foreheads, and on the top of the head a cake or ball of scented unguent in a light framework was placed. This unguent melted by degrees and ran over the head and down into the hair, and besides producing a pleasant coolness in the head imparted to the hair itself a delightful aroma (*see* p. 73).

In figures and statues of the Old Kingdom the hair seems to have been "bobbed," and the appearance of the hair of some of those of the New Kingdom suggests that a mode of treating and dressing the hair closely resembling the "shingling" of the present day was known to the Egyptians. It is not certain whether

Egyptian women knew of or used **depilatories,** but judging by the prescriptions for the hair that are found in the Ebers Papyrus, they must have dyed their hair black when it was turning grey. To increase the thickness of the hair they used many kinds of perfumed oils and scented unguents composed of ingredients that were believed to possess magical properties. Women greatly hoped that they would have masses of hair on their heads in the Other World, and in order to make this certain their hair, under the New Kingdom, was cut off by their relatives and tied up in a bundle, which was placed under the feet of the mummy in its cartonnage case. **Hairpins** were made of wood or ivory, and were ornamented in various ways. The **combs** used for the hair were also made of wood or ivory, and several examples of the small-tooth comb are known. Of the combs that were placed in the hair as ornaments, the oldest known belong to the Late Neolithic Period; many fine examples of those used by Coptic women are to be seen in the British Museum.

The intense heat of the summer, and the bitter cold of the nights, and the blinding glare of the water which covered the land during the Inundation, produced ophthalmia and many other diseases of the eyes, which frequently destroyed the sight. At a very early period both men and women smeared their eyelids with specially prepared unguents, and laid over them powdered **antimony,** or stibium (which the Egyptians called 𓏭𓏤𓐍𓅓𓏥, *mestemt,* and

PLATE III.

A Theban feast.

The guests, male and female, are seated on chairs, with legs made in the form of the legs of lions, and are being served with food and drink by naked female servants. On the top of the wig of each guest we see the cone containing scented unguent, which melts and runs down over the head and body, bringing with it coolness and refreshment.

The inspection and counting of the king's cattle at Thebes. From a tomb wall-painting in the British Museum.

the Greeks στίμμι, and the Arabs كحل, or *kuhl*),
or a powder made from lead or copper or
practically any substance possessing astringent
properties. The unguent was applied by the
finger, but the powder was laid on the eyelids
by means of a short stick made of wood or bone
or ivory or stone, with a flattened end. The
Arabs call such a stick the " needle," إبرة, *ibrah*,
of the *kuhl* pot. **Eye-paint,** as we may term these
preparations, was kept in tubes made of alabaster,
Egyptian porcelain, wood, ivory, earthenware,
etc., and the tube and its needle were often
provided with a leather case. And the Egyptian
women soon discovered that smearing the eyelids
with unguent and stibium not only eased the pain
in the eyes and rested them, but also added to
the natural beauty of their faces. The whiteness
of the whites of the eyes was emphasized by
the darkened eyelids, and the large dark pupils
appeared like black pools in their midst, the
whole effect being very striking. The eyebrows
as well as the eyelids were frequently painted
with stibium, of which several preparations
were known, some wholly black and others
greenish in colour. Whether the custom of
painting the eyelids and eyebrows was indigenous
or of foreign origin is unknown, but there seems
to be little doubt that some kinds of eye-paint
were imported from the East. Under the XIIth
Dynasty a present of eye-paint was brought to
one of the nobles at Bani Hasan by the Åmu
people from Western Asia ; the scene is reproduced in the following illustration.

In the upper register we see the great Egyptian nomarch Khnemu-hetep II accompanied by his dogs and an attendant. The royal scribe Nefer-hetep, [hieroglyphs], presents to him a document on which is recorded the arrival of a company of the Āmu bringing eye-paint. Behind him is the official Khati, [hieroglyphs], and behind him is the

The Āmu bringing eye-paint to Khnemu-hetep II at Bani Hasan.

governor of the land, Absha, [hieroglyphs], who together with his men is bringing wild animals from the desert. The inscription above reads, " The coming to bring eye-paint ; thirty-seven Āmu brought it," [hieroglyphs]. In the lower register are seen the armed men of the company and their women, a boy, and the asses.

Climatic conditions have in all periods made it necessary for the Egyptians to anoint themselves with **oils** and **unguents** of various kinds, and the dead in the various mansions of heaven, as well as the living, found it necessary to make use of them. The oils were obtained from plants and trees, both native and foreign, and were supposed to possess magical as well as medicinal properties ; what kind of fat, or fats, was used in the preparation of salves and pomades is not known. Scented oils and salves were kept in vessels made of stone or alabaster (with closely fitting covers to prevent the escape of the perfume), hundreds of examples of which may be seen in every large museum. Sets of four, six or more, containing the choicest kinds of perfumed oils, were frequently arranged in specially constructed cases, as in Persia, India and other countries at the present day. Anointing the body usually followed bathing, and as the Egyptians attached the greatest importance to **personal cleanliness,** the daily use of oils and salves was general among women of the upper classes ; then as now it brought with it a feeling of physical well-being and restfulness. The hair was perfumed by pouring scented oil on the top of the head, especially during the festivals and other public rejoicings. Anointing with oil had also a ceremonial importance, and under the Old Kingdom the dead were anointed with the **Seven Holy Oils,** the names of which are duly set forth in the Liturgy of Funerary Offerings, and on the alabaster **anointing slabs,** examples of which may be seen in the British

Museum (Nos. 29, 421, 6124, 6125). Women also perfumed their bodies by **fumigation,** for they seated themselves over or near small piles of burning powder made of gums and aromatic substances. One of the principal ingredients was probably sandalwood powder, which is largely used in Egypt and the Sūdān at the present day.

In the matter of washing and anointing, cleanliness and godliness went hand in hand, and the feeling of physical well-being which resulted from them was enhanced by the consciousness that a religious obligation had been discharged. The use of the juice of the *hinna* plant for staining the nails of the hands and feet a reddish-yellow colour was common in Egypt, but whether it had any religious significance, or whether the plant possessed valuable medicinal properties, is not known. Painting the cheeks and staining the lips red was not unknown among Egyptian women, as one of the mummies found at Dêr al-Baharī proves. The breath was sweetened by holding in the mouth small pellets made of aromatic spices mixed with honey, and perhaps the famous *ānti* gum. The **toilet-box,** or dressing-case, of a lady contained tubes of stibium and salve for the eyelids, flasks of scented unguent, a " shell " in bronze or alabaster on which to mix unguents, a pair of sandals, a comb with two rows of teeth, small papyrus cushions, and a **mirror.** The mirror was made of a round or oval plate of fine copper, polished on each side, and was set in a handle of wood, ivory or copper. Some handles are in the form of a lotus column, and others in that of a naked woman, who is probably intended to represent Hathor, the goddess of beauty. Mirrors were kept in wooden or copper cases, but few examples of these have come down to us.

Speaking generally, the Egyptians lived upon the produce of their own country which, except in continuous years of famine, was amply sufficient for their needs. The **food** of the rich and well-to-do folk was more varied than that of the peasants and slaves, and then as now men ate and drank according to their means. The poorer classes had to be satisfied with bread and water and a few vegetables; meat and game and wine and rich pastry were only to be found commonly in the houses of the wealthy.

The most important article of food was **bread,** which was made into cakes and loaves of many shapes and sizes, e.g. ◯ , ◖ , ⬤ , ⬤ . Flour was obtained by crushing and rolling the grain with a stone roller on a slightly concave slab of stone; this grinding was done by the women of the house, who knelt on the ground to obtain the necessary purchase on the roller. When large quantities of flour were required mills with two grinding stones placed one above the other were used. The flour was mixed with water, and the resulting dough was twisted or cut into cakes or loaves, and baked either on heated stones or in ovens. In larger houses the bread-cakes were carried from the oven to the store-house in baskets, as at the present day. Cooks possessing the skill of the confectioner mixed honey with the dough and made dainty rolls and three-cornered cakes for festivals. Many families kept herds of **geese** of the large kind which we see depicted on the walls of tombs. They were roasted on braziers or baked in ovens made of Nile mud. The goose was one of the principal offerings made to the dead, and figures of it are cut upon the *hetep* offering-slabs, ⬚, and drawn on papyri. **Fish** was a common article of food, but, as we learn from the great stele of Piānkhi, the Nubians regarded the eaters of fish as unclean. The **flesh of cows and oxen** was eaten after boiling. The animal was bled to death, and then the head was cut off and the body dismembered. The slaughter of the bull and the presentation of its heart to the deceased form one of the most important ceremonies in the Liturgy of Opening the Mouth.

The **drink** of the community in general was **water** from the Nile, for even if it was drawn from wells, the source of their supply was the river. Water was brought from the Nile in skins (the modern *girbah*), and poured into large porous jars (the modern *zīr*), which stood in the courtyards of houses, presumably in some shady place, or perhaps in a specially roofed-in building. These large jars " sweated," *i.e.* the water oozed through their sides, and the water inside was cooled by the evaporation caused by the currents of air that blew through the courtyards. The texts prove conclusively that the Egyptians loved a " cool drink," ⬚, and more than one deceased person prays that he may drink water drawn from the deep middle part, ⬚, of the river. Nile water must always have had a large quantity of animal and vegetable matter in solution, and yet if drunk fresh it causes the drinker no inconvenience. Year by year the Atbarā brought down in its roaring flood an immense mass of red earth, vegetable refuse, carcases of animals, and sometimes human bodies, and people drank its water and were unharmed. Even to-day, provided the *zīrs* and *kullas* are kept clean, it is a wonderfully refreshing drink.

The Egyptians, like many other African peoples, drank **milk** in large quantities, but their favourite beverage was **beer,** 𓏲 , *heqt.*

The king and every man of substance had his own **brewery,** but the poor man had to buy his beer at the " house of beer," *i.e.* beer-shop, untold numbers of which must have existed throughout the country. Beer was made from almost any kind of grain. The grain was wetted and kept until it began to sprout, then they rubbed it down and made a paste of it, of which they fashioned large cakes. These were lightly baked and then broken up, and the pieces were put into pots which were filled with water. These were left for a day or two so that fermentation might take place, and then the liquid was strained and drunk whilst fresh. It had a slightly bitter, acid taste, probably like that of the beer made in the Sūdān to-day, but if kept for a day or two it became sour and undrinkable. The power of this beer to intoxicate was very great, if we may judge by the warnings against excess in drinking it that are given by the sages,[1] but it was drunk freely by young and old, and by men and women alike. Beer formed one of the most important offerings to the dead, and specially prepared kinds of it were presented to the deceased during the recital of the Liturgy of Opening the Mouth. Curiously enough, offerings of bread-cakes and beer were made to certain of the granite obelisks at Thebes, but this practice must have arisen

---

[1] Here is an example of such warnings from the *Precepts of Ani* :

Make not   thyself helpless   in drinking in the

beer shop.   For will not   the words   of [thy] report repeated

slip out from { thy mouth } without { thy knowing } { that thou hast uttered them ? }

Falling down   thy limbs   will be broken,   [and]

no one will   give thee { a hand [to help thee up] }   as for thy

companions in the   swilling of beer,   they   will get up

and say, " Outside with   this   drunkard."

through the persistence of the belief that the spirit of the Sun-god dwelt in them, for the obelisk was only an elongation of the shaft of the Sun Stone which was worshipped at Heliopolis under the Old Kingdom. The drinking of **wine** in Egypt is as old as dynastic civilization. The hieroglyph for the growing **vine** shows us a vine branch trained over stakes, 🌿, and the hieroglyph for **winepress**, 🍇, which illustrates the pressing out of the juice of grapes into a vessel, proves that the manufacture of wine dates from the earliest times.

The king and every large landed proprietor possessed a **vineyard** and stored the wine in large earthenware jars, the mouths of which were stopped with mud and sealed with seals bearing the name of the owner of the wine. Many districts, *e.g.* Aswān (Syene), Per-Uatchit, the Fayyūm and the country round about Lake Mareotis were famous for their wine, and that made in the Delta, which was a species of *vin ordinaire*, is often mentioned in the lists. Large quantities of wine were imported into Egypt from Libya and Palestine and Syria, and a portion of a wine-jar, inscribed with the words " Rhodian wine," found in the chamber of offerings of a pyramid at Marawi, proves that wine was also imported from the Greek Islands. In some cases the drinking of wine formed a kind of ceremonial function, and it is possible that in certain circumstances it possessed a religious significance. Vases of wine and censers filled with burning incense were offered as very special gifts to the gods at all periods of Egyptian history.   Specimens of the wine-cups used under the New Kingdom are exhibited in the British Museum (Nos. 24680, 26226, 4801). Besides the ordinary beer the Egyptians drank a special kind which was sweetened with honey and resembled **mead.**

CHAPTER III

PHARAOH, King of all Egypt, was, as this title signifies, the "Great House," ⬚, *Per-ā*, in which all his people lived and sought asylum ; with far less reason the Sultān of Turkey also called himself "Bāb al-'Ali," or "the Exalted Gate," which is commonly rendered "Sublime Porte." In prehistoric times each large district of Egypt had its own ruler, and the country was divided into a series of what were practically small kingdoms. In the Late Neolithic Period there was one great king in Upper Egypt and another in Lower Egypt, *i.e.* the Delta, and these two great divisions of the country were known throughout the later Dynastic Period as the "Two Lands," ⬚, Upper Egypt seems to have been divided into two parts, and the capital of the southern half was **Hensu,** which Hebrew writers, *e.g.* Isaiah (xxx. 4), called **Khānēs**, and the Greeks

knew as **Herakleopolis.** At the end of the Neolithic Period war broke out between the kings
of Upper and Lower Egypt, and the king of the
South conquered the king of the North, and so
became the Unifier of the Two Lands and King
of all Egypt. The conquest of Lower Egypt
was probably not effected by one king, and it is
not quite certain which king really earned the
title of " Unifier of the Two Lands," though
on the whole the credit of the subjugation of the
North by the South must be given to **Nārmer,**
who was a mighty warrior and a great conqueror.
Manetho, in his King List, makes **Mēnes** to be the
first king of Egypt, and as this name no doubt

represents the Egyptian **Menà,**   , or Men,   ,

which was also one of the titles of Āha, the
successor of Nārmer, we may assume that the final
unification of Egypt was effected by him. The
power of the king of Egypt at that time was
absolute, and right of conquest made him the
owner of the whole country and the master of
every living being in it, and the religious directors
of the people were his servants. But sooner or
later every king of Egypt has found it expedient
to be on good terms with the ancient priesthoods
of the country, and the early dynastic kings
obtained the support of the priesthood of
Nekhen in Upper Egypt and of the priesthood
of Per-Uatchit in the Delta ; in the former city
the deity worshipped was Nekhebit, the Vulture-

goddess,   , and in the latter the Uraeus-

goddess Uatchit,   . But the king was the

lineal descendant of a god who had reigned upon earth, and was, therefore, a god, even though he possessed a body of flesh ; he was not only the god of his people, but he could present their offerings, together with his own, to himself. The king's will was the god's will, his actions were the outcome of the god's thoughts, and in looking upon the king's person the people looked upon the god. He was worshipped as a god, the " great god," ⌐ ⌐, *neter ā*, the " beneficent god," ⌐ ⌐, *neter nefer*, and even as " lord, maker of things," ⌐ ⌐ ⌐, *neb ari akht.* As man he built a temple to himself as a god, and he worshipped himself in it ; for Amenhetep III built the temple at Sulb in his own honour, and worshipped himself in it, and he built another to his wife Tī as a goddess, and worshipped her as such in it.

The king claimed as his ancestor the god **Her,** or Horus, whose symbol was the hawk, ⌐ , which was in early times regarded as the personification of the spirit of the highest heaven, his right eye, ⌐ , being the sun and his left eye, ⌐ , the moon. His solar character is indicated by the disk on his head, ⌐ . As the son and descendant of Horus the king adopted a **Horus name,** or title, which was written on a rectangular object represented thus ⌐ ; as the king approved by the ancient " mother-goddesses " Nekhebit and Uatchit he assumed a **Nebti** name, or title, , and as the " Horus of gold," , he added a third name to his titulary.   As " Lord of the Two Lands," or perhaps as the Unifier of Upper

Horus, in human form, and wearing the double crown, sailing up the Nile during his conquest of Egypt. He has driven his harpoon into the hippopotamus, the symbol of revolt, rebellion and evil, which is fettered by chains held by Horus, and by Isis, who kneels in the bows of the boat.

and Lower Egypt, he took, at a later time, a fourth title, *i.e.* the **Nesubat** name,  ; in this double character the reed, , is the symbol of his sovereignty over the South, and the bee,

or hornet, 🐝, of his rule over the North.   The
unity of the Two Lands is graphically depicted
in the hieroglyph 🪷, which represents the lotus
of the Delta and the papyrus of Upper Egypt
twined round the symbol of union, and we see it
cut on the sides of the royal throne.   But as a
matter of fact the separate existence of the South
and the North was always recognized.   As lord of
the South the king wore the White Crown, ⚕,
and as king of the North the Red Crown, ♘,
and each is clearly distinguishable in the double
crown, ♙ .

For some time, probably for many centuries,
the king was worshipped as the son of Horus
the Sun-god, but during the rule of the great
kings who built the Pyramids of Gîzah, the
priesthood of An or Anu, the **On** of the Bible
(Gen. xli. 45), succeeded in gaining great power
in the North, and their god **Rā,** a form of the
Sun-god, attained a predominant position among
the gods of Egypt.   The city of On, or Heliopolis,
"the city of the Sun," was founded in very early
times, and it was a large and important town
long before the unification of Upper and Lower
Egypt by Nārmer or Āha.   It was the terminus
of many caravan routes from the east, north,
west and south, and was the greatest centre of
trade and commerce in the north of Egypt.
Men of many nationalities and religions met and
transacted business there, and as a result the

priesthood of On became a very wealthy and
powerful body.   By way of On foreign influences
of all kinds came into Egypt, and the peculiar
form of the worship of the Sun-god that obtained
there seems to have been introduced from some
country in the east coming through Syria and
Palestine.   The priesthood of Rā watched their
opportunity and, having succeeded in dis-
posing of the last kings of the IVth Dynasty,
they were able to set on the throne in succession three of the sons of a woman called
Ruttet, the wife of a priest of Rā of
Sakhabu.   These children were declared to
be the sons of Rā who, in human form, had
companied with her.   The same story is told
about Queen Hatshepsut and Amenhetep III,
who were held to have been begotten by Amen-
Rā, and according to the narrative of the Pseudo-
Callisthenes (Book i. Chap. 8), Alexander the
Great was the son of Amen (Ammon), who took
the form of Nectanebus, the last king of Egypt,
and begot him by Queen Olympias.   The bas-
reliefs illustrating the conception and birth of
Amenhetep III are found in his temple at Luxor,
and those that concern Queen Hatshepsut in her
temple at Dēr al-Baharī.   The priests of Rā,
having placed their nominees on the throne, determined to make an addition to the royal titulary,
and a fifth name or title was added to it describing
the king as the " son of Rā," ⟨hieroglyph⟩, *sa Rā*. From
that time onwards every king of Egypt called
himself the " son of Rā," and the Nubians,
Persians, Ptolemies and Romans who reigned
over Egypt adopted it without scruple.   In

PLATE IV.

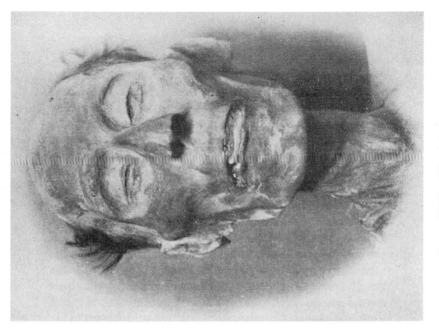

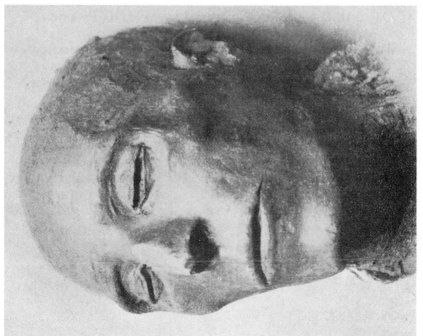

Seti I, King of Egypt, about 1320 B.C.　　Rameses II, King of Egypt, about 1300 B.C.

Photographed from their mummies in the Egyptian Museum, Cairo, by the late Signor Beato, of Luxor.

many cases this name was the personal name of
the king, or an abbreviation of it.   Both fourth
and fifth names of the king were written within

ovals, ⬭, and on many bas-reliefs the oval is

represented as being formed of a rope, of which
the two ends are knotted together.   This oval, or
cartouche, as it is commonly called, was intended
to protect the king's name from evil influences,
for to injure the king's name was to injure the
king himself.   The double knot was believed
to be an amulet of great power.

Of the ceremonies that were performed in the
earliest times when a new king ascended the
throne we know nothing, but the news of his
accession was quickly promulgated.   Under the
New Kingdom four birds were released and sent
each into one of the quarters of the world to
inform all and sundry that a new king occupied
the throne.   The court scribes drew up his
titulary, and despatched copies of it throughout
the country, and the king himself made a royal
progress to all the ancient shrines, and assured
the various priesthoods that he would respect
their privileges and increase them.   In the
first or second year of his reign he set out to
raid some country (in the earlier times the
countries were Sinai and the Northern Sūdān,
in the later Palestine, Syria and Mesopotamia),
in order to show the nations around that he was
a mighty warrior as well as a god.   He fought in
person, and the custom of the country demanded
that he should slay a number of prisoners with
his own hand ; representatives of the vanquished

peoples or tribes were made to kneel before him with their arms tied together at the elbows behind their backs, 𓀒, and the king smashed in their skulls with a stone-headed or metal-headed mace, 𓌂, or cut off their heads with a scimitar, 𓌳. Usually the king was the eldest son of his predecessor by the "king's woman," 𓇓𓏏, or **Queen,** who was sometimes his sister, but many of the kings of Egypt were not of royal birth. In early times it was thought that when the king died he departed to a heaven that was inhabited by the gods alone. The Sun-god welcomed him as his son and equal, and he reigned over the "gods" as autocratically and as absolutely as he had reigned over men upon earth, and hunted at will in the fields of the skies. He forced the "gods" to transfer their power and immortality to him, and he reigned in heaven for ever and ever.

In early times the king lived with his queen and family in a mud-brick house, like his subjects, and his household was very numerous. Though in theory he directed the affairs of the kingdom, and attended personally to every detail of the administration of the laws, etc., in practice the government of the country was in the hands of an official called **That,** 𓍿𓏏, who was the equivalent of the **Wazīr** in modern Oriental Courts. Next to him in importance came the **Keeper of the Seal,** 𓊖. The **seal** itself was a small cylinder made of wood or stone on which were cut the

royal names and titles; it was perforated
lengthwise and was carried on a string, and was
worn on the person of the Keeper of the Seal.
The cylinder was rolled over the soft sealing
material used (mud?), leaving on it a copy of
the inscription in hieroglyphs in high relief.
Several wooden cylinder-seals which were made
and used in the Late Neolithic Period have been
found, and it is doubtful if the use of the cylinder-
seal was introduced into Egypt from Lower
Babylonia, as has been stated.   The cylinder-
seal was superseded by a flat, rectangular stone
seal, and later by the signet ring.   The Wazīr
and the Keeper of the Seal had a staff of **scribes**
and other officials to assist them, and the overseers
of the royal estates and cattle and granaries,
etc., were very numerous.   Certain of the officials
at court were kinsmen of the king and queen,
and these bore the honorific title of **Rekh Nesu,**

, but the king sometimes conferred this title
on a friend who was no relative at all.   Another
title of honour was **Smer,** , or **Smer uāt**

, *i.e.* " Friend " and " Only Friend."

The king's personal attendants were very
numerous, and among them may be mentioned
the bearer of the royal stool or chair, the
sandal-bearer, the fan-bearer, the men of the
bodyguards—each of whom was responsible for
the safety of the royal person—the keeper
of his apparel, the steward of the palace,
the keeper of the king's private chambers,
the butler, the baker, the treasurer, the captain

of the royal barge, the keepers of hunting and fishing equipment, the architect. The **queen's household** was also numerous, and included nurses and tutors for the princes and princesses, keepers of the apartments, keepers of the wardrobe, etc. One of the most valued honours that the king could bestow upon a meritorious official or friend was the gift of a tomb and permission to be buried near the royal tomb. As kings and rulers have done from time immemorial in many parts of Africa, the king of Egypt sent a funerary offering when one of his officials or friends was buried. This offering was not only a proof of his regard for the deceased, but it indicated that he would extend his divine protection to him in the Other World ; in other words, the deceased entered the Other World under royal auspices. When heaven was democratized and the king was believed to share it with the humblest of his subjects, it was generally assumed that he sent a funerary offering at the burial of every one of them. The result of this was that on tombs, sarcophagi, coffins, stelae, etc., the signs ⭰⋀⭤ were prefixed to every inscription in which the deceased prays to the gods and goddesses of the dead for meat and drink for his KA, or personification of his spiritual individuality. The hieroglyphs mean "the king (⭰) gives (⋀) an offering (⭤)," or perhaps a tablet of offerings, and they are found on funerary monuments of the latest period.

The great Babylonian king Khammurabi divided his subjects into three classes, viz., the aristocracy or nobility, the class below, which probably included what we should call the middle and artisan classes, and the slave class. The Egyptian inscriptions make no mention of any such division of the population into classes, but three classes of beings are mentioned which may at one time have represented classes of the people, viz., the HENMEMET, , the REKHIT, , and the APERU, , the first being the gentry, the second the intelligent, instructed class, and the third the peasant labourers and slaves.

In Egypt the hereditary landed proprietors formed a sort of feudal aristocracy, and their power was very great; many of them held high offices under the king as priests and governors of nomes and heads of the departments of the state. The **nomarch** was obliged to have an armed force under his command in order to keep order in his district, and had to equip and supply troops, both for land and river service, when the king ordered a raid to be made. Such high officials sat as chief judges in the Law Courts, and drew up and enforced laws, and assessed and collected the king's taxes. The nomarch was directly responsible to the king for the well-being of the people in his nome, and his authority was well-nigh absolute. Egyptian history shows that the old feudal nobles in places like Nekheb (Hierakonpolis) and Sun (Syene, or Aswān) were practically kings in their districts. It was through Mekhu, Sabben, Herkhuf and other nobles of Sun (Syene) that the Egyptians of the VIth Dynasty made their way into the Sūdān and laid the foundation of their future conquest of that country. The nobles of Nekheb protected the southern frontier of Egypt for some centuries, and two of them, called Aāhmes and Aāhmes-pen-Nekheb, contributed largely to the success of Egyptian arms in Western Asia under the XVIIIth Dynasty. Frequently the interests of the great feudal lords and those of the king clashed, and the officials of the king found it very difficult to perform their duties. The power of the king began to diminish towards the close of the VIth Dynasty, and that of the nobles increased steadily until Amenemhat III, a king of the XIIth Dynasty, forced them to recognize his authority and to obey his laws. But whenever for any reason the central power was weak or lacking in the country, every lord proceeded to do what was right in his own eyes. Robbery and oppression became the order of the day, and the lower classes suffered greatly.

Though there are many examples of men of humble birth attaining high position, either through their great personal abilities, or through marriage with well-born or wealthy women, it is tolerably certain that, speaking generally, sharp dividing lines existed between the classes. The nobleman taught his son to rule and manage the family estates so that he might succeed him ; the handicraftsman taught his son to follow his trade, and the priestly classes and the scribes were the most exclusive of all. The man who was born a **slave** lived and died a slave, and left no memorial of himself behind ; if he was given a wife, or if he took one and had children, they were the property of his master. The Egyptians were a humane people, and it is quite possible that the lot of the slave was not as miserable as has been generally supposed. The inscriptions give us no detailed information on this subject, but, on the whole, I believe that the condition of the slave, in the first half of the XIXth century, under Muhammad 'Alī and his sons, was substantially what it has ever been since the beginning of the Dynastic Period, six thousand years ago. There have always been kind masters and cruel masters, and there must always have been very much worse conditions of life than those under which the slaves of Khnemuhetep lived at Menāt-Khufu under the XIIth Dynasty.

The Egyptian **Soldier.** The history of Egypt shows clearly that the Egyptians as a nation were wholly lacking in military spirit, and that they abhorred war. Whenever it was necessary to do so they were ready to fight in a primitive fashion for their fields and canals and homes, but for the defence of their country as a whole they were by nature and temperament unfitted ; they had no national spirit, at all events under the Old and Middle Kingdoms. And even under the New Kingdom the principal object of all their raids and so-called " wars " was the acquisition of spoil and prisoners, whom they could use as slaves. Though that portion of the Nile Valley which is Egypt, and is 600 miles long, lay open on both sides of the Nile to the attacks of the warlike peoples of the deserts, and invasion from the north and south was always easy for a determined foe, Egypt never possessed anything that could be called an "Army" until the beginning of the New Kingdom. The expulsion of the Hyksos by Aāhmes I, and the successful raids in Western Asia and the Sūdān, and the loot that they obtained, turned the Egyptians into fighters at intervals between 1500 B.C. and 1100 B.C. But after the serious check which Rameses II received from the Hittites, native military ardour evaporated, and with the rise to power of the XXIInd Dynasty the period of domination by the Libyans, Ethiopians (Nubians), Assyrians, Persians and Macedonians began.

Seneferu, having conquered Sinai for the sake of its copper mines, raided the Sūdān for the sake of the gold in its mines and rivers, and brought back 7,000 men (slaves), and 200,000 oxen and goats. The reputation of the fighting powers of the Sūdānī man induced the official Una, ⌇ 〰, who was deputed by Pepi Merenrā to fight against the Asiatics of the Eastern Desert, to "stiffen" his troops with various tribes of the Blacks, 〰 ⌇⌇⌇⌇, *Nehesu.* But Una's "army" was a mixed mob of Blacks and Egyptians, for they robbed the wayfarer of his sandals and food, they ate up the food in every village they passed through, they cut down the fig trees, destroyed the vines, slew the people

Rameses II, in full panoply of war, charging the Hittite forces and their allies at the Battle of Kadesh, and cutting his way through the chariots of the enemy, by which he was surrounded.

who resisted, took prisoner the remainder, and having laid waste the enemy's country returned laden with spoil to Egypt, and were welcomed with cries of joy.   The object of every Egyptian " war," or raid, was loot or, as it was euphemistically called, " tribute."   Great kings like Usertsen (Sen-Usrit) III and Thothmes III established their officers in various towns in the Sūdān and Western Asia, not to teach the natives the secrets of Egyptian civilization, but to collect the tribute and to send it to Egypt annually in order to save their royal masters the trouble of going to fetch it.   The king, every great temple, each governor of a nome, and every feudal noble maintained an armed force to protect their interests, but order was maintained chiefly by the Matchaiu, , who were imported from Nubia.   Under the New Kingdom **mercenaries** were predominant in the army, and Rameses II and Rameses III hired Libyans and other foreigners from the islands of the Mediterranean and the sea-coast to fight their battles. At a later period Greeks, Carians and others, from a military point of view, were masters of Egypt.

The **weapons** of the pre-dynastic Egyptian soldier were :—(1) A stout **cudgel** like that used by watchmen in Egypt to-day ; (2) a **mace** or **club,** ⸢ or ⸤, consisting of a short stick with a lump of bitumen on the top or a perforated stone (later copper) head ; (3) a **spear** made of wood, with a slice of flint fastened to one end ; **(4) bow and arrows,** the latter made of reeds tipped with flints ; (5) a large flint **knife** or **dagger** ; (6) a **battle-axe** formed by tying a slab of stone or flint to a short stout wooden handle or by fixing it in a cleft in the handle, ⊤ .

Sometimes the axe was double-headed, ⊨⊨, the stones being tied to the handle with leather thongs. The stone head had various shapes, *e.g.* ◯, ▢, ◰ ; the holes in the last received the leather thongs which tied it to the handle. Other shapes of axe-heads were ▽ and ⬯ ; each of these was perforated to receive the handle ; (7, 8) a **curved stick**, ⟩, similar to that carried by peoples of the Eastern desert to-day, and a short **pike**, ⟨. The soldier wore a very short tunic with a belt above it, and from this a tail, real or artificial, hung down behind. In his thick hair were one or two feathers of the red parrot (now no longer found in Egypt), and the **standard** under which he fought had for its head the figure of the hawk of Horus, ⬥. The primitive battle-axe with a stone head, ⌐, was probably the original of the hieroglyph which, at a later period, was the sign for "god," ⌐ ; here we have, it seems, a reminiscence of the cult of stones. Under the Middle Kingdom, if not earlier, the soldier defended himself with a **shield**, ⬥, which was made of wood or wicker-work covered with hide and sometimes strengthened with a metal rim and bolts. It was held in the left hand when the soldier was fighting, and on the march he carried it on his back ; it varied in shape, ⚈ or ⚆, and sometimes had a boss. The front was often decorated with tribal marks, etc. The form of the primitive **bow** was ⌐══⌐, from which are derived the later hieroglyphs ⌒⌒⌐ and ⌐══ ; it was held in the left hand, 𓃀 . The arrows were tipped with metal heads and winged with five feathers, ⟵ . The **quiver** was usually carried on the back. The head was covered with a cloth cap, ornamented sometimes with feathers, as the hieroglyphs show, and in later times the king wore a helmet, ⟨⟩, made of leather and metal. The **sling** (or catapult), 𓏲𓄿𓏏𓂋 , *khaā*, was made of leather, and pebbles for it were carried in a little bag suspended from the belt. The **boomerang** was as useful to the soldier as to the fowler. Under the New Kingdom many varieties of the bronze **dagger** and **knife** were used ; they were from 7 to 10 inches in length and were often set in beautifully decorated and inlaid handles. The **battle-axe** had a bronze head and a comparatively short, curved handle, ⌐𓌪 , but other forms were used, *e.g.* 𓌂 and 𓌃═ or ⌐══ . The later kings often used a sort of

scimitar, ⌷⌷ ⟿, *khepesh,* in battle, and a

club or mace, ❘, like their pre-dynastic ancestors.
The **cuirass,** only found under the New Kingdom,
was made of several rows of shield-shaped metal
plates fastened by bronze pins   The use of
horses and **chariots,** ⟼, in war was
borrowed from the Hyksos, Hittites and other
peoples of Northern Syria.   The horse was introduced into Babylonia by the Kassites, and after
the invasion of their country by the Hyksos the
Egyptians quickly realized its importance when
swiftness of attack and mobility were required.

Many men who were eligible for service in the
army were enrolled by the military scribe,
🝔 🝔 🝔❘, of the district, a man of great
power and authority.   The recruits were called
" Neferu," ❘ 🝔 🝔 🝔 🝔, as opposed to the
veterans, ❘ 🝔 🝔 ⟍ ❘❘ 🝔 🝔❘, and until about
1500 B.C. the army consisted of foot-soldiers
entirely.   Under the XVIIIth Dynasty there was
an army of Upper Egypt and an army of Lower
Egypt, and these presumably were the originals
of the Kalasirians and Hermotybians mentioned
by Herodotus (iv. 116).   These were subdivided
into battalions, 🝔❘ , *sa,* each of which had a
special title : thus there was the "*Sa* of Pharaoh,"
the "*Sa* of Amen," and so on.   The **officers** were
usually friends of the king, or noblemen, and

their nominees, and their military and other titles were many. Soldiers seem to have been classified according to their duties as combatants or non-combatants ; among the former were the spearmen, the bowmen, 𓀔𓃀, the men with spears and shields, and the **cavalry**, 𓊪𓈖𓎢𓏏𓀔, *tent hetra*. The Nubians

The Night Boat of the Sun-god on the great river of the Tuat, or Underworld. The god stands under a canopy formed by the body of the serpent Mehen, ⌒✕. At the bows is the beetle of Khepa, 𓆣, or Khepera, and behind him are Up-uatu, Saa, and the Lady of the Boat. Behind the god are Hekan and four gods who form the crew that paddle the boat along. From the Book of Gates.

loved and admired the horse and made fine cavalrymen ; in many of the tombs of the Nubian kings at Nuri the skeletons of horses have been found, showing that these fine warriors wished to have their horses with them in the Other World.

The Egyptian **Sailor**. The Nile being the great highway of Egypt, the Egyptians were from the earliest times compelled to be builders of boats, barges, lighters, war-boats, ferries, etc., and to be skilled watermen. The gods were supposed to sail over the sky in **boats,** and even the Sun-god Rā had his Morning Boat and Evening Boat. Gods and kings alike made their progress through the country in boats, and the nomarch and the nobleman maintained their private ferry-boat and probably also a house-boat of the type of the modern *dhahabīyah.* The current in the Nile carried boats down the river, but to ascend it a sail, ⬚, was necessary.

For the transport of granite from Aswān and stone from the other quarries in Upper Egypt large **rafts** were used, or specially broad **lighters.** **War-boats** carried a crew of about 20 men and a number of armed guards. Seneferu brought large quantities of cedar-wood from Lebanon in sea-going boats, but whether he built them or hired them from the merchants of Kepuna (Byblos) or from the Keftiu (Phoenicians) is not certain. Several kings maintained a fleet in the Mediterranean and a fleet in the Red Sea to bring copper from Sinai and to protect merchant craft. The Mediterranean Fleet of Rameses III co-operated with his land forces and enabled him to win a great victory. The early Egyptians made their river **boats of papyrus,** and worked them with paddles or with steering poles ; they were so constructed that when used as punts the bows could be easily thrust up over the river bank, ⬚. The goddess Isis sailed unharmed over the lakes in the Delta in a papyrus boat, and a belief existed that crocodiles would not attack anyone in a boat made of papyrus. A very early form of boat was made by tying two large bundles of reeds together side by side, and the passenger sat between them and worked a sort of paddle. This kind of boat was called ⟨hieroglyphs⟩, *sekhnui*, and is in use to-day in Nubia under the name of *tōf*; Mr. J. W. Crowfoot and I each crossed the Nile at Samnah on a *tōf* in 1906. River boats of all periods were shallow and broad in the beam. The crews were described generally as " men of the sail," ⟨hieroglyphs⟩, or " men of the steering pole," ⟨hieroglyphs⟩; the sailors in royal service were called ⟨hieroglyphs⟩, *āperu*. The **pilot** or look-out man, ⟨hieroglyphs⟩, sat in the bows, and the **steersman,** ⟨hieroglyphs⟩, *ari hemit,* stood in the stern. The texts show that boat accidents were common on the Nile and that many sailors suffered shipwreck, especially in the Cataracts, where submerged rocks were numerous. When the north wind failed and the boat began to float down-stream, the crew were obliged to disembark and, forming a line along the river bank, to **tow** their boat up the river, a laborious and exhausting task. The divine sailors in the boat of Rā were sometimes obliged to tow the boat of their lord in this fashion. The fare of the ferry-man was called ⟨hieroglyphs⟩, *hamu.*

CHAPTER IV

THE prosperity and wealth of Egypt have always depended upon its **agriculture,** and all the business of the country was arranged in accordance with its demands. But agriculture in Egypt depended in turn upon the water supply, and the water supply was derived from the **Nile** and the annual **Inundation,** for there was no rainfall worth consideration, and there were no fresh-water wells in the country, except those that were formed by the infiltration of the waters of the Nile. The Nile carried down from the highlands in the Sūdān the mud which formed the soil of Egypt, which is, as the ancient writers correctly said, "the gift of the Nile." And the Nile is to-day, what it has ever been, the giver of food and life to every living thing in Egypt. This being so, a few facts about this wonderful river may here be given. The Egyptians called it **Hāpī,** 𒀭 x, from first to last, but the meaning of this name is unknown ;

it must have had a meaning, but it was forgotten at a very early period.   The primitive Egyptians knew nothing about the source, or rather sources, of the river.   Their later descendants wrongly assumed that it was connected with the great celestial ocean, or the sea that surrounds the whole world, and that its springs were under two great rocks near the Island of Philae, at the head of the First Cataract.

As Egypt was divided into two parts, Taui, ⚏, *i.e.* "Two Lands," or the South and the

North, so the river was regarded as consisting of two parts, the Nile of the South and the Nile of the North; the former was supposed to begin at the Rock of Senmit near Philae, and the latter at Heliopolis. Under the Vth Dynasty the Nile was believed to come from Kenset, or Nubia. The **god of the Nile** was called Hāpī,

Hāpi, the Nile-god of the North, in the form of a man with the breasts of a woman ; he has a cluster of lotus plants on his head. The frog was a symbol of fertility and new birth and, with the Christian Egyptians, of the Resurrection.

, like the river, and he was always represented in the form of a man with the breasts of a woman, which indicated the god's powers of fertility and nourishment.   In a fine hymn to the Nile (British Museum, Sallier

Papyrus II, No. 10182), which was probably
sung at the festival of the Inundation, the
people say, "Thou waterest the fields which
Rā created, thou givest life unto the flocks
and herds, all the land drinks thee when thou
descendest in rain from heaven. Thou art
beloved of the Earth-god Geb, thou strengthen-
est the Grain-god Nepra, thou makest prosperous
every workshop of Ptah. . . When thou comest
the whole land rejoices. Thou art the bringer
of food, thou art the mighty one of meat and
drink, thou art the creator of all good things.
Thou fillest the storehouses, thou heapest high
with corn the granaries, and thou hast care
for the poor and needy." A little further on
the hymn says that the Nile-god cannot be
sculptured in stone, he cannot be brought forth
from his secret place, for his place is unknown.
He is not to be found in the sanctuaries—there
is no habitation large enough to hold him—
and the mind cannot conceive what his form
is like. The name he bears in the Tuat is
unknown ; he does not make visible his form, and
to attempt to imagine what he is like is futile.

The principal sources of the Nile are the
three great Equatorial Lakes, which are filled by
the heavy rains that fall between February and
November, namely, **Lake Victoria,** 1,130 metres
above sea-level, with an area of 70,000 sq.
kilometres, **Lake Albert,** 630 metres above
sea-level, with an area of 4,500 sq. kilometres,
and **Lake Edward,** with an area of 4,000 sq.
kilometres. Its tributaries are the Gazelle River,
which flows into it at Lake Nō (west bank),

and the Sobat River, Blue Nile and Atbarā
(right bank); north of the Atbarā the Nile
has no other tributary. The length of the
Nile is 3,473 miles, but if we add the length of
the Kagera (375 miles), which flows into Lake
Victoria, and the length of the Lake itself (250
miles), as many writers do, the total becomes
4,098 miles. The Egyptians did not know the
cause of the **Inundation,** and thought that it
was due to the *swelling* of the river, which was the
result of the falling of a tear of the goddess Isis
into it on a certain night called the " Night
of the Tear-drop," 𓂋𓏤 𓈖𓈖𓈖 𓊪 𓂝 𓏥 𓇋𓇋 𓈗 𓁷.
The Muslims preserved this tradition and kept
their great Nile-festival on the night of the
11th of Paoni, *i.e.* June 17, which they called
" Lēlat al-Nuktah " ("Night of the Drop").
But the true cause of the Inundation is the
heavy rains that fall in the Sūdān and Abyssinia.
The river begins to rise about the middle of
June, when the " green water " appears. The
Blue Nile is in flood at the end of August, and
the Atbarā about the same time. As the result
of the floods of these rivers the Nile continues
to rise in Egypt until the middle of September,
and it attains its highest level in October. It
then begins to subside, but rises yet once more,
then it sinks steadily until the month of June,
when it is again at its lowest level. There are six
Cataracts on the Nile : the Sixth is at Shablūkah,
the Fifth about 30 miles north of the Atbarā, the
Fourth extends from Abu Hamad to Kassingar,
the Third and Second lie between Karmah and

Wādī Halfah, and the First extends from Philae to Aswān. The Seven Mouths of the Nile were called by classical writers the Pelusiac, Tanitic, Mendesian, Phatnitic, Sebennytic, Bolbitic and Canopic. The ancient Nile-gauges, or **Nilo-meters,** cut on the rocks at Samnah under the XIIth Dynasty, show that the floods recorded there were 26 feet higher than any flood of to-day.

The importance of agriculture in Egypt is well illustrated by the oldest **Calendar** used in the country. According to this the year was divided into **three periods,** each of four months, which were called Akhet, Pert and Shemut, and these contained the months of July–October, November–February, and March–June respectively. November–February was the **winter** season, and March–June the **summer** season ; during the period of the Inundation agricultural work came practically to a standstill. During the early months of the Inundation the whole population of Egypt watched anxiously the rising river until it reached its maximum, for on the height of the Inundation the prosperity of the country depended. A " low Nile " meant that the waters would not rise high enough to water all the cultivated land in the country ; crops would be short or light, bread would be dear, and many people would suffer hunger. With a " good Nile " the watering of all the country was possible, and everyone was content ; an abnormally " high Nile " was followed by flooding, and the seed was washed out of the ground and man and beast suffered. A succession of " low Niles " always produced **famine,** misery and ruin to rich and poor alike. An inscription on a rock on the Island of Sāhal in the First Cataract tells of a **seven years' famine** which took place in the reign of Tcheser, a king of the IIIrd Dynasty. " Grain," says the king in his dispatch to Matar, governor of Elephantine, " is very scarce, vegetables are lacking altogether, everything that men eat for food has come to an end, and now every man attacks his neighbour. The men who want to walk cannot move, the child wails, the young man drags his body about, and the hearts of the older men are crushed with despair. Their legs give way under them, they sink down on the ground, and they clutch their bodies with their hands [in pain]. The nobles have no counsel to give, and there is nothing to be obtained from the storehouses but wind. Everything is in a state of ruin." The Book of Genesis mentions another seven years' famine, and the Arab historians mention several famines of like duration in Egypt. The famine of 1066–1072 nearly ruined the country. A loaf sold for 15 dīnārs (£7 10s.) and an egg for 1 dīnār (10s.). When all the animals were eaten men began to eat each other, and human flesh was sold in public. Passengers were caught in the streets by hooks let down from the windows, drawn up, killed and cooked. During the famine in 1201 people ate human flesh habitually. Parents killed and ate their children, and a wife was found eating her husband raw. The graves were ransacked for food (Lane Poole, *Middle Ages*, pp. 146, 216). We have no record of the rise of the Nile flood which, in ancient times, was necessary for the well-being of the whole country, but to-day, if the rise be between 25 feet and $26\frac{1}{2}$ feet, the whole country can be watered.   The **Nilometer** is a pillar or slab, standing in a sort of well, on which is cut a scale divided into cubits (the cubit = $21\frac{1}{3}$ inches) and *kīrāts* (the *kīrāt* = $\frac{1}{24}$th part of a cubit).   There was a very old Nilometer at Memphis, and Strabo and Plutarch mention another famous Nile-gauge at Elephantine.

We may now briefly consider what steps the Egyptians took in order to obtain the greatest benefit from the Nile flood.   Long before it arrived every town and village contributed its number of men to clear out the main and subsidiary canals, and to heap up dykes, which would serve not only to confine the waters within safe bounds, but would also serve as highways during the Inundation on which men and beasts could travel from place to place. In many places the banks of the Nile had to be strengthened, and embankments thrown up, and in certain parts of Upper Egypt, where the distance between the river and the mountains was considerable, large **Basins** to catch and hold the waters of the flood as they rushed northwards had to be constructed.   These basins were sometimes more than one mile long; their width varied according to the width of the river bank.   Their sides were thick, solid, sloping embankments from 12 to 20 feet high, and openings were left in their southern ends.   When the flood waters caught in them were at their greatest height the openings were blocked up, and each basin thus contained a vast quantity of water which would be available for irrigation purposes after the flood had subsided. When needed on the neighbouring ground it was let out by degrees, and when the basin was nearly empty grain was sown in the shallow water, and the crop from it grew up and matured without further watering. The bottom of the basin was covered with a layer of the rich fertile mud that was brought down into the Nile from the mountains and forests of Abyssinia by the Blue Nile and the Atbarā. The soil of Egypt is composed of this mud-deposit, and it is to the thin layer of mud that is added to it annually during the Inundation that it owes its fertility. The Nile is now depositing mud on its bed at the rate of nearly four inches in a century; the thickness of the mud soil of Egypt at Zakāzīk in the Delta is about 110 feet. Muhammad 'Alī introduced a system of Perennial Irrigation into the Delta, and now the Basin System is practically abolished. The **area** of Egypt is about 12,000 sq. miles, but the area of the cultivable land has always varied with the annual Inundation; it increased during a "high" Nile and decreased during a "low" one. The land covered by the Nile deposit was about 7,250,000 acres, but since the building of the **Aswān Dam**[1] 2,000,000 more acres have been irrigated.

[1] The Dam is built across the valley at the head of the First Cataract, north of Philae; the valley is 2,185 yards wide. The Dam holds up water to the level of 348 feet above sea-level, and its storage capacity is estimated at 37,612,000,000 cubic feet. It is filled during the months December–February, and the water is discharged during the months of May, June and July. Between low and high Nile the river rises 26 feet.

From what has been said above it will be seen that the most important **work** to be done in Ancient Egypt was in connection with agriculture, and it seems very probable that the bulk of the population was employed in it. The king's officials watched over the irrigation of the royal estates, the priests safeguarded the interests of the temples, or god-houses, the governor of each of the 42 nomes, or districts, into which Egypt was divided, took care that all the public works in connection with the river were properly done, and the peasant farmer made ready his plots with anxious care. And in every case the slave did most of the work. Most of the seed was sown whilst the water of the Nile flood was several inches deep, and needed no further attention, and that which was sown in the soft mud was generally trodden in by goats. When it was necessary to break up light land the **hoe,** $\flat$, was used ; heavy land required a **plough,** $\searrow\!\!/$, which was drawn by oxen, $\overline{\text{hhh}}$. In reaping the cutting instrument $\_\flat$ was used, and this took the place of the flint knives of early times. The threshing of the grain was done by oxen on a threshing-floor somewhat of this shape $\bowtie$. The preparation of the soil intended for certain crops was carefully studied, and the merits of **top-dressing** were well understood. At the present day the dust from the ruins of ancient and ruined buildings is eagerly sought for by the natives to lay on their fields, and it is most probable that the modern Egyptians are merely following in the steps of their ancestors.

The **principal crops** were wheat, barley, beans, lentils, millet, vetches, lupins, clover, flax, cotton, cucumbers, melons, leeks, onions and papyrus.   In certain parts of Egypt where there was an abundant water supply there were large **vegetable gardens,** in which most of the vegetables known to the modern Egyptians, and beloved by them, were grown. In all periods the Egyptian has eaten largely of vegetables.   And as mention is made in the medical papyri of tinctures and extracts and oils of certain plants, it is clear that the **Physic Garden** was not unknown to the Egyptians, and that a large number of plants were grown because they were believed to possess medicinal properties.   Even at the present day in the purely native markets of Egypt there will be found an old man (or woman) squatting on the ground with a series of little bowls laid out before him containing the dried seeds and leaves of a large number of medicinal plants and woods.   With these are various kinds of powders, lead, antimony and copper, and grease for the eyes, and portions of the dried bodies of crocodiles and other reptiles which are supposed to possess emetic, purgative and aphrodisiac properties. **Arboriculture** in our sense of the word did not exist in Egypt, and exotic trees were only to be found in royal gardens or in the gardens attached to the temples of great gods like Amen-Rā at Thebes.   Under the XVIIIth Dynasty certain trees were brought to Egypt from Southern Arabia, and Punt, and Western Asia, and planted in the palace grounds at Thebes, but the

Egyptians generally preferred to grow trees from which they obtained some solid advantage. The principal trees known to the ancient Egyptians were the thorny **acacia,** 🌿 , in Egyptian 🔲🔽 (, *shentch,* the **date palm,** 〕🌴, *bener,* the **dūm palm,** which flourished best in the southern part of Upper Egypt, the **sycamore,** the **pomegranate,** two or three species of **tamarisks,** the **mulberry,** the **carob, Christ's thorn,** in Egyptian 〰〕 ⋂ (, *nebes,* the **persea,** 🌿 , the **fig tree** and the **oil tree.**

So long as the waters of the Nile flood covered the land the irrigation of the fields and gardens was comparatively easy, for the water flowed into every channel prepared for it, even to the edge of the desert. But when " the land had come forth," *i.e.* when all the water had run off from it, the watering of the fields and gardens became a very serious matter. The Egyptians had no pumps and no mechanical help for watering purposes, and every gallon of water required had literally to be lifted up out of the river and poured upon the land. As the river fell the " lift " became longer, and the work became harder, especially in Upper Egypt, where the Nile banks are very high. In a painting on the wall of a tomb of the XVIIIth Dynasty (*see* p. 234), we see a man drawing water from a hole in the river bank into which the water of the river had flowed. The skin bucket was attached by a cord to the thin end of a long heavy pole, which worked on a pivot in two stout posts driven into the top of the bank. To fill his bucket with water the man drew down the thin end of the pole, and when he had filled it he allowed the end to rise, and the heavy end of it, acting as a weight, lifted up the bucket of water until it reached the level of the channel in the side of the bank, when he tilted out the water in it into the channel, and the water ran on to the plot to be irrigated. This kind of water-raising machine has been in use for thousands of years in Egypt, and the **Shādūf,** which the modern Egyptians use, closely resembles it. The heavy end of the long pole is now often made heavier by plastering it with several hundredweights of Nile mud, especially when the river is very low and greater leverage is required. When the Nile bank is very high it is often necessary to construct a second Shādūf half-way down the bank, and two men are required to work each Shādūf. Whether the ancient Egyptians knew of the **water-wheel** similar to the modern Sākīyah is uncertain, but it is very probable that they had a somewhat similar water-raising contrivance. In the Sākīyah an endless rope passes over the wheel, and to this is attached a series of earthenware pots, arranged at regular intervals, which, as the wheel revolves, dip into a pool, fed by the river, at the bottom of the cutting in the bank, and become full, and when they reach the trough on the top of the bank they empty themselves, one after the other, into it. The wheel is made to turn by means of a cog-wheel arrangement which is kept in motion by an ox or an ass or a camel, or even by a man's wives.

The care of the **live stock** on the estates of the king and the temples and the nobles was also a very important work, and provided occupation for large numbers of peasants and slaves all over the country. The breeding and rearing of cattle were well understood by the Egyptians, and the paintings in the tombs of the Old and Middle Kingdoms attest the importance that was attached by noblemen to the possession of large herds of cattle. One painting even tells us the numbers of the cattle which an official of the Vth Dynasty possessed, viz., 834 oxen, 220 cows and calves, 760 asses, 2,234 goats, and 674 sheep. Under the Old Kingdom two kinds of **sheep** were known, viz., the sheep with spreading horns, 𓃝, which was the symbol of the god Khnem, 𓎛𓃀𓏏, and was worshipped by the people of the First Cataract, and the sheep with the horns curled by the side of its head, 𓃟, which was the symbol of Amen or Amen-Rā. The **bull**, 𓃾, because of his strength and fertility was worshipped at a very early period, and kings were proud to be called "the mighty bull, trampler on his enemies." Even at the present time many an African king is addressed as " Mighty Bull, Bull of bulls " (*see* page 289). The bull was slaughtered and offered as a sacrifice to the gods. The **ox**, 𓃡, did much of the hauling and transport on the farms, and the **cow**, 𓃟, that was a good " milker " was treasured, for the Africans love milk. **Goats,** 🦌, which are often counted with the sheep, were kept in large numbers, and the **pig,** 🐗, was tolerably common. The **ass,** 🐴, was bred on all large farms for transport purposes ; it, like the pig, was probably eaten by the slaves and " swamp-dwellers."

The **herdsmen** belonged to the slave and peasant classes, and were probably, as in many parts of Africa at the present day, mentally or physically deficient. Attached to every herd was an official who watched the feeding of the cattle, and who understood how to treat them medically and to administer boluses, and to prescribe special kinds of food when necessary. The greatest care was taken of cows and sheep that were with young, and according to Diodorus sheep lambed twice a year. Herdsmen were skilled in the **domestication of wild animals and birds,** which were brought to the farms by the hunters and fowlers. Among the animals represented are the ibex, the gazelle, the oryx, the antelope, and among birds the pigeon, the heron, the crane, the duck, and the goose. **Goose-farms** existed in many parts of Egypt, and one district, Chenoboskia, derived its name from the goose-pens for which it was famous. **Bee-keeping** was common, for **honey,** 🐝 ⌒ 𝖔 ͕ ͥ ͥ ͥ, *bit*, was used in making a kind of **mead** and in medicine, and in later times for embalming the dead, and **wax** was valuable for making amulets, and figures of the four Sons of Horus, and the models of men and animals that were burnt during the performance of magical ceremonies. It was sometimes used in mummifying the dead, and in ancient times in Persia mummies were always made with wax ; the word " mummy " means a body that has been treated with wax, though it is often applied to bodies that have been preserved with bitumen. The sign ⟨glyph⟩ that appears in the royal title ⟨glyph⟩ is commonly regarded as a **bee,** ⟨glyph⟩, *āff, i.e.* " fly," or the " honey fly," ⟨glyph⟩, but it more probably represents a **wasp** or **hornet.** As keepers of **poultry** the Egyptians won the admiration of classical writers, and Diodorus (i. 74) says that they used to hatch out large numbers of birds by an artificial process, *i.e.* by the use of the **incubator,** which did away with the necessity of the mother-birds sitting on their eggs. On this matter the inscriptions tell us nothing.

The artisan class formed a comparatively small part of the population of Ancient Egypt, and the most important handicrafts were those of :—

The **Potter.** The pre-dynastic Egyptians succeeded in making very graceful **pottery** without the help of the wheel, the use of which does not seem to have become general until the Dynastic Period. The earliest known coloured pottery is usually red and black, but this was preceded by bowls and pots in monochrome. The art of burnishing was known, as the black, red, and parti-coloured vessels testify. The buff-coloured, unburnished pottery is frequently decorated with designs in red, in which human beings, animals of the antelope class, ostriches, boats with and without sails, mountains and water, are represented. All these vary in size and frequently in shape, and it is quite clear that the potter made no attempt to standardize his work, and that the size and shape of the vessels depended upon the quality, the available quantity of material, and his individual fancy. Some of the pots made during the early period appear to be copies of stone vessels. Under the Old Kingdom many funerary vessels were made of polished red ware, and this reappears in the Ptolemaïc and Roman Periods. The potter often copied the shapes of vessels from Western Asia and elsewhere. The black ware bowls and vessels ornamented with linear designs inlaid with lime, which are often seen in collections, belong to the Hyksos Period, and the false-necked vases, commonly known as " Bügel-kannen," were imported into Egypt from Greece. A considerable amount of Nubian pottery found its way into Egypt under the Middle Kingdom, and the finest examples of what may be called " egg-shell " pottery were made on the Island of Meroë in the Sūdān. The Egyptian potter usually confined himself to making the vessels that were most needed in every-day life—bowls, saucers, flasks for oil and unguents, large wine-jars, oil-jars, water-jars (like the modern *zīr*), and huge amphorae and vessels in which to store grain.   Unlike the Greek, he rarely attempted to invent new forms and shapes, but from first to last was content to follow native custom.   He made vessels to be useful, not ornamental, and most variations in their shape or decoration were due to foreign influence.   A good idea of the general character of Egyptian pottery may be obtained by examining the fine collection exhibited in the Sixth Egyptian Room of the British Museum ; here will be found specimens of all periods, from about 3,500 B.C. to the Meroïtic Period.

The **Brickmaker**. The manufacture of **bricks** gave employment to a great number of slaves and others, for almost every building in Egypt, with the exception of the temple, which was of stone, was made of unbaked bricks.   The muddy soil of Egypt was particularly suitable for brickmaking, for it was free from stones and could be easily mixed with water and kneaded with the hands into a paste of the necessary consistency.   A mass of paste was thrust into a wooden mould of the size of the brick required and the top of it smoothed with a flat stick, and when the brick was dry enough to take out of the mould it was laid in a row with others on the ground to dry in the sun ; in a day or two it was ready for use.   Bricks varied in size from 10 to 15 inches in length, from $4\frac{1}{2}$ to $7\frac{1}{2}$ inches in width, and from 5 to 6 inches in thickness ; some of the bricks made under the New Kingdom have greater dimensions.   Many bricks have, like those of Babylonia, a king's names stamped upon them, and some have thought that such were made by the king's brick-makers for sale to the public. Burnt or **kiln-baked bricks** are not common in Egypt, owing to the scarcity of wood or other material for burning.

The **Weaver.** The products of the looms of Egypt have been famous throughout the world from the earliest times, and **linen, cotton** and **woollen fabrics** must have formed very important items in her export trade. The stalks of flax were soaked in water until the rind became loose, when they were taken out and dried and beaten with mallets on stone slabs. The outer covering of the stalk was made into **lamp wicks,** and the inner fibres were combed out with iron hooks and made into **yarn,** which before being woven into cloth was wetted and beaten with a stone. The greatest care was taken to clean the flax-fibres by heckling them with a large wooden comb (*see* B.M. Nos. 18182, 26740). The yarn was spun by hand, and both women and men were adepts in the use of the **spindle,** which was usually made of wood and had a head made of some heavier material. Two sorts of looms were known, the upright and the horizontal. Linen cloth was calendered by means of wooden rods rubbed over it. and to smooth garments after washing they were rubbed and pressed with a wooden tool which closely resembles a plasterer's wall smoother. Then, as now, linen apparel was worn by those who could afford it or preferred it to wool and cotton, but the swathings of mummies were always made of linen. Under the New Kingdom the city of Apu, the modern Akhmīm, in Upper Egypt, was famous for its textiles, and the Coptic linen weavers to-day perpetuate its ancient reputation. The linen of Pelusium was also famous, and Signor Lumbroso believes that the French word *blouse* is derived from the name of that city. **Cotton** was grown in Upper Egypt, and cotton garments were worn by all classes of people, but it seems that large quantities of cotton were imported into Egypt from the districts near the River Khābūr in exchange for linen fabrics. The weaving of garments made of **wool** obtained among the peasant classes, but the pieces of woollen cloth that have been found in the tombs prove that officials and even priests sometimes wore such.

The **Carpenter** and **Joiner**. The handicraft of **working in wood** was a very general one and, though little wood was grown in Egypt, the carpenter readily found employment. Though there were no wooden floors and no wooden window-frames and sashes in the houses, and the furniture was scanty in most of them, the Egyptians found the carpenter a necessity in almost all their trades. The **woods** principally used by him were the **sycamore-fig,** from which he made coffins, doors, large tables, funerary coffers, etc. ; the **acacia** or **tamarisk,** which, on account of its close grain and hardness, he used for masts of boats, weapons, articles of furniture, etc. ; **ebony,** imported in logs from the Sūdān, and used for making or inlaying ornamental boxes for the toilet, jewel-cabinets, etc. ;

and **cedar,** imported from the Lebanon in large quantities, and used for making the great barges of the gods. Tough woods obtained from the trees in the deserts, and various kinds of **deal,** thought to have been imported from Southern Europe, were also used. The art of **veneering** was known, and inlaying with ivory or glazed porcelain was commonly practised, also a species of **dovetailing** by means of wooden pegs driven through the mitred parts of the sides and ends of boxes. The method of closing coffins and sarcophagi by inserting tongues of wood into slots in the cover and the coffin and driving pegs through them was found to be very effective. The pre-dynastic carpenter used a **saw** and a **chopper** made of flint ; the former was a long flat slice of flint with a beautifully serrated edge, and the latter had a handle, something like ⌇. Later both these tools were made of copper or bronze. Other large tools were the **axe,** ⌐, and an **adze,** ⌐, to the fore part of which was attached by leather thongs a sort of flat chisel made of copper ; the former was used for splitting wood, and the latter for smoothing it, thus in a way serving as a plane. Holes for pegs were made with a **borer,** and slotting work was done with a **mallet** and **chisel.** This mallet was different in shape from that used by the stone-mason. The **plane** was unknown, and was practically unnecessary, for wooden surfaces were smoothed by rubbing with stones. The **drill** was used in working hard woods, and was worked with a cord.

The **Metal-worker.** The principal metals known to the Egyptians were **gold,** 𓈖, *nub*, **silver,** 𓈖𓎱, *nub hetch, i.e.* "white gold," **electron,** 𓈖𓎱, *tchām*, a mixture of gold and silver, or perhaps the pale gold from the Sūdān, **copper,** 𓎡, *hemt*, **iron,** 𓂝𓏤, *baa*, **lead,** 𓏏𓎱, *tchhet*, and **tin,** 𓂝𓏏, *tran*. **Gold** was brought from the Sūdān and from parts of the East Coast of Africa, and from the Eastern Desert. Like honey and wax, it was supposed to possess some special but undefined property, and the blood of the Sun-god was thought to be made of gold. Several qualities of gold were distinguished, the finest and purest being called *katam,* 𓎡𓏏𓅓. It was worked into ornaments in the earliest times, and under the Middle and New Kingdoms very large quantities were used. The mummies of some of the kings were placed in thick gold sheaths, and the funerary vessels—bowls, cups, saucers— of kings like Thothmes III were made of solid gold. As specimens of massive gold work, the jewellery from Dahshūr and the vessels found in the coffin of Queen Aah-hetep may be mentioned. Alluvial gold came chiefly from the Sūdān, gold in the form of rings came from Somaliland and perhaps also from Arabia and Asia. **Silver** was known to the Neolithic Egyptians, and a few of their ornaments made of it have been found. **Copper** was brought in Neolithic times from the ancient mines in the Wādī Maghārah and from Sarābīt al-Khādīm in the Peninsula of Sinai, and in dynastic times from Cyprus and Western Asia. It is possible that the copper deposits near Lake Tanganyika were worked by the Sūdānī tribes. **Iron** was known to the people of the Sūdān at a very early period, and in the Neolithic Period it was imported into Egypt in small quantities. Objects made of it have been found in graves of all periods of dynastic history, but the use of iron never became general. Its red-coloured rust caused the Egyptians to associate it with Set, ⟨ hieroglyphs ⟩, the god of Evil, whose bones were said to be made of iron. The use of **tin** as an alloy for copper was well known to the dynastic Egyptians, for analyses have shown that it exists in **bronze** vessels of every kind, workmen's tools and implements, statues, etc. The large bronze statues of Pepi I and his brother, now in the Cairo Museum, prove that the coppersmiths of the Old Kingdom were very capable handicraftsmen. **Lead** was known to the Neolithic Egyptians, but was little used in the Dynastic Period, except in connection with magical rites ; in late times lead was used for seals.

The **Quarryman** and **Stone-mason.** The tombs and funerary monuments and statues, and the Pyramids of Gīzah, Sakkārah and Mēdūm prove that the quarrymen and stone-masons were great masters of their crafts, and

PLATE V.

The Great Pyramid at Gizah, the tomb of Khufu, a king of the IVth Dynasty. In the foreground is the Sphinx, the age of which is unknown.

suggest that they formed a very numerous and
important section of the artisan classes.   The
principal **quarries** were those of Tura, opposite
Memphis, Kes, in Middle Egypt, Wādī Hammāmāt, those near Abydos and at Jabal Silsilah,
Syene, and there were quarries in many parts of
Nubia.   The stones mostly quarried were fine
white **limestone, alabaster, sandstone,** both
yellowish limestone and crystalline limestone, red,
grey and black **granite, basalt, diorite,** and
porphyry.   For   inlaid   work   **lapis-lazuli,
malachite, carnelian, sard,** red, yellow and
black **jasper,** were commonly used.   The stone
blocks were detached from their bed by driving
wedges into a series of small rectangular slots
cut in a row in the rock to the depth of three or
four inches.   The modern quarrymen used to
make their wedges of the wood of the palm-
tree and moisten them with water, and in
swelling the wedges burst away the block
required.   That this was the method followed
by the ancient Egyptians is proved by the
undetached granite obelisk now lying in the
quarry at Aswān.   The blocks thus quarried were
roughly dressed and shaped with flint and copper
scrapers and chisels and stood ready for removal.
When it was required to take them down to the
river for transport to the site where they were to
be used, they were hauled on **sledges** by men
with ropes, and then sledge and block were
dragged up or down inclined planes to the
river.   Cranes and derricks and even " sheer "
legs were unknown to the Egyptians, and it is
doubtful if they were acquainted with the **lever.**

The only mechanical means they had for lifting stones into their positions in a building was a sort of **cradle,** two models of which (from the tomb of Queen Hatshepsut) are in the British Museum (Nos. 26276, 54991).   The final dressing of the blocks when in position was done by a broad copper chisel, which was tied on the end of a wooden handle held horizontally.   The stone-mason's **mallet** somewhat resembled those now in use among Western nations.

The handicrafts of the artisans briefly enumerated above may be described as the " key industries " of Ancient Egypt ;   other important trades and professions were those of the boat-builder, the wagon-maker and wheelwright, the furniture-maker, the worker in ivory and precious woods, the jeweller, the lapidary, the sculptor, the carver of bas-reliefs, the tanner and worker in leather, the sandal-maker, the coffin-maker, the painter and decorator, the builder, the armourer, the papyrus-maker, the basket-maker, the turner, the butcher, baker, confectioner, and brewer.

THE EGYPTIANS AT PLAY

The average Egyptian was by nature a cheerful, joyous person, fond of amusement and pleasure, and his greatest desire was to " make a good day," ⬅ ☉ ⌿, *i.e.* to eat, drink, and be merry. The pleasures and amusements of the peasant and field-labourer and slave must have been very few and inexpensive. Then, as now, they loved to assemble in the " house of beer," which was the equivalent of the modern café or wine-shop, and gossip with their friends, and many statements in the papyri containing moral aphorisms suggest that the Egyptians were given to **drunkenness.** Whether they were addicted to the use of **narcotics** like opium or hashīsh is uncertain, but it is probable that their **sweet beer** contained an infusion of some plant with soporific qualities. **Acrobats,** conjurers and gymnasts, and **dancing women,** were popular visitors in every town and village, and each community maintained its local troupe of per-formers. These were employed at weddings and on festal occasions, and they even accompanied funeral processions to the doors of the tombs, where they gave exhibitions of their skill to amuse the general body of the friends and mourners of the deceased, whilst the solemn funerary rites and ceremonies connected with the deposit of the body in the tomb were being performed. The **buffoon** was as popular in Ancient as in Modern Egypt, and no local entertainment was complete without the services of the youth who played a single or double **reed-pipe** and sang songs (probably of an amorous character), and the **story-teller** (the Muslim *rāwīyah*). Whether the early Egyptians prac-tised **dancing** as much as the Sūdānī tribes is not known, but we may be sure that when the Nubian peoples came into Egypt as soldiers and watchmen they brought their own tribal dances with them, and that in dancing their steps were regulated by the beat of some kind of **drum** like the modern *darabuka* and by the **clapping of hands.** Children, as we have seen, played with **balls,** and **toys** and **dolls** of various kinds, and youths amused themselves with bows and arrows, wrestling, etc. The Egyptians of all classes played many games of chance and of skill, but nothing is known of the systems on which they were played. The oldest and the favourite of these was **draughts** (*not* chess, as was once thought), and the hieroglyph ⌷⌷⌷⌷, which represents a draught-board with its pieces arranged on it, and which is found in inscriptions of the earliest period, shows that this game is as old, at least, as dynastic civilization. The draught-boards preserved in our museums differ considerably in the arrangement and number of the squares on them, and this fact suggests that the rules and the method of playing the game varied at different periods. The pieces used by the players were at first pebbles or bits of stone, but later they took the form ⋂, and later still the tops of the pieces were made in the form of animals' heads (*see* the set of draughtsmen in the British Museum, No. 24668, some with the head of Bes and others with the head of Anubis). The **draught-board** was as much a necessity for the dead as for the living, and the tombs have yielded many fine draught-boards and sets of pieces, made of ebony inlaid with ivory, the squares being formed sometimes by pieces of beautiful light-blue Egyptian porcelain. In the Vignette to Chap. xvii of the Book of the

Dead we see the deceased seated in a bower in festal attire and "playing at draughts,"

Another popular game was that in which the two players sat facing each other and tried to guess the number of fingers which each in turn thrust out. It was, and still is, common in the East, and may have been the ancestor of the Roman game called "micare digitis" and the Italian game of **mora** or morra. In very early times the **serpent-game** was popular. The board, or stone slab, had on it a representation of a huge coiled serpent, and the pieces were in the forms of lions, dogs, and little balls; how the game was played is not known. From first to last the Egyptians loved **music,** if we may be allowed to use this word to describe their vocal and instrumental efforts. Whether they had written **notation** cannot be said—probably not—and none has so far been found. Certainly modern Central African tribes, who are capable, practical musicians, have none. The Egyptian was a singer by nature. The child sang his lessons, the peasant sang as he worked on the farm, the boatman sang, the fisherman sang, the king and his nobles maintained singing men and singing women, many of whom were blind, and the temples had their great **choirs** to sing litanies and hymns to the gods. Wherever possible singers were accompanied by musical instruments. **Rhyme** was unknown, but **rhythm** was carefully studied and **time** was rigidly marked, either by the clapping of hands

or the beat of a drum of some kind.   The
earliest songs consisted of short statements in
two or three words, often repeated, and often
followed by a jingle of meaningless words;
compare the modern boatmen's "ya bāb

The large Egyptian Harp.

an-nāb."   From these attempts at poetical
composition **folk-songs** arose; it is probable
that the tunes to which they were sung became
traditional.   The principal musical instruments
known to the Egyptians were the **reed-pipe,**
⊸∫ 🦅◗, *sebat,* the **harp,** ∫◠◡ 🍆, *bent,* the

small portable harp, introduced probably from Syria under the New Kingdom, the **Nefer,** $\int$, the **drum** or **tambourine,** � Ⅎ ∿ ○ , *teben,* ⌒ ○ , *ser,* and ⊃Ⅎ○, *teb,* and clappers or castanets, Ⅎ ⍝ » ⌐, *ahui,* or ∿ 🐦 ● ∖∖ ⌐, *mathahhi,* and **cymbals.** The last-named came into use under the New Kingdom. All these instruments were used for secular rejoicings, but there was one instrument the use of which seems to have been reserved for religious services in the temples, viz., the **sistrum,** ☥ , or ♀ , called **seshesh,** ▭▭. This consisted of a broad band of copper, bent almost double, and fixed in a rounded handle of wood or copper, flattened at one end and decorated with heads of Hathor. Through holes drilled in both sides of the copper band bent wires, ⦚, were inserted, and when the instrument was shaken rapidly the wires rattled and produced sharp, ringing noises, which were supposed to drive away devils. The very shape of the wires that rattled had a magical significance.

Dancing appears to have been primarily a religious exercise, by means of which the dancer gave expression to his feelings of gratitude towards the gods and his worship of them. Already, under the Ist Dynasty, on great occasions the king danced before his god, and the man who knew how to dance the " dance of the god " was an honoured and protected person.

King Semti (Ist Dynasty) dancing
before his god.

King Thothmes III, XVIIIth Dynasty, dancing before the
goddess Hathor.

During the processions made by the gods in their boats or shrines, and during royal progresses, it was the duty of everyone to dance. The dance at a funeral was different from the ordinary dance, and it probably dates from predynastic times. Whether special dances like the puberty dance, the initiation dance, the marriage dance and the war dance of the Sūdānī tribes were known to the Egyptians is uncertain. The monuments show that dancing men and women wore little more than loin-cloths, and it seems as if their movements consisted of series of short, sharp jerkings of the legs and arms, and leaping into the air. Under the New Kingdom the character of dancing changed greatly, and the ornaments of the women and the dressing of their hair, and the general *abandon* of their movements, show that the dancing women of the period were the equivalents of the professional dancing women of Kana in Upper Egypt and Cairo to-day. They wore long diaphanous garments which reached to the ankles, and beat tambourines and rattled castanets.

The nobles amused themselves by giving banquets and entertainments to each other, and the paintings in the tombs give us a very good idea as to the way in which they were conducted. The guests, arrayed in festal garments, with plenty of scented grease on their heads and (if women) flowers in their hair, sat on ebony and ivory stools or chairs, and ate course after course of meats, vegetables, and sweetmeats, and drank large quantities of beer sweetened with honey and wine. The host, if a

wealthy man, gave necklaces and other ornaments, and flowers, in wreaths or garlands, to
the ladies, and the servants brought round cups
of wine at frequent intervals.   The stands in
the hall were loaded with fruits and flowers,
the perfume of which filled the air, and meanwhile the band, *i.e.* players on reed-pipes and
flutes and hand-harps, discoursed sweet music
and accompanied singers, both male and female.

A funerary barge with women beating their heads in token of their grief, and singing
dirges for the dead.   The barge is supposed to be crossing from the east to the west
bank of the Nile at Thebes, where the great cemeteries were situated.

Among the selection of songs sung on such
occasions was a **dirge,** the object of which was to
remind the host and his guests that, however
much they were enjoying themselves at that
moment, the day would assuredly come when
they must die ; in some cases, to drive this
lesson home into the minds of the company,
the host had a mummy on a sledge drawn through
the dining-hall.   And whilst mirth and laughter
filled the hall and the wine-cup was circulating,

through the openings in the walls, which served
as windows, came the words of the dirge, which
were addressed by a famous performer on the
harp to Antuf, a king of the XIth Dynasty :—

" O beneficent Prince, it is a decree,
    And what hath been ordained by this
        decree is good :
That the bodies of men shall pass away and
        disappear,
And that others shall abide [in succession
        to them].
I have heard the words of Imhetep[1] and
        Hertataf,[2]
Which, because they wrote them, are
        treasured beyond everything.
Consider what hath happened to their
        tombs :
Their walls have been thrown down,
Their places can no longer be seen ;
It is just as if they had never existed.
[And consider also] none cometh from
        where they are
To describe to us their state,
Or to tell us of their surroundings,
Or to comfort our hearts,
Or to guide us to the place whither they
        have gone.
Anoint thy head with scented unguents,
Array thyself in apparel made of byssus,
Steep thy body in precious perfumes,

[1] A great scribe, physician and architect who flourished
under Tcheser, a king of the IIIrd Dynasty.
[2] Son of Khufu, builder of the Great Pyramid at Gîzah.

Which are indeed the emanations of the
      gods.
Occupy thyself with thy pleasure day by
      day [and]
Cease not to search out enjoyment for
      thyself.
Man is not permitted to carry his goods
      away with him.
Never hath existed the man who, once
      departed,
Was able to return to earth again.
Follow thine heart's desire,
Search out happiness for thyself,
Order thy affairs on earth so that they may
Minister to the desire of thy heart.
For at length the day of lamentation shall
      come,
When the Still-heart (*i.e.* the dead) shall
      not hear the lamentations,
And the cries of grief shall never make to
      beat
Again the heart of him that is in the grave.
[Therefore] comfort thy heart, forget these
      things.
The best thing for thee to do for thyself
      is to
Seek to attain thy heart's desire as long as
      thou livest."

The wall-paintings in the tombs show that
Egyptian noblemen and high officials sometimes
amused themselves with **hunting** and **fishing**,
but it must be admitted that evidence is wanting
that they did so because they were keen lovers

of those sports. Some of the kings of Egypt
seem to have been sportsmen in the true sense
of the word, for Thothmes III, when in Northern
Syria, "hunted 120 elephants" and very nearly

The Nomarch Khnemu-hetep spearing fish in the marshes of Egypt.   In the lower
register we see the boatmen playing games and amusing themselves.   From a tomb
at Bani Hasan.   XIIth Dynasty.

lost his life on one occasion, and in one week,
during the second year of his reign, Amenhetep III
slew with his own hand 96 wild cattle out of a
herd of 190, and during the first ten years of his
reign shot 102 fierce lions. And Thothmes IV

was out in the desert near Memphis shooting
lions and gazelle on the day when the god of
the Sphinx appeared to him during his after-
dinner sleep. Many pictures show us noblemen
fishing and **fowling** in the swamps and marshes
of Egypt, but there are none that suggest that
any of them went to the deserts and forest
fastnesses in the Sūdān where the lion, the
leopard, the elephant, the rhinoceros, the
hippopotamus and other big game live.

The early Egyptians hunted the **lion,**
⛏ 𓊪 𓏏 𓅓 𓄿 𓏏, *ma-hesa*, but he was usually
caught by enticing him to a place where some
living animal was tethered : whilst the lion was
occupied with his prey the hunters and their
dogs attacked him.   The Egyptians admired
the lion greatly and found a way to tame him,
and in the Westcar Papyrus we read of a
magician who could make a lion follow him
like a dog.   Like the late Sultān of Maskat,
Rameses II had a pet lion that drove with him
in his war-chariot and attacked the foe.   Other
wild animals hunted were the **hyena,** the
panther, and the **leopard,** 𓃀 𓃀 𓏏 𓃥 , *abi,* and
the skin of the last-named formed an important
article of priestly attire.   The leopard seems to
have been regarded as a typhonic animal, but
whether the Egyptians thought that the living
and the dead sometimes assumed the form of a
leopard, as many Sūdānī tribes do at the present
time, is not certain.   The **rhinoceros,** 𓃟, the

PLATE VI·

A lion hunt in the desert in the Predynastic Period. The hunters are equipped with double-headed stone-axes, maces, celts in wooden hafts (or boomerangs?), bows and arrows tipped with flints, and spears with metal heads and tails. The creatures hunted are ostriches, jackals, hares, antelopes, and lions. British Museum No. 20792.

elephant, 🐘, or 🏺, *abu*, the **giraffe,**
🦒, *ser*, were well known to the Egyptians,
and the elephant was hunted and killed for the
sake of his tusks at a very early period. The
Vignette of Chap. xxviii of the Book of
the Dead in the Papyrus of Nefer-ubenef
suggests that the existence of large **anthropoid
apes** in the Sūdān was known to the Egyptians.

The **hippopotamus,** 🦛, *tebt,* was
common in Egypt as well as in the Sūdān, and
it was frequently speared with harpoons, and
probably was eaten. This beast was tolerated
in early days because it was supposed to be of a
benevolent disposition, but in the late period
it was regarded as the incarnation of all evil.
In the days of Abbā Benus a hippopotamus used
to come and trample down and eat the crops
of a certain monastery, but when the Abbā in
a gentle voice adjured it to depart in the Name
of Christ, the animal went away and was no
more seen (Palladius, *Paradise of the Fathers*,
i. 337). It is said that the last hippopotamus
in Egypt was killed at Girgā, in Middle Egypt,
in the latter half of the XVIIth century.

Strangely enough the **crocodile,** 🐊,
emsuh, probably one possessing certain marks,
was protected and worshipped as a god, and his
dead body was embalmed and preserved carefully.
Some of the modern Sūdānī tribes revered this
creature, and a sacred crocodile was living in a
tank at Khartūm as late as 1838. The ordinary

crocodile was ruthlessly killed whenever opportunity offered, but certain parts of his body
were dried and powdered and used in medicine,
and even to-day crocodile dust is eaten as an
aphrodisiac.   The Tepi crocodile, ⌐◯ 𓇳 ◖ ,
seems to have been a peculiarly destructive
creature.

The farmer suffered greatly from the attacks of
wolves, foxes, jackals and **wild dogs,** and
these were caught and killed ; many noxious
reptiles, *e.g.* the **scorpion** and venomous
snakes, though regarded as incarnations of gods
and goddesses, were killed whenever possible.
The two reptiles most dreaded were the *cerastes,*
or horned **viper**, ⌢ , and the **cobra,** or hooded
asp, 𓏭 ◠ 𓆙 , *uatchit.* Like many other ancient
nations the Egyptians believed that a number
of composite or **fabulous animals** lived in the
deserts; among these were :—the **Setcha,** 𓏤 𓏤 ,
which has the head and neck of a serpent and the
body of a leopard ; the **Sefer,** 𓏤 ═╲ , which has an
eagle's head and a lion's body, from the back of
which grow a pair of wings ; the **Sag,** —◆— 𓄿 𓊖 ,
which has the head of a hawk, and a body of
which the fore-part is that of a lion, and the
hind part that of a horse with a tail terminating
in a lotus flower, 𓆰 , and with eight teats ; a
leopard with a human head and a pair of wings
growing out of the back ;   the **Sha,** 𓈙 , which

has long square ears, directed backwards like the animal of **Set,** 𓊃𓃩 ; the **Gryphon,** 𓃢, and the man-headed lion or **Sphinx,** 𓃬. The monster **Ammit**, or Eater of the Dead, was part crocodile, part lion, and part hippopotamus.[1]

[1] Two years ago, when the contents of the tomb of Tutānkhamen were being discussed, it was asserted by some writers that the couches had been sent to Egypt as gifts by Mesopotamian kings, and that the method followed in their construction was of Mesopotamian origin. To this statement I objected in a little book on Tutānkhamen, and I showed that the couches were of Egyptian origin and that the beast represented by them was Āmmit. In his book, *A Century of Excavation in the Land of the Pharaohs*, the writer refers to this matter and quotes Sir Flinders Petrie to show that my view was incorrect, but unfortunately this eminent authority, who is no Assyriologist, has made a serious mistake. The Tall al-'Amārnah letter which he quotes to support his erroneous view was not written TO Amenhetep III by Kadashman-Enlil, as Sir Flinders states, but BY Amenhetep III to Kadashman-Enlil. Amenhetep III says, (18) " I have sent you a present (19) for the new house by the hand of Shutti, (20) one bed made of *ushu*-wood (ebony?) inlaid with ivory and gold, (21) three beds of *ushu*-wood inlaid with gold, (22) one litter of *ushu*-wood inlaid with gold, (23) one large throne of *ushu*-wood inlaid with gold, (24) five thrones of *ushu*-wood inlaid with gold, (25) four thrones of *ushu*-wood inlaid with gold—(26) weight of gold of all these, 7 minas 9 shekels, (27) of silver, 1 mina 8½ shekels," etc. (*See* Knudtzon, *Die El-Amarna Tafeln*, vol. i, p. 76, Leipzig, 1915.) Kadashman-Enlil *wanted* gold, and would never send to Egypt what he needed so much. The writer of the letter from which the above is an extract was Amenhetep III and *not* Kadashman-Enlil. Now Amenhetep IV on one ooccasion sent gifts to Burnaburiash, and among the list of them which he gives in his letter to him (Knudtzon, p. 110), he mentions

Among the fabulous creatures of the desert may perhaps be mentioned the animal which was the symbol of the god **Set,** ⚲, or ⚲, and is represented often on the monuments with a head like that of the **camel**, a beast which is never found on any monument and was not known to the Egyptians until the Greek period. The form of the original of the Set animal seems to have been known to the scribes by tradition, and according to some authorities the beast they intended to draw was the **okapi or zebra.**

The Egyptian hunters were armed with bows and arrows, nets, axes and spears, or harpoons. The larger animals were probably caught in pits, or driven into spaces which were enclosed by palisades made of branches of trees or reeds. Gazelle, and animals of the antelope class, were

---

(col. ii, lines 19 and 20), " one bed, inlaid with gold, the feet of which are protecting spirits, one bed, inlaid with gold, [and] one head-rest inlaid with gold." This letter was written BY Amenhetep IV TO Burnaburiash, and the use of the word *lamasse*, " protecting spirits," shows that the legs of the bed were made in the form of those of animals. Thus two kings of Egypt gave beds or couches to kings in Babylonia, and the theory that the couches in Tutānkhamen's tomb were made in Mesopotamia is wholly without foundation. And as Prof. Petrie has obviously made a mistake as to the writer of the letter on which he relies for proof of his theory, further discussion is unnecessary. But whilst expert Assyriologists are able to settle such points for themselves by consulting the cuneiform texts, the general reader cannot do so, and in this case it is necessary to state the facts in detail to prevent further promulgation of errors.

often caught in nets, or with the **lasso,** ⌐□§🐦ℓ, *sephu,* or were brought down with the **boomerang,** ⊿⌐ 🐦, *qemau.* Birds of all kinds, with the exception of the **ostrich,** ∿∿∿ℓ🐦, *nau,* or 🐦, were caught in nets, and fish were speared, or trapped, or caught in nets. During the Inundation and immediately afterwards the fishermen caught great numbers of all kinds of fish, from the large so-called " Nile salmon," which came down from the Sūdān, to the very small fish which were found in the basins and which resemble whitebait. Those that they could not consume at the time of their catches they preserved for future use (as they did also the meat of the animals they killed and could not eat at the time of killing) by storing them in earthen pots, with salt in abundance. The natives of Upper Egypt do the same now and, having filled large earthen pots with alternate layers of salt and fish, they seal their mouths with lumps of Nile mud. Before the railway across the Abu Hamad desert was made, every caravan carried several of these jars of salted fish, partly for the use of the camel-men on their journey, and partly as gifts to their friends at Berber and Shindi.

CHAPTER V

THE earliest **God-house,** or dwelling of the god, in Egypt, was made of reeds or small branches of some tree laced together and held in position by wooden stakes driven into the ground ; it was circular in form and resembled the huts found in many parts of the Eastern Sūdān at the present time and many of the churches in Abyssinia. At a later period, the opening in the hut which served for a door was elaborated, and a rectangular portal was added to the reed or wicker-work structure. On the top of this the symbol of the god within was sometimes placed, and presumably the offerings to him were laid before it. The earliest name for this dwelling of the god was **Er-per,** (in late times Erpi,), "Door of the divine House," *i.e.* "door of the god's house." Next were added a plinth and then steps. The general form of this door was perpetuated in the **shrine,** 🜄, which was placed in every large temple, and was always regarded as the special dwelling-place of the god of the temple. The roof of the " door of the house " projected in front and was supported by two poles, and these in later times were represented by the decorated pillars that support the roofs of the shrines of the great gods and of the state pavilions of kings, who were also gods. In early dynastic times the dwelling of the god was made of unbaked bricks, which in turn were superseded by stone. Then the name, " House of the god," 🜄, or 🜄, was made to describe the shrine, the building in which it stood, and its precincts.

Of the temples of the earliest dynasties nothing is known, for no remains of them exist, and the famous temple of Osiris at Abydos has not been completely excavated. From the ruins of the **Sun - temples** built at Sakkārah by the kings of the Vth Dynasty, which have been excavated in recent years, it is clear that the object of the cult was the **Sun Stone,** which had the form of a pointed

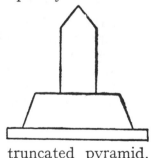

stone, and was set on a truncated pyramid. This stone was called Ben, 🜄 , or Ben Ben, 🜄 🜄 , and the chamber in which it was placed

was called the "House of the Ben Ben,"
. Before it were the vessels for
receiving the blood of the victims, that were
sometimes human beings, and along the sides of
the great courtyard were rows of chambers in
which the sacred properties were kept. The
walls of the passages were decorated with bas-
reliefs. The funerary **temple of Menthu-hetep**
(XIth Dynasty) was built close to the pyramid-
tomb of the king. It had courts to the north and
south, a great fore-court, and a hypostyle hall.
The **temple of Amen,** built at Karnak (Thebes),
under the XIIth Dynasty, was a comparatively
small building ; in the centre of it was a small
chamber, or sanctuary, which probably contained
a statue of the god. It was repaired or rebuilt
and greatly enlarged by several of the kings
of the XVIIIth Dynasty, who turned the temple
of Amen and its precincts into what may
well be styled a "Temple-town," .
From the buildings at Karnak we see that the
worshipper approached the first **Pylon,** *i.e.* a
gateway with a tower on each side of it, by a
wide **dromos,** or pathway, on each side of which
was a row of sphinxes. One statue (or more) of
the king and an **obelisk** stood on each side of
the gate of the pylon. The first pylon led into a
large open court, with **a colonnade** on one side
of it, and passing through a second pylon the
worshipper entered the **hypostyle hall,** where
the offerings were brought and collected by the
temple-servants. To this hall the public had free

access. Beyond it was the sanctuary containing the **shrine of the god,** which was usually kept closed ; round about the shrine were several small chambers in which the dresses and decorations of the god were kept. During certain solemn festivals the doors of the shrine were unbolted and worshippers were permitted to see the face of the statue, which they regarded as that of God Himself.

Attached to the temple was the **sacred lake,** in the water of which every visitor to the temple was obliged to wash, for personal cleanliness was dear alike to gods and men. No man could hope to see the god unless he could say, " I have purified my breast and body with clean water, I have purified my hinder parts with the things that cleanse, and my inward parts have been [dipped] in the Pool of Maāti ; no one member of mine lacks Maāt. I am pure, I am pure, I am pure, I am pure." Both the temple of Hatshepsut at Dēr al-Baharī and the temple of Amenhetep III in Southern Thebes possess special characteristics, but the essential parts are always the same. The **rock-hewn temples** at Kalābshah and Abu Simbel in Nubia stand alone, and the little sandstone temples in that country may be regarded as rough models of the older temples, only made on a small scale. The **priesthoods** of great temples like those of Heliopolis, Memphis, Abydos and Thebes were very wealthy corporations and, to all intents and purposes, guided the destinies of Egypt. Each great god owned estates and lands, flocks and herds, vineyards, vegetable gardens, boats and ships, slaves, soldiers and sailors, and the value of the offerings made to Amen of Thebes and Osiris of Abydos was well-nigh incalculable.

The Temple-town of Amen was the head-quarters of all the best artisans in Upper Egypt, and priests of this god directed the affairs both of the living and the dead. The **high priest of Amen** was the intermediary between the king and Amen, and he performed the ceremonies by which the king received daily the renewal of his life and the supply of the divine essence of the god, which enabled him to rule Egypt. The estates of the god and all business connected with his property were managed by a little army of inspectors and overseers, and the temple accounts were carefully kept by a number of scribes, who compiled lists of the offerings and payments made into the treasury of the god. The king was, of course, the chief contributor to the wealth of the god, and it is clear from the list of the offerings which Rameses III made to the great temples that exact lists of the royal gifts were kept by the scribes. In his Annals Thothmes III says that he gave to Amen 1,578 slaves, male and female, from Syria, four cows of a special breed, three cities in Syria and all the annual taxes taken from them, masses of gold, silver, lapis-lazuli, copper, bronze, lead, ochres, etc., for use in the temple buildings, 1,000 geese for offerings, fields, gardens, corn-lands, bulls, poultry, incense, wine, fruit, bread, honey, beer, etc., and increased existing endow-ments, and established new festivals, and provided the necessary offerings. One very remarkable gift to Amen by Thothmes III was a garden in which he caused to be planted all the shrubs, plants and herbs that he brought from Syria to Thebes. A detailed list of the offerings that Rameses III made to the temples of Thebes, Abydos and Heliopolis is given in the Harris Papyrus No. 1 in the British Museum, and the following extracts from it will give an idea of his munificence in respect of the god Amen of Thebes :—2,844,357 loaves of fine bread, 42,030 jars of wine, 304,093 measures of incense, 110,000 jars of oil, 310 jars of honey, 3,100 measures of wax, 559,500 loads of fruit, 15,500 bundles of figs, 15,110 papyrus sandals, 75,400 bricks of salt, 449,500 measures of the fruit of the dūm palm, 3,029 head of cattle, 126,250 geese, pigeons, etc., 441,000 fishes, 770,200 bundles of vegetables, 1,975,800 bunches of flowers, 18,252 *teben* of fine gold and silver, 112,132 *teben* of copper, lead and tin (?), 18,214 *teben* of precious stones. The employees of the Temple of Amen in the reign of Rameses III numbered 62,626, which shows that the cult of this god was in reality a social system.

Egyptian Gods. The early inhabitants of the Nile Valley worshipped stones, trees, mountains, animals, birds, reptiles, fish and other objects, and the cults of some of these persisted in dynastic times. The stone axe-head with its handle, which became the common symbol for " god," ⌐| or ⌐, is probably a survival of **stone-worship**. The **Sun Stone** in the temples of the Vth Dynasty at Sakkārah was the chief object of the cult of the priests of Heliopolis, and sacrifices were offered up to it; the **obelisk,** which is a development of it, was also an object of worship, and Thothmes III offered to the four obelisks he set up at Thebes large quantities of various kinds of incense, and over 1,000 loaves of various kinds of bread. The persea tree and the tree which was the abode of the goddess Nut were always sacred trees in Egypt, and it has recently been shown that the trees now growing by the tombs of holy men in Egypt are believed to be the abodes of the spirits of Muslim saints, and to be holy (W. S. Blackman, in *Jnl. Eg. Arch.*, vol. xi., p. 57). The tree-trunk, which became associated with the worship of Osiris, is also a survival of **tree-worship.** Bakhau, the Mountain of Sunrise, and Manu, the Mountain of Sunset, were at all times sacred objects. The creatures worshipped by the Egyptians, either for their power or because they were thought to be places of gods and spirits, were many, and among them were : **Animal-gods.**—

The **Hippopotamus-**goddess Taurit, the **Crocodile-**god Sebek, the **Frog-**goddess Heqit, the **Hare-**god Un, the **Bull-**gods Apis, Mnevis, and Bakhis, the **Ram-**god Ba, the **Lion-**god Mahes, the **Lynx-**god Maftt, the **Cat-**goddess Bast, the **Jackal-**god Anpu

(Anubis), ⟨ 𓃡 𓃢, the **Wolf**-god Upuat, 𓃥 𓃢, the **Ichneumon**-god Khatru, 𓏏 𓃭 ⌒ 𓃟, the **Set**-animal god (Okapi ?), 𓃫. The character of the **Ass** is doubtful, but he seems to have been a form of the Sun-god ; the **shrew-mouse** and the **hedgehog** were also sacred animals.

The following **birds** were sacred : the **benu,** 𓃭 𓅦 (phœnix), the **vulture,** ⌒𓆓 ⟨ 𓅂, *nerau,* **hawks** of various kinds, the **ibis,** 𓊖 𓅃 𓃭 𓅂, *habu,* the **swallow,** 𓏏 𓅡, *ment,* and **geese** of various kinds.

The following reptiles and insects were sacred : the **turtle,** 𓆉, the **scorpion,** 𓆸, the **beetle,** 𓆣 ⌒ ⟨ 𓆤, kheprera (*scarabaeus sacer*), the **serpent** called Sata, 𓆙, the cerastes, 𓆑, and cobra, ⟨ ⌒ 𓆗, *aārt.* The "praying" **mantis** and the **grasshopper** are mentioned in mythological texts. The Book of the Dead speaks of two **fishes** that probably were sacred, the Ant, ⟨ 𓏶 𓆛, which announced the rise of the Nile, and the Abtu, 𓋹 𓃭 ⌒ 𓆝 ; and Mehit, 𓂝 𓐍 𓏏 ⌒ 𓅆, was a Fish-goddess. At first all these were drawn in their natural forms, but early in the Dynastic Period most of the animals, birds and reptiles were depicted with human bodies, the heads alone indicating the original forms. Thus the Ram-god 🐏 becomes 𓃘, the Jackal-god 🐕 becomes 𓃥, the Set-animal god ⟋⌐ becomes 𓃩, the Hawk-god 🦅 becomes 𓅉, the Beetle-god 🪲

Khnemu fashioning a man on his potter's wheel.

becomes 𓀭, and so on. The Sun-god ⊙ has a disk on his head, 𓀭, the Moon-god a crescent, 𓀭, the Star-god a star, 𓀭, the Mountain-god a range of hills, 𓀭, the Serpent-god a serpent, 𓀭, and the Nile-god has a cluster of plants on his head and carries two vases, out of which he empties the Nile of the South and the Nile of the North, 𓈗.

The principal gods and goddesses of the Dynastic Period were :—

Khnemu, 𓎸 , was one of the oldest gods in Egypt, and his cult seems to have been in existence in the Predynastic Period. His sacred animal was the flat-horned ram 𓃞. He was the great "builder," 𓎸 , of the universe. He made the gods, and "built up" the cosmic egg from which sprang the sun, and he fashioned the first man out of the material which he created upon a potter's wheel. In a relief of a later period we see him modelling a man on his wheel. Behind him is the ibis-headed god Thoth, who is marking on a notched palm branch the years that the man is destined to live.

Khepera, 𓆣 , the type of matter about to come into a state of activity.

Nenu, or **Nu,** 𓈖𓈖 , the primeval watery mass in which Khepera existed ; his associate was the goddess **Nent,** 𓈖𓈖 , or **Nut,** 𓈖 , a personification of moisture.

Tehuti, or Tchehuti, 𓁟 , *i.e.* **Thoth,** represented the heart and mind of the Creator of the world. By expressing in words the will

of the Creator he made to come into being
everything that exists.   He was the scribe of
the gods, and invented writing and mathematics,
and ordered times and seasons.   His associate

Ptah of Memphis, with
the sceptre of stability
and serenity, the staff of
rule, ⸢?⸣, and the whip.
At the back of his neck is

Thoth, the scribe of the gods, with his
writing-reed, palette, and other implements.

the menat amulet, ⸢♁⸣.

was the goddess **Maāt**, ⸢✍○𓀭⸣, the personification of physical and moral **Law**.

Tem, ⸢𓏏𓅓𓀭⸣, or **Atmu**, ⸢𓏏𓅓𓀭⸣, who
is always represented in the form of a man, was
an ancient solar god, and was adopted by the
priests of Heliopolis as the head of their " Great
Company of the Gods."

Ptah, ⬚𒀭, the great god of Memphis, was a deified man. He was a master-handicraftsman, and was said to have assisted Khepera in the creation of the material world. He often appears in the form of a mummy, 𒀭. He was the first member of the triad of Memphis—Ptah, Sekhmit, Nefer-Temu.

Ptah-Seker, ⬚𒀭, a form of the Sun-god of Night ; a god of death.

Ptah-Seker-Asar, ⬚𒀭, the triune god of the Egyptian Resurrection ; a triad of the gods of death of the district of Memphis.

Ptah-Taten, ⬚𒀭. The creator of the matter of which the world was formed.

Imhetep, 𒀭, the Imouthēs of the Greeks, a native of Memphis who was deified. He was a great architect and a very wise and learned man ; he and Hertataf, a son of King Khufu, were held to be the most learned men in Egypt.

Her, 𒀭, the Sky-god and Sun-god ; as the latter he appears with the solar disk on his head, 𒀭. In the Dynastic Period Horus is often called " the son of Isis," 𒀭.

Herur, [hieroglyphs], " Horus the Elder," one of the oldest gods of Egypt; he personified the face of the Sky, the sun being his right, and the moon his left eye.

Her-p-khart, [hieroglyphs], " Horus the Child " (Harpokrates).

Her-aakhuti, [hieroglyphs], the Harakhthēs of the Greeks, the Sun-god in the two horizons.

Her-em-aakhut, [hieroglyphs], the Harmakhis of the Greeks, a form of the Sun-god.

Her-khenti-khati, [hieroglyphs], Horus in the womb, the unborn Horus or Sun-god.

Her-sa-Ast, [hieroglyphs], Horus, son of Isis, a god who is often confused with Herur, *i.e.* Horus the Elder, or Horus the Aged.

Hether, [hieroglyphs], [hieroglyphs], the **Hathor** of the Greeks, goddess of love, beauty and fertility; a special kind of cow was sacred to her.

Shu, [hieroglyphs], an emanation of Temu or Khepera. He represented the space between the earth and the sky, and separated the Sky-goddess Nut from the embrace of the Earth-god Geb. He was the god of light, heat, air and dryness. He supported the horizon and the solar disk on his shoulders [hieroglyph].

Tefnut, ⟨hieroglyphs⟩, sister and wife of Shu ; she represented rain, dew, the damp heat that produces generation, and moisture generally.

Geb, ⟨hieroglyphs⟩, son of Shu and Tefnut, was an early form of the Earth-god.

Nut, ⟨hieroglyphs⟩ (older form **Nent,** ⟨hieroglyphs⟩), sister and wife of Geb, was the great Sky-goddess.

Asar, ⟨hieroglyphs⟩, or ⟨hieroglyphs⟩, *i.e.* **Osiris,** the judge and god of the dead. The principal seats of his cult were Abydos and Busiris.

Ast, ⟨hieroglyphs⟩, *i.e.* **Isis,** the sister and wife of Osiris and mother of Horus, whom she brought forth in the lotus swamps of the Delta.

Set, Seth, or **Setesh,** ⟨hieroglyphs⟩, ⟨hieroglyphs⟩, the brother and murderer of Osiris, and the great and perpetual Adversary of Herur and all the solar gods ; he was the personification of evil, and the god of calamities of every kind, and of the desert waste and of destruction generally. He was incarnate in some African animal, either the zebra or the okapi.

Nebthet, ⟨hieroglyphs⟩, *i.e.* **Nephthys,** the sister and wife of Set and mother of Anpu.

Anpu, ⟨hieroglyphs⟩, *i.e.* **Anubis,** the divine physician, who embalmed the body of Osiris and was the guardian of all mummies.

Nekhebit, ⸶, the Greek Eileithyia, the oldest " mother-goddess " of Upper Egypt ; she was the great protectress of pregnant women ; her sacred bird was a **vulture.**

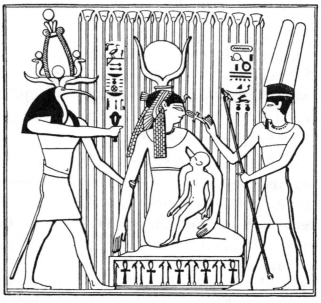

Isis suckling her son Horus among the lotus plants. She wears the vulture head-dress with the horns and disk of the moon. On the right is Amen-Rā, who is holding " life," ☥, to her nostrils, and on the left Thoth, the Twice-great, the lord of Khemenu, the great god, who is presenting to her the magical fluid of life, ☥.

Uatchit, ⸶, one of the oldest " mother goddesses " of Lower Egypt ; the seat of her cult was Per-Uatchit (Buto) in the Delta, and her emblem was a **cobra.**

Net, ⲭ 𓏏, the great " mother-goddess "
of the city of Saïs in the Delta. Though she
existed in four forms or aspects she was called
" One." She was self-begotten and self-produced,
and whilst a virgin gave birth to the Sun-god.

Bast, 🦤 𓂃 𓏏, the " mother-goddess " of
the city of Bubastis in the Eastern Delta, whose
sacred animal was the **cat.**

Taurit, ⲟ 𓅓 𓃗 or ⲟ 𓅓 𓃗, the
Thoueris of the Greeks, was one of the oldest
" mother-goddesses " of Egypt; her sacred
animal was the **hippopotamus.**

Heqit, 𓆸 𓆣, one of the oldest " mother-
goddesses " of Egypt; she was the goddess of
fertility and rebirth. The little green **tree-
frog** was her symbol in Nubia and the Northern
Sūdān, and the ordinary frog in Egypt.

Amen, 𓇋𓏶 𓏏, the " **Hidden,**" a local
god of Thebes, whose cult is as old as dynastic
civilization in Egypt; he represented the
" hidden " powers of generation and growth in
the unborn child. His symbol seems to have
been the **umbilicus ;** if this be so, his cult may
be of Sūdānī origin. Under the XIIth Dynasty
he became the chief god of Thebes, and after the
expulsion of the Hyksos, which was believed to
be due to his power and favour, the attributes of
Rā, the Sun-god of Heliopolis, were merged with

his, and he was called **Amen-Rā,** 〔hieroglyphs〕,
the " King of the gods," 〔hieroglyphs〕.

Rā, 〔hieroglyphs〕, the Sun-god of Heliopolis, whose
spirit was believed to dwell
in the **Ben Ben,** 〔hieroglyphs〕,
i.e. a stone that had the
form of a square pointed
stone set on a truncated
pyramid. He usurped the
attributes of the older solar
gods of Egypt, and his
priests not only made him
the head of the Company
of the Gods, but forced
their nominees on to the
throne of Egypt, and made
them adopt a name as the
sons of Rā. He represented

Rā, the Sun-god of Heliopolis.

the noonday sun, *i.e.* the
sun in his full strength.

Hāpi, 〔hieroglyphs〕, the Nile-god ; he has
the form of a man with the breasts of a woman.

Merit, 〔hieroglyphs〕, the goddess of the Inundation—an ancient goddess ; one of the names of
Egypt was Ta-Mera, " Land of the Inundation."

An-her, 〔hieroglyphs〕, an ancient god of This,
whose attributes were usurped by Osiris.

Menu, ⟨𓏠⟩, ⟨𓏠⟩, a god of generation and fertility; he is usually represented in the form of an ithyphallic man.

Afurā, ⟨𓏠⟩, the body of the Sun-god of Night.

Amset, ⟨𓏠⟩, one of the Four Sons of Horus who protected the viscera of the dead; the other three were **Hāp,** ⟨𓏠⟩, **Qebhsenuf,** ⟨𓏠⟩, and **Tuamutef,** ⟨𓏠⟩. The first had the head of a man, the second that of an ape, the third that of a hawk, and the fourth that of a jackal.

Ami-ut, ⟨𓏠⟩, a dog-headed god of the dead; his symbol was a pied headless bull's skin attached to a rod, ⟨𓏠⟩.

Ani, ⟨𓏠⟩, a form of the Moon-god; his wife was **Anit,** ⟨𓏠⟩.

Ānqit, ⟨𓏠⟩, **Satit,** ⟨𓏠⟩, and **Khnemu,** ⟨𓏠⟩, formed the great triad of Elephantine and the First Cataract; the two goddesses were probably of Sūdānī origin.

Asten or **Astes,** ⟨𓏠⟩, ⟨𓏠⟩, the companion of Thoth.

Baba, 🦅🦅🦅🦅, or **Beb,** , the first-born son of Osiris.

Hāp, , , the **Apis** Bull.

Merur, , the **Mnevis** Bull.

Bekha, , the **Bakhis** Bull.

Hu, , , and **Saa,** , represented **Taste** and **Touch** respectively; they appear in the Judgment Hall of Osiris.

Iusāasit, , an ancient goddess of Heliopolis.

Khensu, , the Moon-god. He and Amen-Rā and **Mut,** , formed the great triad of Thebes; another important form of him was **Khensu-nefer-hetep,** .

Menhit, , a lioness-goddess.

Mentu, , the War-god of Hermonthis and Thebes.

Meh-urit, , a Sky-goddess who took the form of a cow.

Mer-seģerit, , a Theban goddess who is represented in the form of a woman-headed serpent; the name means "lover of silence."

Meskhenit, , a goddess of the birth-chamber.

Mut, , the Mother-goddess of Thebes, wife of Amen-Rā.

Khensu, the Moon-god.

Bes, the Sūdānī god, wearing plumes and a tail. He was the god of mirth and jollity, and as a god of music plays a harp. He also appears in the form of a jovial soldier.

Neb-er-tcher, , " Lord to the [uttermost] limit," a title of Osiris and other gods.

Nefer-Temu, , son of Ptah and Sekhmit of Memphis.

Nehebka, , a benevolent Serpent-goddess.

Pakhit, 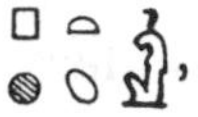, a local Cat-goddess.

Rennit, 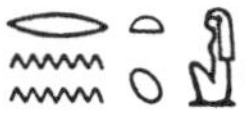, goddess of birth and the harvest.

Sept, , *i.e.* Sothis, goddess of the Dog-star.

Sekhmit, 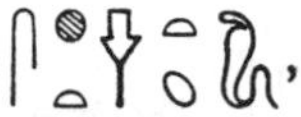, wife of Ptah of Memphis.

Seker, 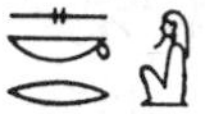, the god of Death of the Underworld of Memphis.

Serqit, 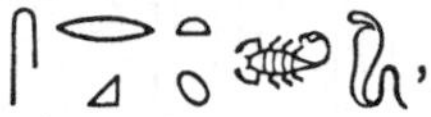, the Scorpion-goddess.

Seshet, , goddess of writing and literature, an associate of Thoth.

Shai, , god of Luck or Destiny.

Tanen, 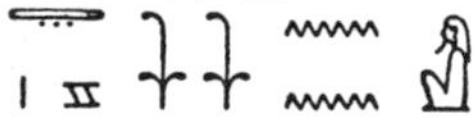, or **Ta-Tenen,** , a cosmic god.

Up-uatu, , the Wolf-god, an associate of Anpu.

Un-Nefer, , the Hare-god, sometimes identified with Osiris.

Āpep, , *i.e.* Apophis, was the perpetual arch-enemy of all the solar-gods; he appeared in the form of a crocodile.

Asar-Hāpi, 𓊮 𓏺 𓎛, Serapis or Sarapis, was the name of the deified Apis Bull. He was identified by the Greeks with their god **Hades,** and both Egyptians and Greeks regarded him as the god of Death, and worshipped him as such.[1]

The following were of Sūdānī origin :—

Ahu, 𓃓 𓏺 𓅡 𓏏 𓅭 , **Bes,** 𓃀 𓊪 𓁫 , **Tetun,** 𓃟 𓏲 𓀭 , **Meril,** 𓅓 𓏤 𓂻 .

The following were of Syrian and Hittite origin :—

Āntat, 𓄿 𓏏 𓏤 𓆇 , a goddess of conception and a daughter of Set.

Ānthreta (?), 𓄿 𓏏 𓆇 , a goddess mentioned with Sutekh.

Āstharth, 𓄿 𓏏 𓆇 , i.e. **Ashtoreth,** " Mistress of horses, and lady of the chariot," 𓏏 𓃒 𓂋 .

Qetesh, 𓆇 , mistress of the gods, the " eye of Rā."

Kent, 𓆇 , lady of heaven.

Āasit, 𓆇 , a goddess of battle.

[1] A list of all the gods and divine beings mentioned in the Pyramid Texts will be found in my *Gods of the Egyptians,* vol. i, pp. 79 ff.

Băr, ⟨hieroglyph⟩, *i.e.* Baal, a god of battle.

Reshpu, ⟨hieroglyph⟩, a god of war and of the lightning.

Sutekh, ⟨hieroglyph⟩, a Hittite god of the same character as Set.

The figures of the gods, made of gold, or silver covered with a thick casing of gold, or bronze inlaid with gold, were kept in small portable shrines, made in the shape of the large shrine, ⟨hieroglyph⟩, and provided with doors, which were closed and bolted and sometimes sealed. When a god desired to make a progress through the city or country, his shrine was brought out and placed in a boat, ⟨hieroglyph⟩, or some other sacred receptacle, and the priests carried it out of the temple into the street. The shrine was followed by a large number of people of all sorts besides the temple staff, and hymns of praise were sung by the priests and the choir of the temple, and probably many laymen joined in. These religious festival processions were highly appreciated by the populace, and when they were allowed to look upon the face of the god they rejoiced greatly, for healing of sicknesses and blessings were believed to follow in his train. The goddess Isis of Philae was carried through the country of Nubia once a year so that women might present their petitions for offspring to her in person. A special barge was kept for the use of the god when he wished to progress up or down the Nile, and the

" boat of the god " was a splendid construction. The barge of Amen of Thebes, called **Userhat,** 𓀀 , was made of cedar-wood and was 130 cubits (at least 200 feet) long, and was gilded all over ; the cabin of the god was made of fine gold inlaid with precious stones, and was decorated with heads of rams in gold, and its prow was in the form of a uraeus wearing the crown of Osiris. The barge of Ptah of Memphis, called **Neb heh,** 𓏴 , was as long as that of Amen, and its cabin and steering-poles were made of gold ; everywhere its approach was greeted with cries of joy and the sound of music. Some figures of the gods had movable limbs, for Amen of Thebes chose Thothmes III as king by touching him with his hand ; Amen of the Oasis of Jupiter Ammon, by touching Alexander the Great with his hand, acknowledged him to be his son and the king of Egypt ; Amen of Napata selected from among the candidates for the throne of Nubia the man he wished to be king by touching him with his hand, and Khensu, a god of Thebes, showed that he approved of the journey of Nefer-hetep to Bekhten by nodding his head. On festal occasions the god was " dressed " by the priests, who placed crowns of gold on his head, an elaborate pectoral on his breast, cases made of gold on his fingers and toes, and the symbols of his power in his hands.

The king, by virtue of his divine origin, was in all periods of Egyptian history the **high priest of the god,** and the priesthood was hereditary in many noble families. As a child and as a youth the son of a nobleman usually occupied himself with duties which were not, strictly speaking, of a priestly character, and did not

The Kheri-heb and his assistants performing magical ceremonies in order to effect the "Opening of the Mouth" of the deceased Hunefer. The words of the "book" are given above in hieroglyphs. On the stele behind Anubis and the mummy is a prayer to Osiris for funerary offerings.

become a priest until he reached early manhood. The ordinary servant of the temple was called "servant of the god," **hem neter,** and served under the direction of a MER, , or overseer ; the custody of the temple generally was in the hands of the " overseer of the temple." Other orders of priests were " father of the god," ⎯⎯, the asperger, or "pure one," ⎯⎯, the " scribe of the holy books," ⎯⎯, and the " Possessor of the book," **Kheri-heb,** ⎯⎯, *i.e.* the priest who arranged the order of the services and recited or sang parts of them. He was usually a man of great learning and was believed to possess magical powers. The Kheri-heb who is mentioned in the Westcar Papyrus is said to have had the power of restoring to life a goose the head of which had been cut off, and of dividing the water in a lake into two parts and making the one part to stand on the other. One of the Kheri-heb's garments was the leopard skin, which conferred upon him the power to deal and treat with the denizens of the Underworld. He was the chief performer in all the important magical funerary ceremonies, especially in those that concerned the " Opening of the Mouth," whereby the deceased resumed the power to think, talk, move and walk, which he had enjoyed upon earth.

There were various grades among the ordinary servants of the god, and a man might be the first or second or third prophet of the god, and he might be a priest of several gods, *e.g.* prophet of Menu, prophet of Isis, prophet of Her-netch-teff. Under the New Kingdom the priests of a temple

were divided into classes, 𓏸𓏸, *sau*, each of which
was under a director.   Several of the priests who
assisted in the funerary ceremonies in the tombs
had special titles, *e.g.* Sa-mer-f, 𓏸𓏸𓏸, and
the priest who undertook duties in connection
with the dead was called " prophet of the Ka,"
𓏸𓏸, *hem ka*.   Under the New Kingdom a great
many priests and servants of the temple of
Amen-Rā at Thebes occupied themselves with
the burial of the dead who belonged to their
order, and coffins, funerary coffers, ushabtiu
figures, scarabs, and all the miscellaneous objects
that were considered necessary for the deceased
in his tomb were prepared under their direction.
Mummification was carried on under their
care, as also were the painting and decoration
of the coffins in which the priests and singing
women of Amen were buried.   The influence of
Amen and his priests at Thebes was felt in every
grade of society, and it culminated when Her-Her,
the high priest of Amen, usurped the throne and
founded the short-lived line of **Priest-kings** at
Thebes, about 1100–950 B.C.   The same thing
had happened about two thousand years earlier,
when the priesthood of Rā at Heliopolis succeeded in making three of their high priests the
first three kings of the Vth Dynasty.

However numerous the official priests may have
been in every temple, they were unable to direct
all the services that had to be performed during
the day and night ; they were assisted in their
work by **lay priests**.   Some of these undertook

to be present and to minister in the temple for a specified number of hours, and were called " hour-men of the house of the god," , and others served for a month at a time. These, with their wives and children, formed the population of the " Temple-town " and were a sort of *imperium in imperio*, a state within the state. The reigning monarch was nominally their king, but the god they served was their real king. The chief of the lay priests was the deputy of the god, and his assistants formed both his Court and his Council. The body of lay priests consisted of soldiers, sailors, handicraftsmen of all kinds, agriculturists, cattle-breeders, merchants, etc., all of whom made offerings to the common fund ; but those who received wages from this fund were not called upon to make offerings. Most of the manual labour required by the lay priests was provided by their slaves, who were very numerous, some temples possessing as many as 682. Rameses III states, in the Harris Papyrus No. 1, that in the course of the 31 years of his reign he gave to the temples of Egypt 113,433 slaves. And the staffs of the various temples enumerated by him in the same document consisted of 5,811 persons.

CHAPTER VI

EGYPTIAN WRITING—HIEROGLYPHIC, HIERATIC, DEMOTIC—AND COPTIC

THE inscribed objects of the Late Neolithic Period which have come down to us show that the Egyptians were able to cut on stone and wood a considerable number of the **pictorial characters** that were used in writing in the Dynastic Period, and that are commonly called **hieroglyphs.** The objects represented by them are all native, *i.e.* African, which shows that the characters were not of foreign origin, but up to the present it has not been proved that the predynastic Egyptians were acquainted with the **art of writing,** as we understand it. They could not construct connected sentences. This art they acquired early in the Dynastic Period, and it is probable that they did so under the influence of some Asiatic or European people. On the other hand, it is allowable to think that the Egyptians themselves turned their pictographs into a syllabary, for they soon found that they wanted to use combinations of them solely for the sounds of the words that they represented, without any regard to the actual objects that they represented. But they went further than this, for they simplified several of the values of the signs in their syllabary and gave them **alphabetic values,** though they never used them as the letters of the alphabet were used by the Persians in the time of Darius I and are used by modern nations in Europe. And down to the latest times in which hieroglyphic writing was used, the inscriptions contain both syllabic and alphabetic characters.

The Egyptians were able to retain the pictorial forms of the characters they used in writing because they found in abundance in their own country a material on which they could be written easily, namely **papyrus.** The Sumerians and Babylonians, whose writing was originally pictographic, had no such vegetable material in Mesopotamia, and they therefore made use of clay. But their scribes very soon found that it was difficult to draw figures of animals and round or curved objects on this material, and little by little the pictorial forms of the characters disappeared, and then was invented the **cuneiform** system of writing, which is so called because each sign is composed of a series of **wedge-shaped** characters. Thus a circle, ◯, which represented the sun, became ⬦, and ✳, a star, became ✳; but from first to last the Egyptian represented the sun by ⊙ and the star by ✳ . The Egyptian might have used Nile mud as the Sumerian used clay, but the former has not the tenacity of the latter and is far less compact.

Kinds of writing. Egyptian writing is known in three forms :—Hieroglyphic, Hieratic, and Demotic.   The oldest form is pictographic, or **hieroglyphic,** and it remained in use from the Late Neolithic Period until the early centuries of the Christian Era.   The dynastic Egyptians said that it was invented by **Thoth,** the scribe of the gods, and they described it as 𓊹𓌃, "words of the god"; and in their opinion it always possessed a specially sacred character.   Hieroglyphs are written in horizontal lines or in columns, and a text may begin either on the right- or left-hand side of a page, as in the following examples :—

1. In horizontal lines :—

2. Beginning on right-hand side of page :—

3. Beginning on left-hand side of page :—

4. In columns :—

In **Hieratic,** *i.e.* cursive hieroglyphic, writing we have only the most salient features of the hieroglyphs preserved, as the following examples from the Tale of the Two Brothers shows. Hieratic writing could be written more quickly than hieroglyphic, and was employed in writing copies of business documents and letters and drafts of inscriptions that were to be cut in stone, and pupils in the temple schools were taught to read it easily and to become experts in writing it by making copies of literary and religious texts.   Under the Middle Kingdom Chapters from the Pyramid Texts and Chapters from the later Book of the Dead, *i.e.* " Chapters of Coming Forth by Day," were written in hieratic on the insides and outsides of coffins. Medical and mathematical papyri, *e.g.* the Ebers Papyrus and the Rhind Papyrus were also written in bold hieratic characters.   Under the New Kingdom copies of extracts from the Book of the Dead were written in hieratic, and sometimes the whole of its Chapters, as in the papyrus of Princess Nesitanebtashru (the Greenfield Papyrus). The following is a specimen of hieratic writing taken from the D'Orbiney Papyrus in the British Museum (Birch, *Select Papyri*, part ii, plates xi and xii), together with a transcript of it into hieroglyphs, which will enable the reader to compare the two writings. The hieratic text is written from right to left, but the hieroglyphs must be read from left to right.

HIERATIC TEXT

HIEROGLYPHIC TRANSCRIPT

Hieratic is usually written in horizontal lines, which are to be read from right to left, but in several papyri of the Middle Kingdom the texts are written in short columns.

Demotic, or Enchorial, the third form of Egyptian writing, is an abbreviated and conventionalized form of hieratic that was much used by business folk and lawyers, but copies of several literary works, funerary compositions and priestly edicts, were written in this script.

Every hieroglyph, or pictograph, could be used to represent a sound or to express an idea, *i.e.* it can be either **ideographic** or **phonetic;** phonetic characters may be either syllabic or alphabetic. Ideographs are to be interpreted sometimes literally and sometimes symbolically; thus ⟨⟩ is a wall, but it may be used as a symbol of building; ⟨⟩ is a seal, but it may be used as a symbol of something sealed up, *i.e.* treasure. Ideographs that have more than one phonetic value are called **polyphones,** and different ideographs that have similar values are called **homophones.** So long as the Egyptians used pictographs pure and simple the meaning of each character was easily understood. Thus in the title ⟨⟩, *hem neter,* ⟨⟩ means " servant " and ⟨⟩ means " god," so we have " servant of the god," *i.e.* priest. In the oft-repeated formula, ⟨⟩, the first sign means " king," the second means " giver " and the third means " gift," or " funerary offering," and the meaning, " the king gives a gift," is obvious. But when the Egyptians began to spell their words with alphabetic signs and syllabic signs they found it necessary to indicate in some way the meaning and even the sounds of many of the words so written ; this they did by adding to the words signs which we call **determinatives.** Thus the word for lily, ⌐🔲, *seshen*, is determined by a picture of the flower itself, 🐝 ; and ≋, chariot, is determined by the picture of a chariot 🐎. These are examples of determinatives that determine a single species, but there is a large class of general determinatives, *e.g.* ⋀ is the determinative of actions performed with the legs, ⌐ is the determinative of " god," and 𝄞 of " goddess," 〰, *i.e.* water falling from the sky, of rain, rain-cloud, dew, etc. These few examples will illustrate the use of determinative signs.

⊿𝄞𝄞🌊, *qebh*, cold water (2 determinatives).

⌐ ⬭ 🐒, *sekher*, to overthrow.

⬜🦅𝄖⋀, *hab*, to send.

🦅⬜🦆, *apt*, goose, duck.

══ ⤳ , *ses*, wooden bolt.

⬭𝄖⬯, *meh*, air, wind.

The Egyptian alphabetic characters are :—

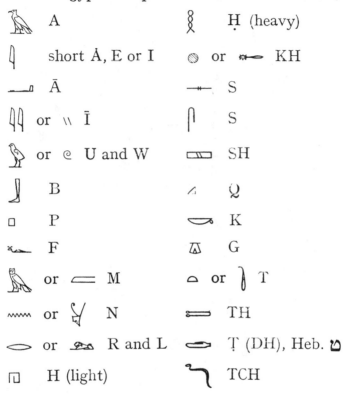

🦅	A	�콰	Ḥ (heavy)
⌇	short Å, E or I	◎ or ⊶	KH
▁	Ā	⊷	S
⌇⌇ or \\\\	Ī	⊓	S
🦆 or ℮	U and W	▭	SH
⌇	B	⟋	Q̇
□	P	⌣	K
⬳	F	◮	G
🦉 or ⊏	M	⌒ or ⌇	T
⌇⌇⌇ or ⑃	N	⊜	TH
⌒ or ⬲	R and L	⌣	Ṭ (DH), Heb. ב
⊡	H (light)	⌇	TCH

The following extracts from texts will illustrate the use of ideographs, alphabetic characters and determinatives in the inscriptions :—

I. □ 🦉 ⌇ 🦆 ⋀   ⌇ ⬳   ⌒   ⌇⌇ ⌇ □ 🦉 ⌢

habu	ḥen-f	er	Åbhat
Sent [me]	*His Majesty*	*to*	*Åbhat*

er	ȧnt	neb ānkh	hen	en	ānkhu
to	*bring*	{ *a lord of life,* *i.e. sarcophagus* }	*and a coffer*	*of*	*the living one*

ḥenā	āa-f	ḥenā	benbent	......
with	*its cover*	*with*	*pyramidion*	*precious* (?)

shepst	en	Merenrā	Khā-nefer	ḥenut
august,	*for the*	*Merenrā pyramid*	[*called*] *Khānefer*	*the royal.*

habu	ḥen-f	er	Abu
Sent [*me*]	*His Majesty*	*to*	*Abu* (*i.e. Elephantine*)

er	ȧnt	math	ārtu	ḥenā	seth - s
to	*bring*	*granite*	*a* [*false*] *door*	*and*	*its libation slab*

math	āau	ruit	er	ȧnt
[*of*] *granite.*	*Doors*	[*and*] *posts*	*to*	*bring* [*of*]

math	khet-nȧ	em	ā	er	Khā-nefer
granite	{ *I sailed down the* *river* [*with them*] }	*at*	*once*	*to*	{ *Khānefer* *pyramid* }

em	usekht	VI	sath	VI
in	*barges*	*six,* [*and*]	*lighters*	*six,* [*and*]

.... III en ...... uàa (?) uā àn sep

boats of eight... three, { [and] for the armed guard } *boat one. Never*

pat àrit Abhat Abu

before had visited Àbhat [and] Elephantine

en .....uàa (?) uā ḥer hau nesu neb.

a ship with an armed guard in the time of king any.

II. àu àrnà ḥesest ret hereret neteru

I have done the behests of men [and] the will of the gods.

ḥeres àu ṭa - nà tau en ḥeqr

Because of it I have given bread to the hungry,

sesau - nà àt àu shes - nà neter

I have satisfied the indigent. I have followed the god

em pa - f àn āa re - à em

in house his. Not did I make great my mouth + against

shenit àn peṭ em nemt - à

superior officers. There is no stretch in stride my,

shem - à	her sa khent	àr - nà	em	maāt
walk	{ *I according to measure.* (*i.e. decorously*) }	{ *I have worked according to the* }		*law*

mer	en	nesu	rekh - kuà	entet	utu - nef
beloved	*by*	*the king.*	*I understood*	*what*	*commanded*

set	res - nà	her àst - à	er	seqa	baiu - f
he it.	*Watched I*	*at seat my*	*to*	*exalt*	*his will.*

ṭua - nà	ṭua - f	hru	neb	erṭa - nà	àb - à	khenti
{ *I sang his praise at dawn* }		*day*	*every.*	*I made my mind to be ready*		

tcheṭ - f	àn	māhi - à	her	sha - nef
for his word.	*Not*	*did I hesitate*	*about what*	*he determined*

kher - à	àth - nà	metrit	henā	metit
{ *with reference to me.* }	*I laid hold on*	*uprightness*	*and*	*justice.*

peḥ nà	enen	her	ger - à	qebb
I grasped	{ *those things* [*about which*] }	*I had to keep silence.*		*Refreshed*

ḥes - nuà	neb - à	her	menkh - à	ma - nef
favoured me	*my lord*	*for*	*my ability.*	*He saw the*

ruṭ	ààui - à	àn	àb-à	sekhent
vigorousness	*of my hands.*	*Lo,*	*my heart*	*made to*

àst - à

advance my position.

The **decipherment** of the Egyptian hiero-glyphs was effected by two men, **Thomas Young** and **J. F. Champollion,** in the first quarter of the XIXth century, through the discovery of the **Rosetta Stone** (now in the British Museum) and the famous Obelisk at Philae (now at Kingston Hall in Dorsetshire). The Rosetta Stone is inscribed in two forms of Egyptian writing (hieroglyphic and demotic) and in Greek, with a decree of the priests of all Egypt assembled at Memphis in the ninth year of **Ptolemy V,** King of Egypt, 196 B.C.   The Obelisk at Philae is inscribed with a petition of the priests of Philae addressed to **Ptolemy IX** and to Cleopatra his wife and Cleopatra his sister.   On each of the four sides of the shaft of the Obelisk is a hieroglyphic inscription giving the titles of the king and mentioning his wife Cleopatra ; on the pedestal are the petition of the priests and Ptolemy's answer to them, written in Greek.   Thus the inscriptions on the Rosetta

Stone and the Obelisk of Philae are two **bilingual** (Egyptian and Greek) documents. The Greek inscriptions on each monument were read without any great difficulty, because Greek was a **known** language ; then scholars set to work to try and decipher the Egyptian inscriptions in the **unknown** language. Many attempts had been made to decipher the Egyptian hieroglyphs, but none was successful until Young began to work at them. It was well known from the hieroglyphic inscriptions available for study in Europe that groups of hieroglyphs were enclosed in ovals, ( ), and Jörgen Zoega, the Dane (1755–1809), guessed that such ovals contained royal names. The Greek text of the Rosetta Stone mentions King Ptolemy, and Young assumed that the Egyptian text would do the same, and that if it did the name would be written in phonetic, *i.e.* alphabetic, characters ; in fact, he was the first to grasp the idea of the existence of a **phonetic principle** in Egyptian writing. He adopted Zoega's guess that the oval ( ), now called **cartouche,** contained the name of Ptolemy, and with the help of the cartouche of Cleopatra on the Philae Obelisk succeeded in proving that it did, and that the beginning of a royal name in a cartouche was always at the rounded end of it. He also identified the name of Berenice from another monument, and obtained the correct phonetic values of several of the hieroglyphs. Thus before 1818 he had deciphered two royal names, **and Mr. Bankes had identified the name of**

PLATE VII.

The Rosetta Stone. On it is a bilingual inscription in two forms of Egyptian writing—hieroglyphic and demotic—and in Greek, containing a copy of the decree promulgated by the entire priesthood of Egypt assembled at Memphis, 196 B.C., directing that special honours be paid to Ptolemy V Epiphanes.

Cleopatra also. Egyptian decipherment was only one of the many abstruse subjects that occupied Young's mind and energies, and after the publication in 1818 of his great article in the *Encyclopaedia Britannica* he practically dropped the matter.

Meanwhile J. F. Champollion in France had been working at the subject and, adopting Young's method and some of his values—unfortunately without acknowledgment—he drew up an alphabet from the names of the Roman emperors and formulated the system of decipherment which has been in part adopted by later Egyptologists. He found a wise and learned helper in his brother, **Champollion-Figeac,** who collected his notes and papers and edited his *Dictionnaire.* Lepsius investigated very carefully Champollion's system in 1835, and it was due to his report on it that its fundamental features were accepted by scholars generally. Champollion, to the deep regret of the learned world in Europe, died in 1832, but the splendid work which he had begun was carried on and developed by Birch, Hincks and Goodwin in England, by Lepsius and Heinrich Brugsch in Germany, and by E. de Rougé and Chabas in France. He who wishes to know the true facts about the part that Young took in the decipherment of Egyptian hieroglyphs should read the third volume of *The Works of Thomas Young* by Leitch (with his *Life* by Dean Peacock), London, 1855. The method followed by Young and Champollion in the construction of the Egyptian alphabet is described in a quarto pamphlet entitled

The Rosetta Stone, published by the British Museum, price 6*d*. This little work contains a good reproduction of the inscriptions on the Stone in collotype. For a fuller account *see* my *Mummy,* Cambridge, 1925.

Coptic is the name given to the form of writing which, it seems, was first used to any great extent by the Copts, or Egyptian Christians, in writing their translations of the various books of the Old and New Testaments from Greek into the Egyptian language. The Egyptian man was called by the Arab " ḳibṭiyy," قِبْطِي, or " ḳubṭiyy," قُبْطِي (whence the name " Copt "), and this appellation was derived from the Greek name for the Egyptian, Αἰγύπτιος. To the Copts " ḳibṭiyy " was the Egyptian Christian who had embraced the Monophysite form of Christianity, as opposed to the " Melkite," or " Royalist," who accepted the ruling of the Council of Chalcedon, but the epithet was probably applied by the Semites to every indigenous Egyptian long before Christianity was introduced into Egypt in the Ist century of our Era. The language of the " ḳibṭiyy," or " Copt," was called by the Arabs " ḳibṭiyyah," whence our " Coptic." Some of the papyrus manuscripts containing copies of Books of the Bible are certainly as old as the beginning of the IVth century, and probably are a century older, and there is every reason to think that they were copied from manuscripts in Upper Egypt. At the beginning of our Era it seems that the demotic script was in general use in Egypt, but the Egyptian Christians decided to adopt the Greek alphabet, and all the Coptic translations of the Scriptures that have come down to us are written with Greek uncials. There were, however, some sounds in the Egyptian language that could not be expressed by any letter in the Greek alphabet, and the Copts added to it modified forms of the hieroglyphs that represented them. These additions are ϥ, ϩ, ϧ, ϫ, ϭ and ϯ. The following is the Coptic version of St. Matt. vi. 19 and 21 in the dialect of Upper Egypt :—

19. ⲙ̄ⲡⲣ̄ ⲥⲱⲟⲩϩ, ⲛⲏⲧⲛ̄ ⲉϩⲟⲩⲛ ⲛ̄ϩⲉⲛⲁϩⲟ
    Do not   gather   for you   in   treasures

   ϩⲓⲝⲙ̄   ⲡⲕⲁϩ,   ⲡⲙⲁ   ⲉϣⲁⲣⲉ
   upon   the earth, the place in which are wont

   ⲧⲭⲟⲟⲗⲉⲥ ⲙⲛ̄ ⲑⲟⲟⲗⲉ ⲧⲁⲕⲟ ⲛ̄ϩⲏⲧϥ̄,
   the rust   and the moth destroy in it,

   ⲁⲧⲱ ⲡⲙⲁ   ⲉϣⲁⲣⲉ   ⲛ̄ⲣⲉϥϫⲱⲧⲉ ϣⲟⲭⲧ̄
   and the place where are wont the thieves   to dig

   ⲉⲣⲟϥ ⲛ̄ⲥⲉϫⲓⲟⲩⲉ.
   into it   to steal.

21. ⲡⲙⲁ   ⲅⲁⲣ ⲉⲧⲉⲣⲉ   ⲡⲉⲕⲁϩⲟ   ⲛⲁϣⲱⲡⲉ
    The place for   wherein thy treasure shall be

   ⲛ̄ϩⲏⲧϥ̄ ϥⲛⲁϣⲱⲡⲉ ⲙⲙⲁⲩ ⲛ̄ϭⲓ ⲡⲉⲕⲕⲉϩⲏⲧ.
   in it,   shall be   there   thy heart also.

CHAPTER VII

THE WISDOM OF THE EGYPTIANS

GREEK writers tell us that their own sages and philosophers, *e.g.* Archimedes, Hecataeus, Plato, Pythagoras, Solon, Thales, went and studied in Egypt in order to become acquainted with the wisdom and learning of the Egyptians, but in what that wisdom and learning consisted none of them has told us. Stephen the Martyr, in his dying speech (Acts vii. 22), says that Moses was "learned in all the wisdom of the Egyptians," and we shall perhaps be not far wrong if we assume that he thought Moses had read and studied the native Egyptian works on magic and religion and had acquired a special knowledge of the Egyptian doctrines and beliefs concerning the origin of the world and of "gods" and men, and the resurrection and the world and life beyond the grave. We shall see later on that the Egyptians did not possess the great and exact knowledge of mathematics,

chemistry, and other sciences with which they
have been credited, but it is impossible to think
that their reputation for learning and wisdom
and the knowledge of " mysteries " was wholly
undeserved.   To the Egyptians " mysteries,"
SHETAT, ⌐⌐ 🦅 ⫯⫯, meant the secret rites that
were performed by specially initiated persons
only, and also religious doctrines which seemed
to be above or beyond ordinary human com-
prehension. The Egyptian priests and sages and
teachers of theoretical and practical magic *must*
have possessed some knowledge that was not
to be found out of Egypt, and, if they did, it
concerned spiritual matters rather than material.
The texts make it quite clear that the Kher-heb
priests   and   the   learned   in   Egypt   studied
matters that are now called " occult," and that
some of them possessed psychological powers of
a   remarkable   character.   There   must   always
have been in Egypt a limited class of thinkers
who tried to probe mysteries and wanted " to
know," ⌐ ⫯, and to whom knowledge was its
own reward. They probably wrote books on the
subjects that they studied, but if they did none
of them has come down to us.   For the ordinary
Egyptian the road to success and prosperity
could only be traversed by knowing how to read
and write ;   hence the extraordinary respect
which was paid to the profession of the scribe
and to the scribe himself.   The unlettered man,
● 🦅 ⌐⌐, was regarded everywhere as a fool

and of no account.   The principal branches of Egyptian learning were :—

Mathematics.   The Egyptians were not naturally great mathematicians, and they owed their knowledge of the higher branches of the subject to the Greeks.   They used the **decimal system,** but traces of a duodecimal system are found in the 12 hours, the 12 months, perhaps in the 12 Signs of the Zodiac, and in the 36 (12 × 3) Dekans.   The numbers 1 to 9 are represented by strokes I, II, III, II, III, III, IIII, IIII, III, 10 is represented by ∩, 100 by ℮, 1,000 by ⌇, 10,000 by ⌇, 100,000 by ⌇, 1,000,000 by ⌇, and there are signs for 10,000,000 and 100,000,000.   Thus 1,765,949 is expressed by ⌇ ⌇⌇⌇⌇⌇⌇ IIIIII IIIII ℮℮℮℮ ∩∩ III ℮℮℮℮ ℮ ∩∩ III, and 10,000,000 years by ⌇⌇⌇.   **Addition** and **subtraction** were often used ; **multiplication** and **division** were difficult, for the **multiplication table** was unknown.   **Ordinal numbers** were formed by the addition of ⌣ to the number, *e.g.* ⌣, *fifth*.   **Fractions** are expressed by the addition of ⌔, meaning a " part " ; thus ⌔ = ¼, and ⌔ = ⅔, but many fractions, *e.g.* ⅝, were expressed in a clumsy fashion.

Geometry. In measures of length the royal cubit, ⟩ ⌒ ⌐ (·525 m.), and the little cubit, ⌐ 𓅱 (·450 m.), were used. Other measures were the finger-breadth, the hand-breadth, the palm, the span, and the length of the upper arm. In **land measure** there was the *arura*, 𓅜, with its divisions ½, ¼, ⅛, $\frac{1}{16}$, $\frac{1}{32}$; the chief liquid measure was the *hen*, 𓎼 ☉. The two principal **weights** were the *teben*, ▭ ▥ (9·09591 gram.), and the *qet* (90·9591 gram.).

Astronomy. Until the Egyptians came under the influence of Asiatic nations and the Greeks their notions of astronomy were very limited, and their star-gazers were unable to define the length of the year correctly. The oldest year known to them contained 12 months (divided into 3 seasons, **Akhet,** 𓇳, **Pert,** 𓇳, and **Shemut,** 𓇳), each containing 30 days ; to these they added at a later period the 5 epagomenal days, and the year then contained 365 days, and was nearly a quarter of a day shorter than the solar year. It was not until the reign of Ptolemy III that any general attempt was made to reform the **Calendar,** but a year of 365 days with an intercalated day every fourth year was not adopted by the Egyptians until nearly two centuries later.

The modern Egyptians begin to sow their winter crops some time in October, generally towards the end of the month, and these are all reaped by the middle of February, when they begin to sow their summer crops. At this time the *fallâhîn* take up their abode in the fields, and they stay there until the summer crops are grown and reaped, say about the middle of June. In this month the swelling of the Nile begins, and the waters from the great Equatorial Lakes make their appearance in Egypt. The final rise of the Nile takes place in October, and it seems that the period from the middle of June to the middle of October represents the old season of the Inundation called Shemut, 𓇳. If this be so, Akhet, 𓈍, the " season of growing," began in October and ended in February, and 𓈖, the " season of coming out," began in February and ended in June. The natural agricultural year began at the end of the period of the Inundation, which probably varied slightly in length. Some Egyptologists think that Akhet began on July 19 and ended on November 15 ; that Pert began on November 16 and ended on March 15 ; that Shemut began on March 16 and ended on July 13 ; and that then followed the five epagomenal days.

There is no proof that the Egyptians ever used the **Sothic Period,** or the **Phoenix Period.** They had no **Era** like that of the later Christians and the Muslims, and at first only dated their years by events ; later they used the regnal years of their kings. Each month was dedicated to a god, and every hour of the day (12 hours) and every hour of the night (12 hours) had its deity. The early Egyptians divided the **stars** into groups in which they thought they saw the forms of men and beasts, and parts of beasts and other objects, and they seem to have thought that these ruled the destinies of men. It is probable that the **star cult** is the oldest in Egypt. The five **planets** known to them were Jupiter, Saturn, Mars, Mercury, and Venus. The **36 Dekans** were known to the Egyptians of the New Kingdom, but the **Signs of the Zodiac** were introduced into Egypt by the Greeks, who borrowed them from the Babylonians, who in turn had borrowed them from the Sumerians. The texts mention two sets of stars, " the stars that never rest " and " the stars that never set "; the last are probably the circumpolar stars. There is no proof that the Egyptians systematically observed the stars over a period of many thousands of years, like the Babylonians, and material at present available suggests that their knowledge of astronomy was very limited.

Astrology. Such knowledge of the stars as was possessed by the Egyptians they devoted to building up the science of astrology, which existed in Egypt from the earliest times ; in pure astronomy they were not interested, for they regarded the stars merely as arbiters of their destinies, and as things that expressed the Will of the Creator. This view being general in Egypt, as in Babylonia, the development of astronomy was impossible.

The stars were gods, and from their appearances, colour, movements, and positions the astrologers made predictions and divinations concerning the outcome of events in Egypt generally, and the future actions of their kings, and the affairs of private individuals, and every circumstance of life. As they ruled the heavens, so they ruled the earth and times and seasons. Every hour of the day and night throughout the year, and every month, had its regent, and according as the events which had happened to the gods at certain hours of certain days of certain months were good or bad, parts of days and whole days were lucky or unlucky. In the Calendars of **Lucky and Unlucky days and hours,** the days are divided into three parts: thus a lucky day is described by 𓏤𓏤𓏤, and an unlucky one by 𓎟𓎟𓎟, and when a part of a day is lucky and the other two parts are unlucky, we have 𓏤𓎟𓎟, or 𓎟𓏤𓎟, or 𓎟𓎟𓏤, and so on. There were many kinds of astrologers, diviners, interpreters of dreams, casters of nativities, etc., but the aim of all of them was the same, *i.e.* to direct, or modify, or annul the wills and operations of the Star-gods. The **horoscope** and the **astrolabe** were not known to the Egyptians, as some have supposed, for the former was invented by the Greeks, and the latter by the Persians ; but it seems that the Egyptian astrologer drew up tablets of the positions of planets and used them for foretelling events in the lives of men. The doctrine of the sacredness of certain numbers must have formed a part of the science of astrology, among such being 3, 4, 7, 9, 27, 42, 75, 77, 110, etc. Thus we have **three** gods (the triad), and three divisions of the world, heaven, sky, and Tuat ; **four** sons of Horus, four quarters of the world, four blazing flames (Book of the Dead, Chap. cxxxvii*a*), four altars, four doors of heaven, four rudders of heaven, four vessels of blood, four vessels of milk ; **seven** Ārits, seven hawks, seven-headed serpent, seven Scorpions of Isis, seven Spirits ; **nine** gods in a Company, nine chiefs, nine Ennutchis, nine nations who used the bow ; **twenty-seven** gods (three Companies, 9 × 3) ; **forty-two** nomes, forty-two Assessors ; **seventy-five** Addresses to Rā ; **seventy-seven** in magical papyri ; **one hundred and ten** years, the limit of a man's life.

Scientific instruments. No remains of any such things have come down to us. Nothing like the tube of a telescope has been found, and though the Egyptians knew how to make glass paste under the Old Kingdom the **lens** was unknown to them. They had no mechanical instruments for measuring time, whether **sundial, gnomon** or **clock** ; the **water-clock** was introduced by the Greeks. There is no truth in the statements that they lighted their tombs by **electricity** and protected their buildings by **lightning conductors,** for the metal cases of the pyramidions of the obelisks and the metal caps of poles had no contact with the earth. The Egyptians never made and never could make any advance in physical science because they considered natural phenomena to be due directly to the operations of the gods.

Alchemy. The Egyptians possessed great skill in the working of metals, gold, copper, iron, etc., under the Old Kingdom, and the crafts of the goldsmith, blacksmith, smelter and metal engraver attained a high pitch of perfection in the later periods of their history. But no evidence exists in the inscriptions that they were adepts in the art of alchemy, which is generally understood to have had for its object the transmutation of the baser metals into gold and silver. The word alchemy comes to us through the Arabic *al-kīmīā*, الكِيمِيَاء, *i.e.* " the kīmīā," (*al* being the article *the*) ; kīmīā, it is said, means the art and knowledge of Chēmē, or Kēmi, which is the Coptic form of Kamt, ⌒ 𓅭 ⊗, Egypt. Now the name " Kamt " means the " black land " of the Delta as opposed to the " red land " or deserts of Upper Egypt, so " kīmīā " is the " Black Art of Egypt." In the Middle Ages this Black Art was often regarded as Black Magic, of which Egypt was the home.

Medicine. From the days of Homer downwards the Egyptians were famous for their skill in surgery and their knowledge of the art of healing. The practice of the art of mummification must have taught them something of **anatomy,** and there seems to be no doubt that they possessed much knowledge about the **properties of certain herbs and their effect on**

the human body. But it is impossible for modern medical experts to decide how great or how little was their knowledge of the art of healing, because we have no papyri that can be seriously regarded as Books of Medicine. Several papyri inscribed with long series of **prescriptions** are known, and those who are competent to pass an opinion upon the value of the few **diagnoses** given in them regard them as rudimentary and unscientific. It is well known that they used many vegetable and mineral substances in their medicines, but what these were cannot always be said, because in our present state of knowledge it is impossible to identify them. Besides these they used the excreta of men and of many kinds of animals, and other substances which we consider loathsome. Many of these disgusting prescriptions resemble those that were in use in Babylonia and Assyria and northern lands at a later period, and some of them found their way into the books of English herbalists.

The Egyptians thought that sickness and diseases were caused by demons and devils, who sometimes made their way into the limbs and members of the sufferers and could only be expelled by the help of spells and incantations, or by the direct assistance of Isis, or Thoth, or Imhetep. The help of the gods could be obtained by offerings and sacrifices, and the goodwill of the physician by liberal payments. The efficacy of the prescription depended upon the magical power, ⚱︎⊔, *heka,* which he could invoke, and the might of the god who could be persuaded to come and vanquish the demon of disease. The physician sometimes sprinkled the patient with holy water, or anointed him with holy oils, and the value of **massage** was well known. Amulets laid on the body or hung up in the sick man's room were used as means of healing. The physician and the magician and sorcerer held in his hand a short rod when reciting spells and exorcisms, from the time of the Old Kingdom to the days of Nektanebos, the last native king of Egypt ; sometimes a hooded cobra was substituted for the rod. By pressing a part of the neck of the cobra it could be made to straighten itself out like a rod, and when the pressure was removed the creature assumed its normal form. This trick was practised by Pharaoh's sorcerers in the presence of Aaron and Moses (Exodus vii. 12), and the snake-charmers of Egypt perform it at the present day. The Egyptian could easily have become a scientific physician, but in medicine, as in astronomy and physical science, all development was made impossible by his belief in demonology and religious magic. The following is a prescription for headache from the Ebers Papyrus :—

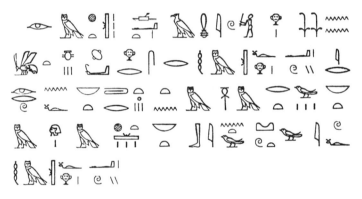

" Another [prescription], the sixth, which
was made by the goddess Isis for Rā himself
to drive out the pain which was in his head :—

Coriander seed	..	..	..	I
Seeds of the *khasit* plant (poppy ?)				I
Sāam leaves..	..	..	..	I
Seeds of the *shames* plant ..		..		I
Juniper berries	..	..	..	I
Honey	..	..	..	I

" Make these into a single substance, rub down with honey, smear it over [the patient's head] so that he may get relief quickly. If all these remedies be applied to the patient suffering from pain of any kind in the head, or from any discomfort and trouble of any kind, he will obtain relief immediately." (*Ebers Papyrus*, Pl. 47, lines 5–10.)

CHAPTER VIII

THE EGYPTIAN RELIGION

THE religious texts found on the walls of the chambers and corridors of the pyramids of the Old Kingdom, and on the walls of innumerable tombs and sarcophagi and coffins of the Middle and New Kingdoms, and on the rolls of papyrus inscribed with the texts of the various Recensions of the Book of the Dead, prove that the Egyptians, in the long course of their history, at different times worshipped stones, trees, wells, mountains, beasts, birds, reptiles, their ancestors, and men whom they deified. Of the religion of the predynastic Egyptians and their methods of worshipping the various objects of their cult we know nothing, but the monuments of the Dynastic Period make it clear that from first to last the fundamental religious beliefs of the Egyptians never changed, though at different times, owing to changed circumstances, they were differently expressed.

The Egyptian was always, both by nature and habit, a moral and religious man, but he was always extremely practical, and the end and aim of all his moral and religious efforts was to secure for himself ease, comfort, and prosperity in this world, and a life of everlasting joy and happiness in the next. The oldest graves known to us supply proofs that he believed in a future life, though where and how he thought it was to be lived we have no knowledge. His descendants in the Dynastic Period had many theories and views on the subject, and however childlike and absurd they may seem to us, they were preserved in their religious literature down to the Roman Period. Some of these theories flatly contradict each other, and this the Egyptian knew as well as ourselves, but he clung to them all and abandoned nothing, for in matters appertaining to the future life he considered no belief, however old or fantastic, to be unimportant. As a result of this attitude on the part of the Egyptian his religious texts contain a mixture of beliefs of all periods, which it is extremely difficult to classify and arrange chronologically.

The Pyramid Texts show that the Egyptian believed there was a time when the heavens and the earth and death did not exist, and when even the gods had not come into being. The number of the " **gods** " **of the Egyptians** whose names are mentioned in the Texts is between two and three thousand, but among them were many who were in reality only " spirits " of different kinds, and who are only mentioned once. Every town, village, hamlet, and settlement had its local god, and some more than one, with whom each community had to keep on good terms; hence the large number of the gods is not surprising ; but the Egyptian made all these " gods " in his own image, and he assumed that they ate and drank, and made love, and wore clothing, and that their feelings, passions and emotions resembled his own. He thought that they could be flattered, cajoled and wheedled into granting his requests, and even on occasions into assisting him to break the laws of the community and to acquire unlawful things. Such " gods " could be bribed by gifts and offerings of sweet-smelling incense, oils, meat, flowers, fruit and vegetables, beer and wine, and the presentation of such things formed one of the principal acts of worship of any and every god at all periods of Egyptian history.

Though the god of a nome had a greater reputation than a provincial or village god, and the national god of the Delta or of Upper Egypt was more important than the nome-god, the nature and dispositions of all of them were one and the same, and it was believed that under certain circumstances they could suffer like men. An interesting example of this fact is furnished by the well-known **Legend of Rā and Isis.** According to this Rā, the self-created god and the creator of the world and everything in it, maintained his sovereignty over gods and men by means of a great and secret name which was hidden within himself and was known to none. The great goddess Isis, who possessed extraordinary magical power of speech and action, wished to become as great and powerful as Rā, and she wanted to rule over the earth jointly with him ; she thought scorn of the powers of the gods and men. She decided in her mind that she could only attain to this power by getting possession of the great and hidden name of Rā. Now at this time Rā was old and feeble, and he dribbled at the mouth, and he had little or no control over his body. Then Isis took some earth in her hand and, kneading it up with the spittle which dropped from Rā in the sky, she fashioned it in the form of a serpent and, having endowed it with her magical power, she laid it down by the side of the path along which Rā was wont to journey every day.

In due course Rā, accompanied by his gods, came along, and as he passed close to the serpent that Isis had made, the reptile hurled itself at him and drove its fangs into his body. Immediately after this attack the god began to feel his vital power leaving him, and as the poison flowed through his veins his strength began to fail him, and His Majesty uttered a shriek which penetrated all heaven and reached the ears of the gods, who rushed to him, saying : " What is it ? What is the matter ? " But the action of the poison had been so rapid that Rā could not answer their questions and tell them what had happened. His jaws rattled together, his limbs quaked as with ague, for the poison had flooded all his members, just as the Nile during the Inundation floods all the land of Egypt. At

length the god managed to control himself
sufficiently to speak, and he cried out to the
gods who were accompanying him : " Come ye
to me, O ye gods who came forth from my
members and have been created by me, and I
will tell you what hath happened. I have been
wounded by some deadly thing. I feel and know
that it is so in my heart, but mine eyes have not
seen what thing did it. I did not make that
thing with my hand, and I know not any one
who would do this thing to me. I have never
suffered pain such as this before, and there is no
pain greater than that which I now suffer. As
for me, I am King, the son of a King, my essence
proceeded from a god. I am a mighty god, the
son of a mighty god. My father did not remember
the name I was to bear. I have many names
and many forms, and my substance existeth in
every god. Temu and Horus, who bestow
names, have proclaimed me, and my father and
my mother have uttered my name. My name
was hidden inside my body by my begetter so
that the words of power of those who would
work magic upon me might not obtain dominion
over me. I had come forth from my chamber
to look upon what I had made, and was passing
through the Two Lands (*i.e.* Egypt) which I
had created, when something aimed a blow at me,
but what it was I know not. Can it be fire ? Can
it be water ? My heart is on fire, my limbs shake,
and my members are full of twitchings. Let the
gods who are lords of enchantments, and are
skilled in uttering spells, and whose powers reach
to heaven be brought to [my help] forthwith."

Then his children—all the gods—came to him there, weeping as they came, and Isis, with her enchantments, in whose mouth is the breath of life, whose commands (?) destroy diseases, and whose words bring the dead to life, also came. And Isis said: "What is the matter, O Father-god? What is it? A serpent hath shot poison into thee, a thing that thou hast made hath lifted up its head against thee. But it can be overthrown by efficacious words of power. I will make it to retreat from thee whilst thou lookest on."

And the august god opened his mouth and said: ". . . I was bitten by a serpent which I did not see. Is it fire? Is it water? I am colder than water. I am hotter than fire. My limbs sweat, I quake, my eye hath no stability, I cannot look at the sky; my face is drenched with water even as in the time of summer." Then said Isis to Rā: "Tell me thy name, O divine father, for the person liveth who repeateth (?) his name." This, however, Rā was not willing to do, and he proceeded to describe his works thus: "I made the heavens and the earth. I knitted together the mountains, and created whatever is upon it (the earth). I made the waters, taking the form of Meht-urit. I made Ka-en-mut-f, the author of love-joys. I made heaven and I furnished the two horizons, and I set the Soul of the gods in it. I am he who openeth his eyes and light cometh into being, and when he closeth them there is darkness; when he uttereth the command the Nile riseth. The gods know not his name. I made the hours, I created the days, I open the festivals

of the year, creating the waters. I am the
maker of the fire of life, causing the works in
the houses to be performed. I am Khepera
in the morning, Rā at noon-day, and Temu in
the evening." But though Rā spake all these
words the poison did not cease to flow through
his body, and the god obtained no relief from
his pain. Then Isis, who saw that the god
had not uttered his name, said: "Among the
words which thou hast spoken thy name is not
mentioned. But only tell me thy name, and the
poison shall come forth from thee. The person
liveth who repeateth his name." Meanwhile
the poison burned in the body of Rā, and the
inflammation was greater than that caused by
burning with fire.

At length Rā said: "I will allow myself to
be searched through by Isis, and will let my
name come out from my body and pass into her
body." And the divine one hid himself from
his gods, and his seat in the Boat of Millions of
Years was empty. Then Isis called her son
Horus to help her, and she took the divine
name of the god Rā from him. This done,
she pronounced the following spell: "Discharge
thyself, O poison, and come forth from Rā.
O Eye of Horus, come forth from the god. . . .
I, I work, and I make to fall on the ground the
poison which hath been vanquished. Verily the
name of the great god hath been taken from
him. Rā shall live, for the poison is dead ; the
poison dieth and Rā liveth."

But though such views about the human nature
of the gods were general in Egypt, passages in

the Books of Moral Precepts written by scribes and others show that at least some of the Egyptians did believe in the existence of a great and Supreme Being. Though, like the ancient Egyptians and Nubians, many modern peoples in the Sūdān adore demons of every kind, they also believe in the existence of a Supreme Being. But it seems that both the ancient and modern dwellers in the Nile Valley thought that this Being was too great and mighty to concern Himself with the affairs and destinies of human beings, and that He had permitted the management of this world and the destinies of human beings to fall into the hands of hordes of " gods " and demons, and good and bad spirits. They troubled themselves little about the good spirits, but they passed their lives in a state of fear and trembling, dreading the malignity of the bad ones, whom they tried to placate by gifts and abject adoration and service.

The Egyptian word which may be translated by " God " or " god " is " Neter," or " Nether," ⌓, ⌓, or ⌓, in the plural ⌓, ⌓, ⌓, ⌓; the meaning of the word is unknown. The Egyptian Christians, or Copts, adopted this name for God in their translations of the Scriptures, where it appears under the form of ⲛⲟⲩⲧⲉ, Noute. In the Books of Moral Precepts the article is often prefixed to Neter thus :

⌓, pa-Neter, " the God," just as the Arabs always speak of " Allâh," i.e. Al-Allah, "the God." One sage wrote: "Seat thyself (*i.e.* repose) on the two arms of the God " (words which at once call to mind " the everlasting arms " in Deut. xxxiii. 27) ; " Commit thyself for security to the hand of the God " ; it is " He Who bringeth a man into Amentt (*i.e.* the Other World), where he is safe in the hand of the God." Another sage wrote : " The things that God doeth cannot be known " ; " Daily bread is according to the dispensation (or planning) of God " ; " God loveth obedience, He hateth disobedience " ; " A good son is indeed the gift of God." Another sage wrote : " Noisy, vain repetitions are an abomination to the sanctuary of God. Pray thy prayer with a loving heart in secret. He will do for thee all that is necessary for thy daily needs ; He will hearken to thy supplications, receiving thine offerings." Some think that the God referred to in these passages was the local god, Rā or Amen-Rā, but, even if this be so, it does not do away with the fact that the writers of them conceived of the existence of an Almighty Being who possessed some of the attributes and power of God.

In the Precepts which King Khati wrote for his son in the third millennium B.C., he says : " God hath hidden Himself, knowing the dispositions [of men]; none can resist the lord of the hand. . . . The disposition of him that is right of heart is more acceptable than the ox of the evil-doer. Work for God. He will work for thee in like manner. . . . Regulate men and women, who [are] the flocks and herds of God. He made heaven and earth for their pleasures. He scattered the darkness (?) on the waters. He made the breezes of life for their nostrils, [for] they are the images of Him who came forth from His members. He mounteth up into the sky for their gratification. He hath made fruits and herbs, flocks and herds, fowl and fish for their subsistence. He slew His enemies, He destroyed His own children because they conspired against Him and rebelled.[1] He made the daylight to please them, He journeyeth in a boat that He can look upon them (or, can be seen by them). He lifteth himself up in a shrine behind them. [When] they weep He heareth [them]. He gave them a Governor who was a ruler before his birth, a Captain to stiffen the back of the feeble man. He made for them **Magic** (, *hekau*) to be a weapon wherewith to destroy the power of [untoward] happenings [and terrifying] visions by night as well as by day."

The mention above of the god who mounts up into the sky and travels in a boat certainly points to Rā, the great Sun-god, as the god who created men and things, and who sailed across the sky daily in an indestructible boat. But though the Egyptians made offerings to him in his temple, and hailed with joy the processions through the streets during which his statue was carried by the priests, it is impossible to believe

[1] The allusion is to the old tradition that Rā destroyed the men who came forth from his eye, because they reviled him; another legend says that Hathor, who was the eye of Rā, destroyed mankind.

that they thought that it was the jewel-studded gold figure which they saw who had created the heavens and the earth and themselves. The sun was the dwelling of the god in the sky, and his statue can only have been regarded as a temporary habitation for the occasions when he appeared on earth. Egyptian theologians in the earliest period asserted that Rā was the offspring of Temu, who proceeded from the primeval waters Nenu or Nu ⟨hieroglyphs⟩, and that Nenu was the " Father of the Gods," including Rā. And Temu is made to say in the Book of the Dead (Chap. xvii), " I was alone (or, one). I came into being from Nenu," ⟨hieroglyphs⟩. In the same Chapter the " gods " are said to be only the **names** of Temu and Rā, and as Rā was only a name of Temu the Egyptians, from this point of view, had reason for saying that Rā, who appeared in the form of the sun, was the **one and only** God, and therefore the creator of everything that exists.

The oldest **Company of Nine Gods** in Egypt was that presided over by **Temu ;** in addition to him it consisted of four gods and four goddesses, viz. Nu and Nut, Hehu and Hehuit, Keku and Kekuit, and Gerh and Gerhit. The first pair were the male and female properties of water, the second pair represented its everlasting existence, the third pair its darkness, and the fourth pair the night which enveloped it. This was the teaching of the priesthood of Thoth of Khemenu (Hermopolis), and is probably older than dynastic civilization in Egypt. The gods of Thoth's Company had the heads of frogs, and the goddesses the heads of serpents, but the horrible and monstrous creatures that inhabited Apsū, the primeval waters of Babylonian mythology, are wanting. Under the Old Kingdom the priests of **Anu,** 𓉼𓊖 (the On of the Bible, and the Heliopolis of the Greeks), who were worshippers of the Sun-god Rā, invented another Company of Nine Gods, and made their god its president instead of Temu. These Nine Gods, 𓇳𓏥, *pestcht*, also written 𓇳𓏭 and 𓏥𓏥𓏥, consisted of Rā, Shu, Tefnut, Geb, Nut, Osiris, Isis, Set, Nephthys and Anubis or Horus, for the Nine, or Company, often contained more than nine gods, and sometimes as many as thirteen are mentioned. This was the " Great Nine " gods of heaven, 𓏥 𓏥 𓏥 ⌒, but there was also a " Little Nine," 𓏥 𓏥 𓏥 𓅿, who were the gods of earth. The Pyramid Texts mention Three Nine-gods, 𓏥𓏥𓏥; the Third Nine were probably gods of the Tuat, or Other World. The last five gods and goddesses of the Great Nine, namely, Osiris, Isis, Nephthys, Set and Anubis, were all the children of Nut, who is said to have brought all of them forth at a single birth ; the gods married their sisters and begot sons before any of them were born.

The magical and religious texts tell us much about the gods and their deeds, but there is only one text that helps us to understand the views of the Egyptians about the **Creation of Heaven and Earth,** and this, strangely enough, forms part of a magical ritual which was performed in the temple of Amen-Rā at Thebes. The object of the ritual was the destruction of **Āpep,** a terrible monster that lived in the nethermost parts of heaven and endeavoured daily to prevent the rising of the Sun-god Rā, and to stir up lightning, thunder, tempests, storms, hurricanes and rain, and to obscure the light of the sun by filling the sky with clouds, mist, fog and blackness. He was symbolized in the ceremonies that were performed in the temple by a **waxen crocodile,** on which the name of Āpep was cut. This was wrapped up and placed inside a papyrus case on which the name of the monster was written in green ink, and then burnt in a fire of *khesau* herbs. Whilst it was burning the priest stabbed it with a knife, and spat upon it, and poured filthy water on it, and stamped upon it with his left foot. This ceremony was repeated several times during the day and night, and various Chapters of the **Book of Overthrowing Āpep** were recited at the same time.

The text that describes the **Egyptian Cosmogony** is called the " Book of knowing how Rā came into being, and how to overthrow Āpep." The story of the Creation is put into the

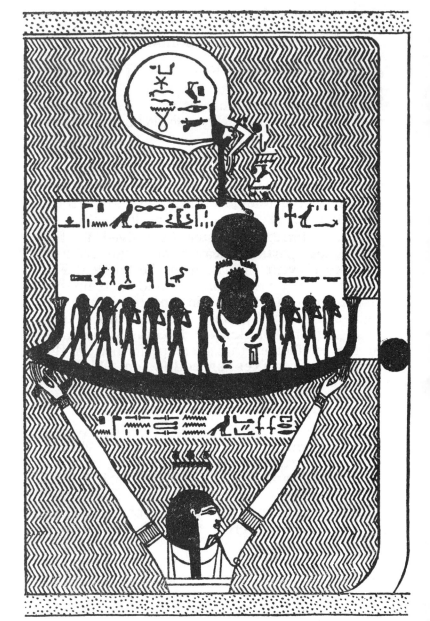

THE CREATION. Nenu, the god of the primeval waters, lifting up the Ātet Boat of the Sun into the heavens. The solar disk is being rolled up into the sky by the Beetle-god Khepera; on one side is Isis and on the other Nephthys. The gods in the boat are Geb, A (Thoth), Hek, Hu and Saa. Beyond is the Tuat, or Kingdom of Osiris, which is circular in form and is surrounded by his body.

mouth of **Nebertcher,** the god who is the "Lord
to the uttermost limit [of the universe]." He says:
"There was no heaven, no earth, no serpents,
no reptiles ; all these I produced out of the inert
watery mass Nenu. There was no place for me
to stand upon. I uttered a spell over my heart
(or, mind), in which I laid the foundations
with strict exactitude of everything that I
made [afterwards]. I was alone—for I had not
then fashioned Shu and Tefnut, and there was
no other being to work with me. I laid the
foundations in my own heart (or, mind) of all
the multitudes of things that came into being,
and of all the things that were produced by them,
and of everything to which they gave birth.

I had union with my own shadow, ⌒ 𓂺,
khaibit, and I begot in myself offspring, viz. the
god **Shu** (*i.e.* the atmosphere and light and
heat) and the goddess **Tefnut** (*i.e.* humidity and
moisture). From being one god I became
three gods, 𓆣 𓏤 𓃀 𓅝 𓏏𓅱 𓏏 𓏏𓅱 ⦀·
I lifted up Shu and Tefnut out of Nenu in which
they existed, and my Eye (*i.e.* the Sun) followed
after them. Then I joined my members together,
and I wept over them, and a man (or, men) came
into being from the tears that fell from my Eye
upon my members. My Eye was wroth with me
when it came and found that I had made
another [being] in its place. But I requited
it with the gift of the spell which I had made,
and I brought it forward to the place that it
hath in my face, and since that time it hath

ruled the whole earth, and the power which I bestowed upon it falleth on vegetation and on the things that creep upon the earth. Shu and Tefnut brought forth **Geb** (the Earth-god) and **Nut** (the Sky-goddess), and Geb and Nut brought forth **Osiris, Her-khenti-an-maati** (*i.e.* the Blind Horus, or the Night sky without a moon), **Set, Isis,** and **Nephthys.''** In the other version of this narrative the god Khepera says : " My name is Ausares,'' ⌐ᴇ⌐ 🗝 🜨, or Osiris.

The account of the Creation summarized above is found in a papyrus in the British Museum (No. 10188) which was written towards the close of the IVth century B.C., but the ideas and beliefs described in it are as old as dynastic civilization. The creation of Shu and Tefnut by Temu or Khepera from his own body is mentioned in the Pyramid Texts of the VIth Dynasty, and the fact that the oldest **Trinity** known consists of two gods and one goddess is noteworthy. The statement that the forms of every created object were depicted in the mind of the Creator before they existed is specially interesting, for it is reproduced in the writings of several of the early Fathers of the Christian Church. On the matter of how the Power of Evil, which is symbolized by the crocodile Āpep, came into being, the papyrus is silent. The Christian Fathers identify him with Satan, or the Devil, and hold that he was the general of the hosts of heaven who rebelled against God, and was hurled headlong to earth

and destroyed. The Egyptian texts show that
Āpep was never destroyed, and that the utmost
that Rā could do to him was to paralyse him
by a glance of his eye, and to drive his spear-like
rays into his body and shrivel him up, but
Āpep recovered from these injuries, and though
rendered impotent to-day was able to threaten
the power and existence of Rā on the morrow.
On another subject Nebertcher is silent, viz. the

Tuat, ✕ ⌂, or Other World, or Underworld,
that is, the abode of departed spirits, but as this
region formed the kingdom of Osiris, a brief
description of it will follow the account of this
god. **Rā,** the Sun-god (the midday sun), was
undoubtedly the national god of Lower Egypt
during the Old and Middle Kingdoms, and his
priesthood at Anu-Resu, " the Southern Anu "
(the Hermonthis of the Greeks and Armant, or
Erment, of the Arabs), possessed considerable
power.

But the greatest of all the gods of Upper
Egypt was **Osiris** (at one time the moon-god),
the centres of whose cult were Abydos and
Pa-Asar (Busiris) in the Delta. When Amen
was chosen to be the national god of all Egypt,
Rā was associated with him, only his name
came second and followed that of Amen ; but
from first to last neither companion nor counterpart was given to Osiris who, even under the
Old Kingdom, ousted Rā from his supreme
position in the funerary texts which his priesthood had assigned to him as the Great Judge in
heaven. The position of Osiris as the god of the

dead, *par excellence*, and their Judge was never usurped by any other god. The Egyptians regarded Rā as the provider for their existence in this world, and Osiris as the cause and source of their lives in the next. It was, as the monuments

Osiris, in the form of a mummy, wearing the Double Crown and Menat, ⌐⅄, and holding the emblems of "rule," ⌐, and "life," ⚲, seated on a chair of state, set upon a platform having nine steps. He, in the form of a mummy, is the support of the Great Scales. His Company of Nine Gods watch the working of the Scales. The two dog-headed apes (baboons) of Thoth are taking away Set (*i.e.* Evil), in the form of a black pig, in a boat. Anubis looks on. From the Book of Gates.

show, their duty to make offerings to the "gods" of their country and to honour the local god, but the wise man, in accepting the gifts of Rā, lived his life in such a way as to secure the acquittal of his soul at the trial to which it would be subjected in the Judgment Hall of

Osiris. In spite of their ancient universal trust in demonology the Egyptians, from the earliest times, believed that men would be rewarded or punished for the deeds done in the body, and that there would be a **Last Judgment.** The oldest description of this Judgment is found in a papyrus at St. Petersburg, and in it King Khati (about 2800 B.C.) says to his son :—

> " Know thou that the Tchatchaut, who judge wrongdoers, will show no pity on the day of judgment of wretched man, in the hour when they are performing their appointed duty. It is a terrible thing for the man who knows [his sin] to be charged with it. Buoy not up thy heart with the idea that length of years [will excuse thee]; they look upon a whole lifetime as a single hour. They make their trial after a man's death ; his actions are [set] near him as evidence (?). In the Other World existence is everlasting, and he who puts this [fact] out of his mind is a fool. He who being guiltless attains to that place has an existence there like that of God, and like the Everlasting Lords he moves unfettered from place to place."

The Tchatchaut, ⌁ ⌁ ⌁ ⌁ ⌁ ⌁, *i.e.* " Chiefs " or " Assessors," are well known from other texts. From the Book of Gates we learn that they kept the Registers of Osiris which contained the names of all those who are in the Other World, and the Book of the Dead (Chap. **xxx***b*) shows that they watched the weighing of the heart of a man in the " Great Scales " and stood ready to intervene and bring forward any proof of its sinfulness. A very ancient tradition asserted that Osiris was judged by the great gods of Heliopolis, and that he was declared innocent of the charges brought against him by Set, his brother and enemy, chiefly through the good offices of Thoth, the scribe of the gods, who acted as his Advocate. The description of the Last Judgment by King Khati makes no mention of any Advocate, so we may assume that the introduction of such a helper of the deceased is a characteristic of the system of Osiris.

There is no text known at present which gives us in a connected form the history of **Osiris,** but the work of Plutarch (*De Iside et Osiride*), and the facts that can be collected from the inscriptions, enable us to construct one with considerable accuracy. Osiris, in Egyptian

⬧, 𓀀, ⬧, was a king of Egypt, and was therefore part man and part god. He reigned wisely, taught his subjects law, order, and religion, and by the introduction of cereals and the vine, and a superior form of agriculture, made his country prosperous. Having ordered his own kingdom he set out to visit other countries, and he instructed foreign nations, to their great advantage. During his absence his wife Isis administered his kingdom, but she was greatly troubled by her brother Set, who tried to undo all the good that Osiris had done. When Osiris returned Set determined to kill him and to seize his wife, with whom he was in love. By a stratagem he made Osiris to lie down in a box, and when he had done so Set and his friends nailed the top of it down and covered it with lead, and Osiris was suffocated. They then threw the box into the Nile, and its waters carried it through the Delta and across the sea to Byblos (?), where a large Erica tree grew up round it. Isis found the box and hid it, but Set discovered it and, tearing it open, dragged out the body of Osiris and broke it into 14 pieces. Isis set out and collected these pieces, and wherever she found one she buried it and built a sepulchre over it. Osiris returned from the Other World and urged Horus to fight Set. He did so and vanquished Set, whom he handed over to Isis. To the chagrin of Horus she released Set from his bonds, and Horus was so angry that he tore the crown off his mother's head. Set accused Horus of being illegitimate, but the gods, at the instance of Thoth, non-suited Set, and Horus succeeded to the throne of Egypt. Later Isis companied with her dead husband Osiris, and the child Harpokrates was the result of the embrace.

The persecution of Osiris did not end with his murder by Set and his companions, for, hearing that Osiris was risen from the dead, Set brought a series of charges against Osiris, which were so grave that the Great Company of the gods decided to bring Osiris to trial in their abode in the heaven of Anu (Heliopolis). Whether the heart of Osiris was weighed in the Great Scales or not we do not know but, as already said, Thoth investigated the charges made against Osiris by Set, and proved to the satisfaction of the gods that Set was a liar and that Osiris was " maā-kheru," 〔hieroglyphs〕, *i.e.* " a speaker of the truth." Osiris, as said above, had in some form visited this world, and must therefore have vanquished the powers of Death and the grave ; and now that he had obtained a verdict of innocence from the gods of Heliopolis, the whole Company of the gods of heaven and of earth decided to make him the **Judge of the Dead.** They therefore assigned to him a kingdom in the Other World, though where exactly that was situated it is impossible to say.

Osiris is always represented in the form of a bearded mummy, 〔sign〕 ; he sometimes wears the White Crown, 〔sign〕, and sometimes the Atef Crown, 〔sign〕, *i.e.* the White Crown with two plumes and a pair of horns attached to it, and he holds the sceptre, 〔sign〕, in his right hand, and the whip, 〔sign〕, in his left. His beard is in the form of the beard worn by the men of Punt, and this and the White Crown together suggest that in his oldest form Osiris was a god from the South. He sits upon a throne which has the form of a funerary coffer with bolted doors, and it is probable that this was believed to contain a special portion of the body of the god. His grandsons, the four sons of Horus, usually stand on a lotus flower near him, and behind him are

Isis and Nephthys; close to his throne the pied bull skin attached to a pole, 𓎺 , is often seen. The bodies of kings and chiefs were often buried in the hides of bulls, and instances of bull-skin burial are common in the Sūdān at the present day. This skin was called " Meska," 𓉔𓈖𓂧𓅡𓆲 , which is the name for the place of resurrection in heaven. The throne of the god was set upon water which came from the great celestial ocean, the walls of his shrine were flames of fire, and on its cornice was a row of the " Living Uraei " (i.e. sacred cobras).

The supreme position of Osiris was only challenged once, and the man who was bold enough to attempt to abolish the god was Amenhetep IV, king of Egypt about 1350 B.C., who endeavoured to make **Aten**, 𓇋𓏏𓈖 , the national god. According to his views Aten, that is the **Disk** of the sun, was the source of all life, and was the Sun-god, who manifested himself in solar heat. In other words, he made **Heat** his god, and called it " One," even as his predecessors had called Rā and several other gods " One." As an incarnation of Aten he believed himself to be the " One god," and therefore all the " gods " of Egypt, including Osiris and his Company, were impostors and nonentities. He ordered the name of Amen, the great god of Thebes, and the word for " gods " to be cut out from the inscriptions; he abolished the priesthood of Amen and confiscated their revenues, and swept away, so far as he was able, all the ancient beliefs in the resurrection of the dead and immortality. He abandoned Thebes and built a new capital, which he called **Aakhutaten,** changed his name from Amenhetep to **Aakhuenaten,** built many temples to Aten, and for a time officiated as high priest. But he failed to establish Aten as the One, self-created, self-subsisting and self-existing god, and in less than 25 years after his death his capital, now known as Amārnah, or Tall al-'Amārnah, was in ruins, and he was only remembered with contempt. Amen, Lord of the World, triumphed, and Osiris, Lord of Heaven, retained his sovereignty unimpaired. Under the last Ramessid kings of the XXth Dynasty the priests of Amen obtained very great power, and when the last Rameses died Her-Her, the high priest of Amen, proclaimed himself king, and founded a line of **priest-kings** (Dynasty XXI, ruling at Thebes). Some of the princesses regarded Amen as more powerful than Osiris in the Other World, but they were all buried with the rites and ceremonies which the religion of Osiris prescribed, and all expected to receive from him the gift of resurrection and, with it, everlasting life.

The belief that a being, part god and part man, had died and risen from the dead seems to have been in existence among the predynastic Egyptians, but it is uncertain if that man was called Osiris. The religious views of the Egyptians underwent many changes under the kings of the Ist Dynasty, who built their tombs at Abydos, and some think that both the name of Osiris and certain elements of his religion were brought into Egypt by the invaders who conquered the country. No satisfactory meaning has been proposed for the name, and it is possible that ☽, *Asar*, is a transcription of the

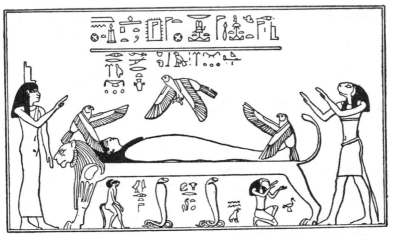

The mummy of Osiris Khenti Amenti, great god, lord of Abydos, lying on his bier with his soul, in the form of a hawk, hovering over him. Isis, Heqit (the Frog goddess) and Thoth are reciting spells to bring about the resurrection of Osiris. The hawks at the head and foot of the bier represent Isis and Nephthys.

name of a foreign god. The similarities in the history of Osiris and the history of Bel-Marduk of Babylon are too striking to be dismissed lightly without consideration. Whether the Babylonians borrowed from the Egyptians, or the Egyptians from the Babylonians, or both peoples from a common source, remains to be decided. The cult of Osiris absorbed within it that of **Anher,** 𓀭 ═ 𓀭, an important local god of the Abydos nome, and under the Ist Dynasty Osiris became the representative *par excellence* of the earlier African man-god who had died and suffered mutilation and had risen from the dead. The cult of Osiris flourished greatly under the Old Kingdom, but became unimportant under Dynasties VI–X ; it revived

The soul of Horus (or Osiris ?), which stood waiting above the sacred tree at Abydos, has been made by Horus to enter the body of the god, and Osiris is raising his body from the bier, having returned from the abode of the dead.

under the XIth and XIIth Dynasties and resumed its earlier importance under the XIXth and XXIInd and XXVIth Dynasties. At Busiris and Mendes in the Delta the cult of Osiris absorbed the cults of the old sacred tree and the Ram-god, and the Book of the Dead shows (Chap. xvii) that the souls of Osiris and Rā became merged in each other in Tetu,

𓏏𓏏𓄿 ⊗ . In Ptolemaïc times the theologians joined Osiris to Hāpi, the sacred Bull-god of Memphis, and formed the new composite god of the dead, **Serapis,** and so satisfied Egyptians and Greeks alike.

The kingdom of the man-god Osiris was in Upper Egypt, and the place of his burial was Abtu, 𓊪𓃀𓈒𓄿⊗, *i.e.* **Abydos,** in the Thinite nome. The sacred symbol of the " Great Land," as the place was called, was 𓊖, or 𓊖 . The first of these represents a box, or case of some kind, from which the head of a serpent projects ; above the box are two plumes ; in the second the serpent is wanting, and two horns are added. The box presumably contained a portion of the body of Osiris, probably his head ; both these symbols are very old, and when the White Crown, 𓋓, was assigned to the god the plumes and the horns were added to it.

The tomb of Osiris and the tombs of the earliest dynastic kings are on the left or west bank of the Nile at Abydos, in the region called Amentt, 𓇋𓏠 or 𓊪 𓈖, and thither for many centuries the bodies of the dead from all parts of Egypt were taken to be buried. Here Osiris reigned over the dead, and one of his oldest titles is Khenti Amentt, 𓁶 𓄿 𓇋𓈖𓏠, " President of Amentt," or 𓁶 𓄿 𓊪𓄿𓈖𓏥,

Khenti Amentiu, " President of those who are in
Amentt." As a god Osiris was identified with
many gods—water-gods, vegetation-gods, vine-
gods, animal-gods, *e.g.* the Bull-god and the
Ram-god—but here only his character as god and
judge of the dead can be considered.

The religion of Osiris promised to those who
followed it faithfully both **resurrection** from
the dead and **eternal life,** but to obtain these
the Osirian had to lead a moral and upright life,
to avoid lying speech, deceitful actions, and
duplicity of every kind, and to observe the laws
of the national god and the local or town-god.
Under the Old Kingdom all breaches of the
Moral Law, which was of a very high character,
had to be paid for by gifts and offerings to the
local shrines, but Osiris expected his followers
to avoid all breaches of the Moral Law and sins,

𓇋𓈖𓅮𓏤, *asfet,* so that he might not be obliged to

call them to account when he judged them. He
expected a man to have a clean **conscience** as
well as clean hands and a clean tongue. And
though the judgment of Osiris is described as a

" weighing of words," 𓀁𓂡𓇋𓏤𓍿𓏤𓏤𓏤, it

included the weighing of intentions and motives
and the actions prompted by them.

Between the XIIth and the XVIIIth Dynasties
a great development of the moral and religious
views of the Egyptians took place, and we find
them admirably summarized in the second part
of Chap. cxxv of the Book of the Dead, which
may be described as the Moral and Religious

Code of Osiris. It contains a series of 42 statements which the deceased was expected to make to 42 gods, one statement to each god. In each of these he asserted that he had not committed a certain sin. This Code was considered to be of such importance that it was drawn up in a tabular form, with a picture of each of the 42 gods addressed by the deceased, and was supplemented by Vignettes representing the weighing of the heart, ☩, against the feather, ⌡, the symbol of the two Truth-goddesses of Upper and Lower Egypt, the god Thoth, etc. In the great Codices of the Book of the Dead a large Vignette of the Judgment Scene is placed at the beginning of the work, and from this we are able to get an idea of the method of procedure at the " Weighing of Words."

The Judgment Chamber was called the " Hall of Maāti." Along each side of it were, either seated or standing, 21 of the Tchatchau, or Assessors, to each of whom the deceased made his statement that he had not committed such and such a sin. In the fore-part of the Hall were set the Great Scales, with a dog-headed ape seated on the top of the pillar. This animal was chosen by Thoth as his associate because of the keenness of its vision and its great faculty of watchfulness. A pointer was attached to the beam of the Scales, and its markings were scrutinized by Anpu (Anubis), the great physician who embalmed the body of Osiris.

The deceased, having recited the names of the doors and door-posts of the Hall correctly,

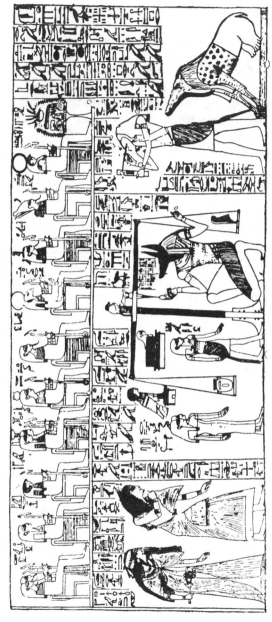

The weighing of the heart of the scribe Ani in the Judgment Hall of Osiris. (From the Papyrus of Ani. About 1500 B.C.)

entered the Hall and stood with bowed head near the Scales. Close to the Scales stood his **soul,** in the form of a man-headed hawk, 🦅¹, *Ba,* the god Shai, *i.e.* destiny of the deceased, Meskhenit and Renenit, the two goddesses of birth and the birth-chamber, together with the man-headed object 🦅⊏⊐, which rests on a funerary building. In one pan of the Scales was a feather, ∫, symbolic of Law and Truth, and in the other was the heart of the deceased. Whilst these things were being done the deceased prayed the prayer which tradition asserted was composed by the god Thoth, presumably for the use of Osiris when, in pre-dynastic times, he was being tried in the divine Court of the gods of Heliopolis. This prayer was in use throughout the Dynastic Period, and even in the time of Cleopatra ; it must be one of the oldest prayers in the world ; it forms Chap. xxx*b* of the Theban Recension of the Book of the Dead, and is entitled " The Chapter of not letting the heart of the deceased be driven away from him in the Underworld." It reads : " [O] my heart (*áb*) from my mother, O my heart from my mother ! O my heart (*hati, i.e.* foremost part) of my being ! Stand not up against me in the Judgment. Thrust me not back among the Tchatchau. Make not to be a turning aside [of the Scales] in the presence of the Guardian of the Scales. Thou art my KA, the dweller in my body, the god Khnemu who endows with strength my members. Go forth

thou to the happiness whither we [would] go.
Make not my name to stink with the Shenit
gods [of the House of Osiris], who make men
to stand firm. May we hear joyfully glad
tidings at the Weighing of Words. Let not lies
be told about me before the god [Osiris], the
Great God, the Lord of Amentt. Verily exalt
thyself rising up (?) at [the words] ' Maā-kheru '
(*i.e.* true of voice, or truth-speaker)."

Meanwhile **Thoth,** the scribe of the gods,
the great Advocate of Osiris, has taken up
his position on the other side of the Scales,
and with him is the monster **Ām-mitu,** the
Eater of the Dead, which was part crocodile,
part lion and part hippopotamus. Then
Thoth, holding in his hands his writing reed
and palette, received from Anpu the report
that the heart of the deceased had been
weighed in the Scales, that his soul had
testified to its integrity, and that it had been
" found true by trial in the Great Scales."
The god added the statement that the deceased
was no wicked man, no filcher of divine
offerings, no evil-doer, and no calumniator of
men. He then read this report to the gods,
who declared forthwith that they had no ground
of complaint against the deceased, and decreed
that he should not be given to the Eater of
the Dead, but should be led before Osiris, who
would give him his reward. Thereupon Horus,
taking the deceased by the hand, brought him
into the presence of Osiris, and reported to
him the result of the weighing of the heart of
the deceased, and confirmed all that Thoth and

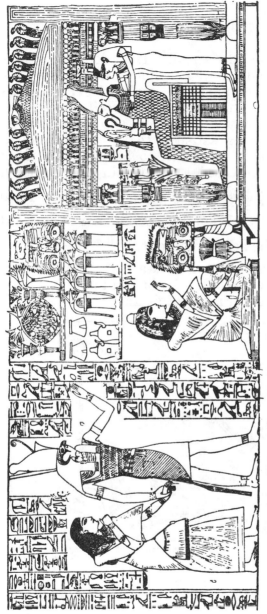

The scribe Ani, being declared to be a "truth-speaker," is being led by Horus, the son of Isis, into the presence of Osiris. (From the Papyrus of Ani. About 1500 B.C.)

the gods had said. This done the deceased
advanced and, kneeling before Osiris, said :
" There is no sin in my body.   I have neither
told lies nor acted with deceit ; make me one
of those favoured beings who are in thy train."
Osiris, being satisfied that he was admitting a
speaker of the truth to his kingdom, assigned
to the deceased an estate in the Sekhet-Aaru,

, or " Fields of
Reeds," and gave him permission to draw rations
from the Sekhet-heteput,　　　　　, or " Field
of Offerings," which was kept supplied by the
faithful on earth, who brought offerings regularly
to the sanctuaries of Osiris.

Picture of an ancient Egyptian Shâdûf being worked by a
farm labourer.   From a wall painting in a tomb at Thebes.

CHAPTER IX

WE owe our knowledge of Egyptian Literature to the inscriptions on pyramids,
temples, historical and biographical
stelae, rolls of papyri, etc. ; these are written
in the hieroglyphic, hieratic and demotic scripts,
and cover a period of about 3,500 years. The
language employed is Egyptian, of which there
appear to have been three **dialects,** if not more.
The foundations of the language are African, but
at a comparatively early period additions to them
were made as a result of the influence of the
Semites. At a later time words were borrowed
from the Libyans and the peoples of the Eastern
deserts, and from Arabia and the countries
beyond. The **style** is rhythmic, rhyme being
unknown ; the use of parallelism of members is
frequent, and is often employed with very fine
effect. The **Literature** of Egypt may be divided
into two classes, **Religious** and **Profane,** and

at least three-quarters of it belong to the former class.

History.—No complete native history of Egypt exists, and it is probable no king was anxious to preserve a record of the doings of his predecessors. Good specimens of the historical documents are : the **Annals** of the campaigns of Thothmes III, copied from a leather roll, on the walls of the Temple of Amen at Karnak ; the **Acts of Rameses III**, as found in the Harris Papyrus No. 1 in the British Museum ; the account of the **Battle of Kadesh,** written by the court scribe Pentaurt ; the account of the **Invasion of Egypt** by Piānkhi the Nubian ; the **Annals of Nastasen** describing the defeat of Cambyses (?). Good examples of biographical inscriptions of a historical character are found on the tomb stelae of Una, Herkhuf, Antef, Amasis and other feudal lords of Al-Kāb, and in other places.

Chronology.—The most important documents are the **Stele of Palermo,** the **King-lists** of Sakkārah, Abydos and Karnak, and the **Turin Papyrus,** which, when complete, contained a list of about 300 kings of Egypt, with the lengths of their reigns given in years, months and days. **Astronomy.**—Lists of the risings of stars were kept under the New Kingdom, and at a later period lists of the 36 Dekans and the 12 Signs of the Zodiac. **Astrology.**—On this subject much literature probably existed, but little of it, except the **Calendars** of Lucky and Unlucky Days and Hours, has survived. Much of the ancient astrological lore is to be found in the almanacks in use among the peasant population of Egypt at the present day. **Mathematics** (Geometry and Arithmetic) are represented by the Rhind Papyrus in the British Museum (No. 10057). **Geography** as a science was unknown, but we have a map of the gold-mines in the Sūdān, and a map of the sacred localities of the Fayyūm. **Medicine.**—Several books of collections of prescriptions are known, *e.g.* those in London, Paris, Leyden, Berlin and California, the longest and most important being the **Ebers Papyrus,** but no treatise on anatomy has come down to us. **The Law.**—Many documents of this class of literature exist, and they suggest that the Egyptians were fond of litigation. They deal with funerary endowments and benefactions, political and other adoptions, reports of law proceedings, etc. ; the record of the prosecution of tomb-robbers by the Crown in the reign of Rameses IX is one of the most interesting of the last-named class of legal documents (B.M. Nos. 10053, 10054). **Songs.**— Fragments of a few songs of the folk-lore class have come down to us, and several **Love-songs** are preserved in the Harris Papyrus in the British Museum (No. 500). The latter closely resemble in phraseology the Song of Solomon. A translation of the **Song of Antuf** (Song of the Harper) has been given above (p. 135) ; it is a remarkable composition.

Narratives or **Short Stories.**—Among these may be mentioned as of special interest : The **Story of Sanehat.**—Here we have the story and adventures of a young man who,

for some reason not quite clear, flees from
Egypt into Palestine, where he is welcomed by
the natives. He marries and begets a family,
and gains great renown by defeating and slaying
a mighty man of war who had challenged him
to combat ; this part of the story resembles
that of the killing of Goliath by David. At
length he yearns for his native country, and
finally he returns there and is warmly received
by the king and his family ; there he dies and is
buried in a tomb provided for him by the king.
In the **Story of the Shipwreck** we read of a man
who is shipwrecked and cast up on a phantom
island, where he found an abundance of fruit and
fish, and having used the fire-stick he made a
fire and offered up a sacrifice to the gods. In
due course he met the Genius of the island, *i.e.*
a snake nearly 50 feet long with a beard over
3 feet long. It received him in a most friendly
manner, conversed with him, and eventually
loaded him with gifts and sent him away on a
ship which happened to visit the island. A
very interesting set of **Stories of Magicians**
is found in the Westcar Papyrus in Berlin ;
the contents of some of these have already been
alluded to. The **Tale of the Two Brothers**
gives us a series of very short stories which
originally had no connection with each other ;
a brief summary is given further on in this
Chapter. The **Story of the Doomed Prince,**
which unfortunately is incomplete, shows that
there is no way of escaping from one's Fate.

As **Historical Romances** may be mentioned the story of the **quarrel** between the

Hyksos Rā-Apepi, king of Lower Egypt, and
Seqenen-Rā, king of Upper Egypt (B.M.
No. 10185), and the **Capture of Joppa** by an
officer of Thothmes III. The latter romance has
resemblances to the Arab story of Alī Bābā and
the Forty Thieves. The literature of **Travels** is
represented by the story of **Unuamen,** who was
sent to Syria to obtain cedar-wood wherewith
to build a new barge for the god Amen. He was
robbed on his journey into Syria, and on his way
back found himself in Cyprus. The story is
incomplete. As examples of contemplative and
semi-prophetical literature we have : 1. The
Dialogue between a man and his soul ; though
he is tired of life, he nevertheless advises his
hearers to " pursue the day of happiness and
forget care," 𓅱𓏏𓏤𓌳𓂝𓏤𓆓𓏏𓇳𓏤𓄿𓍿𓏏𓈖𓅓𓏏𓀁.
2. The **Admonitions of a Prophet,** found in
a papyrus at Leyden ; some of his utterances
have been thought to be Messianic in character.
3. The **Lamentations** of Khākheperrā-seneb,
found on a wooden tablet in the British Museum
(No. 5645). 4. The **Prophecy** of Nefer-Rehu, in
a papyrus at St. Petersburg. 5. The **Lament
of the Peasant**, found in papyri in Berlin.
Religious Magic is illustrated by the works
found in the Salt Papyrus (B.M. No. 825)
and in the Harris Papyrus (B.M. No. 10051),
and by the **Book of Overthrowing Āpep**
(B.M. No. 10188).

Legends of the Gods.—Among these may
be mentioned the Legends of Rā and Isis (summarized above, p. 203 f.), the Creation of the

World by Khepera, the Destruction of Mankind, Horus of Edfū and the Winged Disk, Khensu-hetep and the Possessed Princess, Khnemu and the Seven Years' Famine, the Resurrection of Osiris and the Birth of Horus, the Death and Resurrection of Horus, the Wanderings of Isis, as told in the Metternich Stele. **Rituals.**—The oldest of these are the "Book of Opening the Mouth" and the "Liturgy of Funerary Offerings," whereby the transmutation of foods and drink took place. Of divine Rituals the longest and best known is the Daily Service used in the Temple of Amen at Thebes. **Comic Caricature** is illustrated by a papyrus in the British Museum (No. 10016). **Books of Moral Precepts.** — Several of these have been preserved, and the series now available for study enable us to follow the development of moral ideas in Egypt from about 3000 B.C. to the end of the Dynastic Period. The authors were Kagemna, a Wazīr of King Huni (IIIrd Dynasty), Ptah-hetep, a Wazīr of King Assa (Vth Dynasty), Tuauf, a royal official (VIth Dynasty), King Khati (IXth or Xth Dynasty), Amenemhat I, Sehetepabrā, an officer of Amenemhat III, Amenemapt, a minister of Agriculture, and the scribe Ani.

Religious Literature.—The oldest collection of Magical-Religious texts is found inscribed in hieroglyphs on the walls of the chambers and corridors of the Pyramids of Sakkārah, which are the tombs of kings of the VIth Dynasty. These form the Heliopolitan Recension of the Book of the Dead. Another collection, containing

Chapters from the above-mentioned Pyramid Texts and several others, probably of a more recent date, was inscribed in hieratic on wooden sarcophagi and coffins of the XIth and XIIth Dynasties. Fine examples of these are the sarcophagus of Amamu and the sarcophagi and coffins from Al-Barshah. The texts on these form the Recension of the Book of the Dead in use in Upper Egypt under the Middle Kingdom. Some time after the XIIth Dynasty the **Theban Recension** of the Book of the Dead came into being. The oldest papyri containing it are written in hieroglyphs, *e.g.* the Papyrus of Nu, the Papyrus of Nebseni, the Papyrus of Iuaa, the Papyrus of Ani, etc., but under the XIXth Dynasty collections of Chapters from it were written in hieratic, and in the Papyrus of Nesitanebtashru (XXIst Dynasty) the whole work is in hieratic. The Theban Recension is illustrated by a long series of Vignettes, painted sometimes in monochrome, and sometimes in many bright colours. In the **Saïte Recension** the Chapters are written both in hieroglyphs and hieratic, and the Chapters have a fixed order; the Vignettes are drawn in black outline. The Book of the Dead contains a large number of spells and incantations which the deceased was supposed to repeat if he found himself in trouble or danger on his journey from this world to the Kingdom of Osiris. Besides these we find in it hymns, litanies, prayers, exegetical texts, plans of the mummy-chamber, the Judgment Hall of Osiris, the Elysian Fields, with explanatory texts, drawings of the Gates and Divisions of the

Underworld, the Ritual of the Lamps (Chap. cxxxvii), drawings of the Boats of Rā, and a great mixture of miscellaneous mythological texts and traditions, belonging to all periods and emanating from many different parts of Egypt. All were intended to help the deceased, and the whole book was regarded as an amulet of great power. Parts of it, *e.g.* the texts relating to the Judgment of Osiris, were in use in the Roman Period.

Later funerary works based on the Book of the Dead were the "Book of Breathings," the "Book of Traversing Eternity," the Book "May my name flourish," etc. Works recited in connection with the **Miracle Plays** of Osiris were the "Lamentations of Isis and Nephthys," the "Festival Songs of Isis and Nephthys," the "Litanies of Seker," etc. During the process of embalming the dead the "Book of Embalmment" was recited. At one period of Egyptian history the theologians wrote **"Guides"** to the Underworld, the most interesting of these being the "Book of Gates," and the "Book of him that is in the Tuat." These supplied the deceased with a full description of the places through which he would pass and the names of the beings he would meet, and gave him the words of power necessary for him to complete his journey safely. **Hymns** to the gods form a large section of Egyptian religious literature; the most important are the Hymns to Osiris, Rā, Rā-Harmakhis, Amen and Thoth. The literature written in demotic is considerable, and consists of works of magic, tales illustrating the power of magicians, collections of moral precepts, various kinds of legal documents, marriage contracts, etc.

Magic. — The Egyptians in all periods believed that earth, air, fire and water were filled with spirits, each one of which was able to inflict injury upon them. Some were found by them to be kindly and well-disposed towards man, but the greater number of them were believed to be malicious, vindictive and hostile to man and all his works. The great god who had made the universe was thought to be indifferent to the affairs of mankind, and to have permitted the spirits to obtain almost unlimited power and authority over man and his possessions. The Egyptians troubled themselves little about the good spirits, though they made offerings to them, and addressed words of respect and even of affection to them. But they were horribly afraid of the evil spirits, and they spared no pains in placating them and in trying to annul their power. The art of dealing with spirits of all kinds, *i.e.* magic, was carefully studied by the priests, who were to all intents and purposes in the earliest times **magicians** pure and simple. The Egyptians of all classes esteemed magic highly, and King Khati stated, in the work that he wrote for his son, that

Heka, ↑ ⎵ , *i.e.* **Magic,** was invented by Rā himself (*see* p. 210). Rā apparently did not care to trouble himself about mortal affairs, and therefore gave to man the gift of **Heka,** so that he might be able to control the invisible

Harpokrates, wearing the lock of youth and standing on crocodiles within a canopy made of the body of the serpent Mehen, and held in position by Isis and Thoth. Above him is the head of the Aged Sun-god. His mastery over noxious animals is shown by his holding scorpions and serpents and savage animals in his grasp.

Polytheistic figure representing the "Old man who renews his youth," *i.e.* Rā, the Sun-god, who comprises in his own person all the powers, attributes and forms of every kind of living creature. The text contains a series of spells which were intended to break the power of the Seba fiends, and of the crocodiles and other evil reptiles.

and supernatural powers, both good and bad, for himself. When **Heka** was used by man to benefit his fellow-man, we may term it **White Magic ;** and when it was employed to slay or injure man or beast, **Black Magic.** The men who became professional magicians no doubt possessed psychological powers above the ordinary, and were persons of ability and great shrewdness. They were skilled in all the learning of their time, and wrote the spells and incantations and charms which they used ; their assistants performed the rites and ceremonies that were the necessary accompaniments of the spells. The chief instrument of the magician was the **spell.** To use this effectively he had to be a properly qualified person, and to wear the garb and bear the equipment of such. He had to recite the magical formula in a certain tone of voice, clearly and correctly, for if he forgot any part of it, or garbled it, the spell was inoperative. And the rites and ceremonies had to be performed with scrupulous care. Ceremonial purity of both person and place was absolutely necessary. The magician wrote amulets for his clients on papyrus, leather, wood and stone plaques, and figures made of wax, wood, and stone, using names of power, magical diagrams, etc., and strings of meaningless syllables of somewhat similar sounds. The most curious of all the monuments left by the Egyptian magician are probably the little tablets, rounded at one end, that were placed in the walls of houses and under the floors to protect their owners from the attack of evil spirits, fiends, demons, hobgoblins, and every kind of baleful influence that the Egyptians could imagine. Such a tablet is commonly called a **Cippus** (*i.e.* pillar) **of Horus,** and the finest example known is that which was published by Golénischeff (*Metternichstele*, Leipzig, 1877). It is figured on pp. 244 and 245. On this monument are sculptured nearly 300 figures of the gods of heaven, earth, and the Tuat, or Underworld. On the sides and Reverse are cut a series of magical legends in hieroglyphs ; for descriptions of the figures and translations of the texts *see* my *Legends of the Gods*, London, 1912. This Cippus originally stood in a prominent place in some building, probably a temple, and was intended to protect it and those who were in it every moment of the day and night. On it are figures of all the gods and goddesses of the cults of Rā and Osiris, and the gods of the seasons of the year, the months, the weeks, the days of the week, the hours, the planets, the Signs of the Zodiac, the Dekans, etc. It was believed to protect Psemthek-Ānkh, who had it made, from the attacks of Set, Āpep and other gods of evil, and from every injury that noxious reptiles and Typhonic animals had the power to inflict upon man.

The following extracts illustrate some of the characteristics of Egyptian Literature :—

Hymn to Osiris.—Homage to thee, Osiris, Lord of eternity, king of the gods, whose names are many, whose forms are holy, whose attributes are hidden in the temples, whose Ka is august, President of Tetu (Busiris and Mendes), mighty one, dweller in Sekhem, the praised one in the nome of Ati (?), President of Ánu, the Lord commemorated in Maāti, the Hidden Soul, the Lord of the Circle of the Underworld, the holy one of Memphis, the Soul of Rā, whose very body rests in Hanes, beneficent one, who art hymned in Nart, the raiser up of his soul, the Lord of the temple in Khemenu, the mightily feared one in Shashetep, the Lord of eternity, President of Abtu (Abydos). The path of his throne is in the Holy Land, his name is established in the mouths of men, he is the substance of the Two Lands (Egypt). . . . He is the President of the Company of the gods, the beneficent Spirit among spirits, for him Nu pours out his waters, to him approaches the wind at eventide, the breeze comes to his nostrils to the satisfaction of his heart, he renews his youth. . . . The heights of heaven and the stars obey him. He makes the mighty gates to open before him, he who is praised in the southern heaven and adored in the northern heaven. The never-setting stars are under his rule, and his abodes are the stars that never rest, offerings come to him by the command of Geb. The Companies of the gods praise him, the stars of the Tuat adore him, the ends of the earth bow before him, the boundaries of the sky pray to him [when] they see him, the holy dead fear him, the whole earth praises him [when] it meets His Majesty. He is the glorious Master at the head of the masters, endued with higher rank, stablished in dominion. He is the Beautiful Sekhem (*i.e.* Power) of the Company of the gods, gracious of face and beloved by those who see him. He has set his fear in all lands, and through their love for him they exalt his name above every other name. All nations make offerings to him, he is commemorated in heaven and upon earth. He is greatly acclaimed in the Uak festival, the Two Lands with one voice utter cries of joy. He the great one is the first among his brethren, he is the Prince of the Company of the gods, and the stablisher of truth throughout the Two Lands. He has set his son [Horus] upon the great throne of his father Geb. He is the darling of his mother Nut. Great of might he overthrew the Seba fiend, he stood up, slaughtered his enemies and set his fear in his foes . . . firm of heart (or, will), his legs stand firm. He is the heir of Geb and of the sovereignty of the Two Lands. Geb has seen his excellence and has entrusted to him the ruling of the world so long as times and seasons last. With his hand he made this earth, and the water, air, vegetation, cattle, feathered fowl, fishes, creeping things and beasts of all kinds. The desert belongs by right to the son of Nut (*i.e.* Osiris), and the Two Lands rejoice to crown him upon the throne of his father like Rā. He rises in the horizon, he lightens the darkness, from his plumes he shoots forth light and brilliance like Athen (*i.e.* the solar disk). He floods the Two Lands with splendour in the early morning. His white Crown pierces heaven, he is a brother of the gods, the guide of every god. He is gracious in command and speech, he is the favoured one of the Great Company of the gods, and the beloved of the Little Company of the gods.

[**The Birth of Horus.**] His sister [Isis]
protected him, driving off his enemies, turning
aside evil happenings with the spells of her
mouth, the weighty utterances of her tongue, the
infallibility of her speech, and the effectiveness
of her command and word.   Isis the enchantress,
the avenger of her brother [Osiris], sought him
untiringly, and travelled about over this earth
sorrowing, and rested not until she had found
him.   She produced warmth from her hair, she
caused air to come by [the beating of] her wings,
and she uttered doleful cries for her brother.
She caused movement to take place in what was
inert in the Still Heart (*i.e.* the dead Osiris),
she drew essence from him, she made flesh and
blood, she suckled [her] babe in loneliness, no
man knowing where he was.   The child grew
up, his hand became mighty in the House of Geb
(*i.e.* the earth), and the Company of the gods
rejoiced greatly at the coming of Horus, the son
of Osiris, stablished of mind, true of voice, son
of Isis, heir of Osiris.   (From a stele in Paris.)

Hymn to Aten.   Thy rising is beautiful
in the horizon of heaven, O Aten, ordainer
of life.   Thou risest in the eastern horizon,
filling every land with thy radiance.   Thou
art beautiful, great, splendid and raised up
above every land ; thy rays, like [those of]
Rā, deck every land thou hast made.   Thou
hast taken them (*i.e.* the lands), however many
they may be, and hast made them subject
to thy son.   Thou art far away, but thy beams
are on the earth ;   thou art on [men's] faces,
they [admire] thy goings.

[When] thou settest in the west, the earth is dark as with death. Men lie down in their cabins shrouded in wrappings ; one eye (*i.e.* person) cannot see his companion, and if all their goods that are under their heads be carried off they cannot see [the thief]. The lion comes out of his den, creeping things bite (*i.e.* eat), the darkness is their shelter. The land is silent [for] their maker hath set in his horizon. Thou risest up in the horizon at dawn, thou shinest in the Disk in the day, thou scatterest the darkness. Thou sendest out thy rays, the Two Lands rejoice, [men] wake up and stand on their feet, for thou raisest them. They wash, they dress themselves, they give thanks for thy rising, they do their work. All beasts and cattle turn into their pastures, the grass and herbs flourish, the water-fowl fly over their marshes, their feathers praising thy Ka. As soon as thou risest all the beasts stand up, and feathered fowl and reptiles of all kinds spring into life.

At thy rising the boats sail up and down the river, every road opens out, the fish swim up towards thy face, thy beams go down into the seas. Thou createst seed in men, thou fashionest it into offspring in women, thou makest the son to live in his mother's womb, making him to be silent and not to cry out. Thou art a nurse in the belly, giving breath to sustain life in what thou hast created. When the child is born, and on the day of his birth openeth his mouth after the manner [of babes], thou providest food for him. The chick cheeps inside the egg, thou givest it air so that it can live. Thou perfectest its body, it breaks the shell from inside, it comes out of the egg, it chirps with all its might, having come forth it walks on its two feet. O how many are the things which thou hast made! they are hidden from [one's] face, O thou God One who hast no counterpart! Thou, existing alone, didst by thy heart (or, will) create the earth and every thing that is thereon—men, cattle, beasts and creatures of all kinds that move on feet, all the creatures in the sky that fly with wings, the deserts of Syria and Kesh (Cūsh), and the Land of Egypt.

Thou hast assigned to every one his place, providing the daily food, each receiving his destined share ; thou decreest his span of life. The speech and characteristics of men vary, as do [the colours of] their skins, the dwellers in foreign lands having their distinguishing marks. Thou hast made the Nile in the Tuat, thou bringest it at thy will to make men to live. Since thou didst make them for thine own purpose, it is for thee, their Lord, to support them. . . . O Lord of every land, thou shinest upon them, O Aten of the day, thou mighty one of majesty. Thou createst the life. Of the foreign desert, and of all deserts, O Lord of the way (?) thou createst their life. Thou hast set a Nile in heaven, it descends upon them. It makes on the mountains (or, hills) a flood like the Great Green Sea, it waters the fields about their villages. How perfect, wholly perfect, are thy plans, O Lord of Eternity!

Thou art a Nile in the sky for all those who dwell in the deserts of foreign lands, and for all the beasts of the plains that move upon feet. The Nile comes from the Tuat for the Two Lands of the Inundated Country. Thy beams are the nurse of every plantation ; thou risest, they live, they flourish through thee. Thou makest the Seasons to develop every thing that thou hast created ; the season of Pert (*i.e.* November–March), that they may enjoy refreshment, and the season Heh (*i.e.* March–November), so that they may taste thee (*i.e.* feel thy heat). Thou hast made heaven which is remote that thou mayest rise up therein and look upon everything that thou hast made. Thou art he who is the One, the one who rises up among the things thou hast made as the **Living Aten,** rising, shining, departing afar off, returning. Thou hast made millions of forms from thy Oneness—cities, towns, villages, roads and river ; every eye (*i.e.* all men) has them in front of it. Thou art **Aten of the Day** in the highest. . . . (From the Hymn of Ai to Aten.)

A Prayer of the steward Nu to Osiris and the Forty-two gods of the Judgment. Homage to thee, O Great God, thou Lord of Truth. I have come to thee, O my Lord ; I have come hither to behold thy beneficence. I know thee. I know thy Name. I know the names of the Forty-two gods who are with thee in the Hall of Maāti, who keep ward over sinners, who feed upon their blood on the day when the lives of men are judged in the presence of the god

Un-Nefer. . . . Verily I come to thee, I bring
Truth to thee, I have destroyed sin for thee.
I have done no evil to mankind. I have not
wronged my kinsfolk. I have not committed
sin in the place of Truth. I have not known
worthless men. I have not done evil. I have
not insisted that excessive work should be done
for me daily. I have not thrust forward my
name for honour. I have not entreated servants
cruelly. I have not thought scorn of God.
I have not robbed the poor of his goods. I
have not done that which is hateful to the
gods. I have not caused a master to injure his
slave. I have not inflicted pain. I have allowed
no man to suffer hunger. I have made none to
weep. I have not committed murder. I have
not made any man to commit murder for me.
I have not cheated the temples of their offerings.
I have not stolen the bread of the gods. I
have not stolen the bread of the blessed dead.
I have not committed fornication. I have not
defiled myself in the sanctuary of the god of
my city. I have not cheated in measuring the
bushel. I have not stolen land. I have not
seized wrongfully the fields of others. I have
not cheated with the scales. I have not
declared the weight wrongly. I have not
taken milk from the mouths of babes. I have
not driven cattle from their own pastures.
I have not snared the fowl in the preserves
of the gods. I have not caught fish with
bait made of fish of their kind. I have not
stopped the flow of water [on the fields]. I have
not made a breach in a canal. I have not

extinguished a lamp (or, fire) when it should burn.
I have not defrauded the gods of their meat
offerings. I have not driven off cattle from the
pastures of the gods. I have not thrust back
the god when he would come forth. I am pure,
I am pure, I am pure, I am pure. . . . O
declare ye me righteous in the presence of
Nebertcher, for I have done what is right in
Ta-Mera (Egypt). . . . I live upon truth, I feed
upon truth. I have performed the command-
ments of men and the things that please the
gods. I have made the god to be at peace with
me by doing his will. I have given bread to the
hungry man, and water to the thirsty man, and
a boat to him that was shipwrecked. I have
made offerings to the gods, and given sepulchral
meals to the Spirits (*i.e.* the dead). Therefore
deliver me and protect me, and bring no charge
against me in the presence [of the Great God].
I am clean of mouth and clean of hands ; therefore let it be said [by the gods] when they see
me, Welcome ! Welcome ! I have testified
before Hrafhaf (*i.e.* the Divine Ferryman), and
he has acquitted me. I have prayed to the
gods, and I know their persons. I have purified
my breast with clean water, and my back with
the things that make clean, and I have steeped
my inward parts in the Pool of Truth ; there is
no member of mine lacking in truth. (From
the Book of the Dead, Chap. cxxv.)

A Prayer to Osiris. Homage to thee, O
my divine Father Osiris ! Thou livest, having
thy members. Thou didst not decay, thou
didst not become worms, thou didst not crumble

away, thou didst not become corruption, thou didst not putrefy. I am the god Khepera, and my members shall have an everlasting existence. I shall not decay. I shall not rot. I shall not putrefy. I shall not turn into worms. I shall not see corruption before the eye of the god Shu. I shall have my body, I shall have my body ; I shall live, I shall live ; I shall germinate, germinate, germinate ; I shall wake up in peace ; I shall not putrefy ; my reins and inward parts shall not perish ; I shall not be lacking in any member. Mine eye shall not be dimmed ; my features shall not be changed ; my ear shall not be deaf ; my head shall not be removed from my neck ; my tongue shall not be cut out ; my hair shall not be cut off ; my eyebrows shall not be shaved off ; I shall suffer from no damaging defect. My body shall be established perfect and shall neither be ruined nor destroyed on this earth. (Book of the Dead, Chap. cliv.)

Precepts of Amenemapt, who says : Lend me thine ears, I pray ; hearken to the things that I am about to say. Give thy mind to the difficult matters that I am about to unravel for thee. It will be to thy advantage to set them in thy heart, to reject them will be a calamity for thee. Set them in the treasury of thy belly, for they will enable thee to keep a right heart, and they will be a guide for thy tongue. If thou wilt live and keep them in thy mind daily, they will help thee in the time of adversity. Thou wilt find my words to be a storehouse of life and a source of strength and safety [so long as thou art] upon the earth.

Take heed not to rob the poor, and be not cruel to the destitute. Turn not thy hand from the old man, pretending to be a great man. Send not on a mission of danger the man for whom thou hast affection. If thou canst answer the man who attacks thee do him no injury. Let the evil-doer alone ; he will destroy himself. We must help the sinner, for may we not become like him ? Set him on his feet, give him thy hand, commit him to the hand of the God. Feed him with bread, give him drink, for it is in the heart of the God to show another act of compassion. Join not thyself to the chatterer ; avoid him ; leave him to the God who knows how to requite him. Encroach not on the property of the God, and make not a servant of His to neglect his duty for the benefit of another man. Say not, To-day is even as to-morrow. Encroach not on the lands of the blessed dead. Steal not land from the widow when marking out fields for cultivation. Break not down landmarks. Make offerings to God, take interest in the estates of the dead. Plough not the land of another. Six feet of land given thee by God are better than thirty thousand which thou hast stolen.

Pass not thy day in beer-houses and eating-houses, or thou wilt become a mere mass of food. The beggar in God's hand is better off than the rich man in his palace. Crusts of bread and a loving heart are better than rich food and contention. Hanker not after dainty meats. Mind thy business, and let every man do his when he wishes to do it. Learn to be content with what thou hast. Treasure obtained by fraud will not stay with thee ; thou hast it to-day, to-morrow it has departed. It will either disappear of its own accord, or the earth will swallow it up, or it will waste away, or take wings like the goose and fly away. If thou sailest with a thief thou wilt be left in the river. Get into the habit of praying sincerely to Aten (*i.e.* the solar Disk) as he rises in the sky, saying, " Grant me, I beseech thee, strength and health." He will give thee all that is necessary, and thou shalt be saved from anxiety. Approve what is good ; spit upon what is bad. Avoid lying (or, slander). Be kind to the poor. Get thee a seat in the sanctuary. Be strong to do the Will of God. Hide the flight of the runaway slave.

Disregard what thou hearest, whether good or bad ; it is not thy business, heed it not. Speak only what is good, what is bad hide in thy belly. Avoid the scandal-monger. His lips are date-syrup, his tongue is a deadly dagger, and a blazing fire is within him. Avoid converse with evil men, for that God hates. Make thy plans wisely. Be dignified. Place thyself for safety in the hand of God. The liar is an abomination to him. Falsify not the registers of land ; it is an abomination to God. Support not the liar by word or deed. Undervalue nothing. The approval of men is better than riches. Do right and thou shalt do well for thyself. Cheat not with the scales, and obliterate not the stamps on the weights and measures of capacity. Help the man who stumbles. Covet not gold. Use not a land measure marked with two different scales of measurement. Indulge not in morning slumber whilst the day breaks majestically in the sky. What can be compared to dawn and daybreak for beauty ? To what can the man who knows not the dawn be compared ? For whilst God is performing His splendid work that man is wallowing in slothfulness. Say not, " Evil should not be permitted to exist " ; there is neither good nor evil in the hand of the God. A man's tongue may be his steersman, but it is Nebertcher (*i.e.* the God of the Universe) who is the Captain. Cause not the giving of a wrong verdict in the Law Courts by hiding the truth. Accept no bribe. Truth is the great support of God (or throne-bearer). Seek not to penetrate the Divine Will, for Destiny and Fate are established.

Waste not the early hours of the day in sleep. Haste not to be rich, but be not slothful in thine own interest. Laugh not at the blind man, and make not a mock of the dwarf. A man mixes the mud and straw for his house, but it is God who is the architect. Give no orders to thy superior. Be courteous to the man thou dislikest. Help the old man who is drunk, and treat him with respect before his family. Follow not the cult of the wine-cup, for it will encourage thine enemies. The love of God is better than the reverence of the nobleman. If thou art asked to help to work the ferry-boat, take a paddle and do so ; God will not be offended thereby. If thou hast a ferry-boat on the river, take not the fares of the passengers, but let the ferryman keep them. These Precepts will please thee and teach thee. They will make the fool wise, and the man who hears them read will assuredly steer his course by them. Steep thyself in them, and set them in thy heart. Learn them well, think about them and understand them. By following them the scribe who would make himself a master of his craft will become a nobleman.

The Tale of the Two Brothers. Anpu, a peasant, lived with his wife on a small farm, and his granary and cattle byres were close to the house ; in his work he was assisted by Batau, his younger brother, who was to all intents and purposes his slave. Anpu's wife fell in love with her brother-in-law, and one day when he came back to the farm to fetch a further supply of seed corn for his brother, who was then ploughing in the fields, she stopped him at his work and told him of her admiration of him and her love for him. Batau despised her compliments and refused to carry out the plans she had made, and taking up the measure of grain on his shoulders, fled from the farm, leaving her very angry. She then untied her hair, rent her garments as if she had been engaged in a severe struggle with a man, and threw herself on the ground, pretending that she had been badly beaten, and was suffering greatly. When her husband came back to the farm in the evening he found the house in darkness, and on going inside he saw his wife lying on the floor and having the appearance of having been seriously ill-treated. In answer to his questions she told him that when Batau came to fetch the grain he endeavoured to force her, and that having beaten her he took the grain and departed. She went on to say that she was afraid he would kill her when he returned in the evening and found that she had told Anpu what he had done. Anpu did not suspect that she herself had torn her garments, and had made herself sick by eating some nauseating substance, but having heard her story he took a large reed-cutting knife and hid himself behind a door in the byre, intending to kill his brother when he should arrive. In due course Batau drove his cattle to the farm, walking behind them and carrying a heavy load of vegetables on his back. When the cattle were entering the byre the foremost ox looked back to Batau and told him that Anpu was standing behind the door with a knife in his hand waiting to kill him ; and the other oxen said the same. Batau looked under the door and saw his brother's feet, and believing the words of the oxen, he set down his load of vegetables and fled for his life from the farm. Anpu rushed out and followed him, but Shu, the Sun-god, seeing that he was gaining on Batau, caused a river full of crocodiles to come into being, and Anpu was on one side and Batau on the other. The following morning Batau told Anpu the facts of the case, and as a proof of his words mutilated himself, and leaving the river he departed to the Valley of the Acacia ; Anpu, filled with sorrow for his brother and anger with his wife, went home and cut up his wife and threw her limbs to the jackals. Batau passed his time in hunting in the Valley of the

Acacia, and the gods gave him a very beautiful wife, but she was sent for by the king and brought to Egypt, where she became his wife. Subsequently Batau's heart was discovered by Anpu, who was searching for it, and he revivified it, and Batau, having thereby recovered his powers, took the form of a bull, and then, after several transformations, begot a son by his wife, who had become Queen of Egypt, and this son succeeded to the throne.   (From the D'Orbiney Papyrus.)

A Legend of Khensu Nefer-hetep.   Now behold His Majesty Rameses was, according to his wont, in Mesopotamia, and the chiefs of all the lands there came to pay homage to him, and to entreat his good-will and favour.   And the people of the countries brought to him offerings of gold, lapis lazuli, turquoise, and every kind of thing which the hand of God produces, on their backs, and every chief sought to outdo his neighbour.   When the Prince of Bekhten brought his gift and tribute, he set his eldest daughter in front of it as a proof of his reverence for His Majesty and to gain his favour.   Now the maiden was beautiful, and His Majesty thought her the most beautiful girl he had ever seen, and straightway he bestowed on her the title of " King's Woman, lady in chief," and called her " Neferu-Rā " (*i.e.* the Beauties of Rā).   And when he came to Egypt she became the " King's Woman " in very truth.

When the king was in Thebes, in the temple of the Southern Apt (*i.e.* Luxor), on the 22nd day of the second month of Shemut (August or

September), in the 15th year of his reign, it was reported to him that an envoy had arrived from Bekhten with many gifts for the King's Woman. And when he had been brought before His Majesty with his gifts, he said : "Praise and glory be to thee, O Sun of the World ; let us live before thee." And prostrating himself, with his head on the ground, he said : "O Sovereign Lord, I come to thee on behalf of the lady Bent-Resht, the young sister of Neferu-Rā, the King's Woman. An evil disease has laid hold on her body, and I beseech thee to send a physician to see her." His Majesty said : "Let the sages and their books be brought to me"; and when they came he said : "Select for me from among your company a man who is wise of heart and cunning with his hands." [They did so] and when the royal scribe Tehuti-em-heb came, His Majesty ordered him to set out with the envoy and go to Bekhten. When the wise man arrived in Bekhten he found that Princess Bent-Resht was possessed of a devil, against whose power he could do nothing.

Then the Prince of Bekhten sent his envoy a second time to His Majesty, saying : "I beseech thee to command that a god be brought [here]." Then the king went into the temple of Khensu Nefer-hetep in Thebes, and said : "O my fair Lord, once again I come to thee on behalf of the daughter of the Prince of Bekhten." Then the god was brought into the temple of Khensu, and in the presence of Khensu Nefer-hetep the king said : "O my fair Lord, turn thy face upon Khensu, and grant that he may go to Bekhten.

And let thy saving power go with him to deliver the Princess of that land from the power of the devil that possesseth her." And Khensu Neferhetep granted the king's request, and he bestowed his saving power upon Khensu. Then His Majesty sent Khensu in his boat, and five other boats, and chariots and horses, and the god arrived in Bekhten after a journey of seventeen months, and was welcomed with great joy by the Prince. When Khensu came to the place where the Princess was, he worked upon her with the magical fluid of life $\left(\text{\Large ?}, sa \right)$ and she was healed straightway. And the devil who had possessed her cried out, "Welcome, indeed, is thy coming to us, O great god, conqueror of the hosts of darkness! Bekhten is thy city, its people are thy slaves, and I am thy servant. I will depart unto the place whence I came to gratify thee, as for this purpose thou hast come. But [before I go] I beseech thee to command that a festival be made at which the Prince of Bekhten and I may rejoice together." And Khensu assented to this request and ordered his priest to tell the Prince of Bekhten to make a festival in honour of the devil. And the Prince of Bekhten made a feast in honour of Khensu and the devil, and they all passed a happy day together, and then the devil departed to the place which he loved.

Then the Prince of Bekhten determined to keep Khensu in his country, and refused to allow him to return to Egypt; and the god remained there for 3 years, 4 months, and 5 days. And one day

the Prince, whilst lying on his bed, saw in a vision
Khensu come forth from his shrine in the form of
a hawk with feathers of gold, and he flew up
into the air and departed to Egypt. The Prince
awoke in terror, and when he spoke to the priest
of Khensu, he replied, saying: " The god hath
left us and departed to Egypt. We must now
send back his chariot to Egypt." Then the
Prince gave the command, and the [statue of the]
god set out for Egypt, with multitudes of gifts,
accompanied by a host of soldiers and horses.

The following account of the hunting of wild
cattle by Amenhetep III is taken from the great
scarab, the base of which is reproduced on
Plate VIII. (1) In the second year of the reign
of His Majesty, (2) the Living Horus, the mighty
Bull, diademed with Maāt (*i.e.* Truth), the
Stablisher of Laws, (3) the Pacifier of the Two
Lands (*i.e.* Upper and Lower Egypt), Mighty
one in arm (or, thigh), Smiter of the Nomads, the
Lord of the Two Lands, ⎡ Neb-maāt-Rā ⎤, (4) the
son of Rā, ⎡ Amenhetep, Governor of Thebes ⎤,
giver of life (the King's Woman, the Great
One, [being] ⎡ Tī ⎤, living one like Rā), a
marvellous thing took place (5) through His
Majesty. One came bringing a report to His
Majesty, saying: " The wild cattle are in the
hilly ground (6) of the district of Shetep." His
Majesty set out by boat and sailed down the
river in the royal barge called " Khā-em-
Maāt " (7) during the night. And having made
a successful journey he arrived safely in the

district of Shetep (**8**) early the following morning. His Majesty mounted his horse and rode off with all his bowmen following him, and the head men, and all the captains of the bowmen, (**9**) were commanded to keep a strict watch on the wild cattle, and all the children (**10**) of the neighbourhood to do the same. And His Majesty gave orders for all the wild cattle (**11**) to be driven into a stockaded enclosure with a ditch (?) round about it. (**12**) His Majesty commanded a counting of all the wild cattle to be made, and their total number was 170. (**13**) The number of the wild cattle which His Majesty hunted and slew on this day was 56 head. His Majesty remained idle for four days (**14**) in order to allow his horses to recover their fieryness. Then His Majesty mounted a horse, and (**15**) the number of wild cattle which he hunted and slew was 40 head. (**16**) The total number of the wild cattle [slain by him] was 96 head.

The following transcript of the text will help the reader to decipher the text on the Plate.

¹ Lord of the Vulture, Lord of the Uraeus.
² Horus of gold (?).
³ Man of the reed, man of the bee (or, hornet), *i.e.* King of the South and North.

PLATE VIII.

Steatite scarab inscribed on the base with an account of the hunting and slaughter of 96 wild cattle by Amenhetep III in the second year of his reign, about 1448 B.C.

4.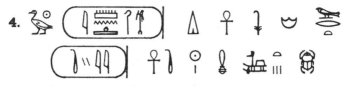

5.

6.

7.

8.

9.

10.

11.

12.

13.

14.

15.

16.

CHAPTER X

THE Egyptians of the Neolithic Period believed that their existence would not come to an end with the death of their bodies, and they appear to have thought that the renewed life which they would live in some unknown region would closely resemble that which they were accustomed to lead in this world. This is proved by the fact that in the oldest known predynastic graves pots containing food, flint weapons for war and the chase, flint tools, etc. have been found in considerable numbers. The belief in **immortality** which is attested by these objects never diminished, but, on the contrary, developed and increased throughout the whole period of dynastic history. The Neolithic Egyptians who could afford to bury their dead and did not cast their bodies out into the desert for wild beasts to devour, dug oval shallow graves for them on the edges of the desert. The cultivable land was then, as it has been in all periods, far too valuable to devote to the dead. The body was buried in the bent, or pre-natal, position, and was wrapped sometimes in a reed mat and sometimes in the skin of some animal, perhaps a gazelle, and the grave was covered over more or less carefully. The dryness of the soil and the absence of wind enabled the body to retain its form as it gradually dried. In some graves the unfleshed bones of the skeleton are found, but by what means they were unfleshed is unknown. Many modern African peoples take their dead out into the forests and, when the ants have cleaned the bones, collect them and bury them or otherwise preserve them. Other graves were covered over with large earthenware pots, and later still bodies were laid in boxes of various shapes, which were the prototypes of the coffin.

The predynastic Egyptians made no attempt to mummify their dead ; there was no necessity for them to do so, for the dryness of the soil preserved the body sufficiently for their purpose. Under the early dynasties parts or the whole of the dead body were wrapped in linen cloth, and before the end of the Old Kingdom attempts were made to preserve it with natron or by covering it with plaster of some kind. The burial of bodies in the pre-natal position was common under the first three or four dynasties, and then the custom arose of burying them lying on their backs and stretched out at full length in their

PLATE IX.

Dried body of a Predynastic Egyptian in the pre-natal position. From Gebelén. British Museum, No. 32751.

coffins. This was probably due to the development of the cult of Osiris, the priests of which
preached the resurrection of the body with all
its powers and members complete.   They
proclaimed that the body of Osiris, who was

slain on the dyke bank at Netât, ⌇⌇ 𓎛 𓈗, near

Abydos, had been reconstituted, and made
incorruptible and immortal.   By treating the
dead body of a man as that of Osiris had been
treated by Anpu (Anubis), the divine physician
and embalmer, and reciting the same spells of
Thoth that Isis had uttered, the priests proclaimed their power to enable it to rise from the
dead and become immortal.   The art of mummification reached its highest pitch of development
under the XVIIIth Dynasty, and although from
about 1300 B.C. it steadily declined, mummification was practised in Egypt until the IVth or
Vth century of our Era.

The religious texts show that many different
views were current about the **resurrection of
the body.**   The material body was called *khat*,

𓍼 𓅃 𓎼, a word meaning " something that

decays," " corruption," etc., and Osiris had a
material body of this kind.   One view was that
the very substance of this corruptible body was
re-made and re-born by means of mummification, and by the magical and religious spells
that were recited by properly qualified priests
whilst the various processes were being carried
out, and that the body of every man who
appeared before Osiris was the actual body in

which he had lived upon earth. Another view
was that the mummification and spells made to
spring from the natural body **another body**
which was identical with it in shape and form,
but was so immaterial in character that it
might be called a " spirit body." This body was
called **Sāh,** ⌐⌐, and many passages in the
Pyramid Texts prove that it lived in heaven
with the gods, and that the soul dwelt in it.
We read less about it in the texts of the New
Kingdom, and their general evidence suggests
that the later Egyptians preferred to believe in
the resurrection of the man's natural body.

When a man was born there was born with
him the **Ka,** ⊔, a word very difficult to render
by any one word. It is usually translated by
"double," but at times it seems to mean
character, disposition, individuality, mind, personality, etc. It was ever present with a man
during life, and after death it dwelt in the tomb
with his body. It needed food and drink, it
delighted in the smell of the meat offerings and
the perfume of flowers, and in all periods men
prayed to Osiris and the gods of his Company
to give an abundant supply of offerings for the
benefit of their Kas. The Ka had its chapel,
⌐⌐⊔, and there existed a body of priests
called " ministers of the Ka," ⌐⌐ ⊔. In many
a tomb of the Old Kingdom is found a painted
stone portrait figure of the deceased seated or
standing in a specially prepared walled-off

chamber, with an opening in one of the walls, through which it might see the offerings and enjoy the smell of them. This has often been called the " Ka statue," but there is a possibility that it had nothing to do with the Ka, and that it was only regarded as a memorial statue.

Horus presenting Amenhetep III, when a babe, and his Ka to the god Amen-Rā, who acknowledges the child to be his son and blesses him.

Other nations have set up such statues or effigies of the dead *over* their tombs, but the Egyptians set their statues *inside* the tombs of their beloved ones. Pictures of offerings of food, drink, flowers, etc., were often painted on the inside of coffins and on the walls of tombs with a very definite object, viz. as a means of supplying the Ka with nourishment. Circumstances might arise when it would be impossible to continue to supply material offerings to the Ka. In such a case the Ka would be expected to recite the spell, " I am master of my heart, and my breast (?), and my hands, and my feet, and my mouth, and all my members, and my funerary offerings " (Book of the Dead, Chap. lxviii). The words here rendered " funerary offerings " are PERT ER KHERU, 𓏁𓏲𓊵, or 𓊪𓂋𓏏𓊵, and their literal meaning is " offerings of bread, meat, geese, incense, wine, that appear at the word " ; and when these words were pronounced either by the Ka or his kinsfolk offerings straightway appeared.

We have seen above that the heart of the deceased was weighed in the Great Scales, and that his soul stood by and testified on its behalf. The

The soul of the scribe Nebseni visiting its mummified body in the tomb.

Soul, BA, 𓃩, is often depicted in the form of a man-headed hawk, 𓅽. When a man died it left him and went to heaven, where it lived with the gods and with the souls of the righteous, but it was believed to descend from time to time to visit the body in which it formerly dwelt, and a passage was always prepared through which it might enter the mummy-chamber. The conception concerning the Ba associated it with the heart, and for this reason it has been called the " Heart-soul " to distinguish it from the AAKHU, 🦤, or **Spirit,** or " Spirit-soul," the exact functions of which are not known. The **name,** ⌒, *ren,* and **shadow,** 🇹, *khaibit,* also formed important elements of a man, and each accompanied him after his resurrection into heaven.

According to one view the souls of the blessed dwelt with the gods in a **heaven** situated above the sky. The floor of this heaven formed the sky, which was rectangular in shape and was supported by four pillars, ||||, the " four pillars of Shu," one at each corner. Each pillar was kept in its place by one of the Four Sons of Horus, whose names were Amset, Hāpi, Tuamutef and Qebhsenuf. Other views represented the sky in the form of a woman with bowed body, whose hands and feet touch the earth, 🇫, and in the form of a cow, the four legs of which formed the four pillars of the sky. The souls that wished to ascend to the floor of heaven were obliged to use a **ladder,** and in the Papyrus of Ani this ladder is depicted. Osiris himself had recourse to a ladder, 🇪, and Set and Horus stood by and held it firmly whilst the god ascended it. An ancient tradition states that

souls set out on their journey to heaven through
the gap in the mountains at Abydos, called
Pega, ▢🐦↝. Near this gap was the famous
well into which offerings to the dead were put.
It was connected by means of a subterranean
passage with the kingdom of Osiris, and offerings
made by the faithful were transported through
it to their kinsfolk in the Other World. According to the Book of Gates the Judgment Hall of
Osiris was situated at Abydos, and the judgment
of the dead took place here daily at midnight.

The oldest name for the place of departed
spirits is **Tuat,** ✶🐦▱, or ✶▱, the meaning
of which is unknown. According to some texts
it was situated under the earth, and contained
the kingdom of Osiris, a region where the gods
of the dead lived, and a series of the Under-
worlds of great towns and cities like Memphis,
Heliopolis, Saïs, Herakleopolis. To reach the
kingdom of Osiris the deceased had to cross a
great river, the waters of which, when drunk by
the righteous, were cool and sweet, but when
drunk by the wicked were boiling hot and
bitter. Osiris kept a ferryman called **Herfhaf,**
🜨🐦, a god whose " face was
[turned] behind him," and who, therefore, had
eyes in the back of his head, so to speak. If
this being and his magical boat were satisfied
that the souls that came to him to be ferried
across were right and true, he would transport
them to the land of Osiris ; if they were not,

the ferryman and boat refused to take them.
The ferryman's head was turned behind him so
that he would be able to see any souls that tried
to board his boat as he was pushing off, and
could thrust them away.   Once across the river
the soul had to pass through the **Seven Ārits,**
or great gates, each of which admitted it to a
large Hall and was guarded by three gods—
the Gatekeeper, the Announcer and the Watcher.
The arrival of every soul was announced to
Osiris, and without his permission no soul was
admitted.   It is uncertain whether these Halls
were all on the same level or whether they were
placed one above the other.   Some papyri
mention Twenty-one Gates, in which case each
hall would have three gates, and some give the
number as ten or twelve.   The whole question is
difficult, and the Egyptians themselves were as
much puzzled by it as we are.   In every case
each Gate was guarded by three gods of terrifying
forms and aspects.   Besides these Gates and
Halls there were **Twelve Circles,** four
of which are described in a papyrus in the British
Museum (No. 10478), but where and how they
were situated cannot be said.   Dante probably
derived his idea of the Circles from Egyptian
tradition.

Different views about the situation of the
kingdom of Osiris also existed.   According to
the Vignettes on the sarcophagi of the Middle
Kingdom, Osiris dwelt on an island surrounded
by several islets, but the papyri of the New
Kingdom show that the beatified lived in a place

intersected by canals, and that they ploughed and harrowed the ground between them, and sowed grain, and reaped their harvests and threshed wheat and barley there. The wheat was 8 feet high, the ears were 3 feet long, and the stalks 5 feet ; the barley was about 12 feet high, the ears were 5 feet long, and the stalks 7 feet long. The spirits who reaped the crops were 15 feet high. Several boats, which were self-propelled, were moored to steps, and in these the beatified sailed about at will.

The Book of Gates shows that the Tuat was a circular valley formed by the body of Osiris himself, and that it was on the plane of the land of Egypt or of the sky. The Sun-god traverses the valley each night, and sails over the whole length of the river in it in his boat with his gods. As he advances he gives light and air to the dead who are in the various sections of the Tuat ; the righteous are on the right bank of the river and the sinners on the left. As he passes along he rewards the righteous with celestial food and drink, and the wicked are punished and condemned by him to utter destruction. In the Fifth Division of the Tuat we find the souls of foreigners—the Libyans, the Asiatics and the Negroes—each nation being separated from the Egyptians. In the Sixth Division is the Judgment Hall of Osiris. The god sits on a chair of state placed on a throne with nine steps, and at midnight he judges all the souls who have come there during the day. To the righteous he awards estates in Sekhet-Aaru, and the wicked he hands over to

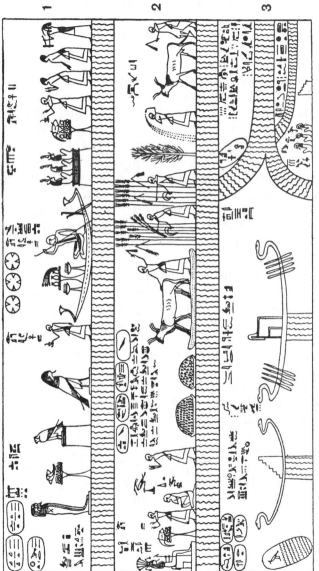

The Sekhet-Aaru, or Field of Reeds, where the blessed dead lived.

1. The deceased adoring the gods, paddling a boat, and censing a divine soul in Sekhet-hetep.
2. The deceased sowing, reaping, threshing the grain, and adoring the Nile-god.
3. The magical boats of Rā, and Un-Nefer, which move themselves, and the abode of the gods and perfect souls who reap the celestial crops.

his headsman Shesmu, who hacks their bodies in pieces, which fall down into a pit of fire, where they are consumed.

The righteous have the choice of two heavens in which to live, viz. the Sekhet-Aaru of Osiris and the Boat of the Sun-god Rā. The followers of Osiris, *i.e.* the greater number of the Egyptians, preferred his Elysian Fields, where they could enjoy spiritualized pleasures and an existence that closely resembled their life upon earth. Those who chose the Boat of Rā sailed with him over the skies, they fed upon light, and were arrayed in light, and were finally absorbed into the light of the god himself. On the other hand, the Osirians assisted Osiris in cultivating the plant of Truth, Maāt, which was of the substance of Osiris himself, and as they lived upon Maāt, they finally became absorbed into Osiris and lived by and in him for ever. The Boat of Rā passed on, and the ministers of the god gathered together his enemies in a place at the eastern end, or side, of the Tuat, where they were to be destroyed in the fire-pits prepared for them. When Rā arrived, he passed sentence of death on them, and they were thrust head downwards into pits full of red-hot sand forthwith. The pits were fed with a constant supply of fire which the goddesses of destruction vomited continually into them, and the bodies, souls, and shadows of the enemies of Rā were utterly consumed in the sight of those beatified souls that had chosen his boat as their heaven. Some have adduced the Vignettes of the Book of Gates as

Diorite ushabti figure made for Amenhetep II, King of Egypt, about 1450 B.C., now in the British Museum. The ushabti figure was supposed to do agricultural work for the deceased in the Other World. No. 35365.

Cover of the outer coffin of Hent-mehit, a priestess of Amen-Rā, about 1000 B.C., now in the British Museum. No. 51101.

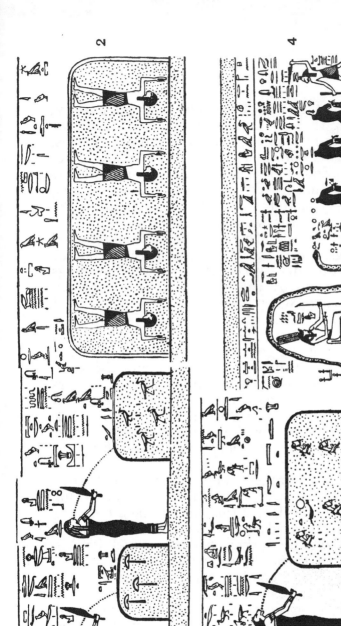

The annihilation of the damned in the Tuat (Underworld).

1. The shadows, ⌒⌒⌒, and souls, ⍦⍦⍦, of the wicked being burned in pits of fire.
2. The wicked, head downwards, being burned in a pit of fire.
3. The enemies, ⍦⍦ ⍦⍦ ⍦⍦, of Osiris being burned in a pit of fire.
4. Osiris seated under a canopy formed by a serpent which spits fire on to the decapitated bodies of the damned and consumes them. (From the Book of Gates.)

proofs that the Egyptians believed in **purgatory,**
thinking that the bodies and souls and shadows
in the fire-pits represented those of human beings.
But this is not the case, for the enemies of Rā
were the devils and fiends of mist, cloud, darkness
and rain, that tried to prevent the sun from rising
in the sky, and the fate of these, as also of the
enemies of Osiris, was **annihilation.**

Under the Old Kingdom heaven was reserved
for kings alone, and the texts on the pyramids
of the Vth and VIth Dynasties show us how kings
were received by the gods, and what they did
in heaven. When Unas arrived in the Other
World, heaven dropped water-floods, the stars
quaked, the bow-bearers ran about in terror,
the bones of the god Aker trembled, and all the
beings there fled when they saw him rising up
as a Soul, and as a god who lived upon his fathers
and mothers. Unas hunted the gods, Herthertu
lassoed them, Khensu cut their throats and took
out their intestines, Shesmu cut them up and
cooked them in his fiery cauldrons, Unas ate
them, and so absorbed their spirits and vital
powers. The largest and finest of the gods
he ate at daybreak, the smaller ones he ate for
his evening meal, and the smallest he ate during
the night ; the old and worn-out gods he rejected
entirely and used their bodies as fuel for his
furnace. The cauldrons containing the thighs
of the gods and goddesses were heated by gods
who projected fire from their bodies into the
cauldrons beneath them. In his hunting expeditions Unas journeyed over every part of the
day sky and the night sky. The strength he

derived from eating the gods enabled him to become the chief of the oldest gods of heaven, and the equal of the giant of Orion.   His power and his will were absolute, for the spirits and souls of the gods were in him, and he had absorbed the wisdom of them all, and the property of everlasting life which especially belonged to them.   Thus he possessed the power to live longer than any god, and to live as long as the heavens endured.   If the description of the life led by Unas in heaven is to be believed we must conclude that when upon earth he lived the life of a savage African cannibal, whose chief delights and occupations were fighting and the carrying off of men's wives.

The later texts of the pyramids supply many interesting details concerning the existence of the beatified in heaven.   The early conception of heaven was at once material and spiritual, and it never disappeared from the mind of the Egyptian.   The body of the king in heaven was the body of the god, and his flesh and bones were those of the god.   He walks among the " Living Ones," ☥☥☥, and he becomes a god, the son of a god, ⌐⅋⌐.   Each of his features— eyes, nose, mouth, cheeks, etc.—is the feature of a god, the gods elect him to be a member of their Company, and the other two Companies invite him to take his seat among them.   He becomes not only Horus, the son of Osiris, but Osiris himself.   He is the brother of the moon, the son of Sothis (Sirius), and he strides over the heavens like Orion. The gods bow their heads to the ground before him, and he rules them all. Rā will not allow him to walk, but lifts him up on his shoulders and carries him about from place to place. He absorbs the power and wisdom of Thoth, who was the mind of Rā and the Advocate who obtained the verdict " Innocent " for Osiris at the Great Trial, and so becomes the Judge of the Dead. Side by side with the god he sits on a great throne made of translucent material, which is decorated with the heads of lions and has feet in the form of the hooves of bulls. He is arrayed in glorious apparel of the finest texture, similar to that worn by those who sit on the Throne of Living Truth. On his head he wears the greatest of all crowns, which the god set upon his head. He does not hunger, or thirst, or feel sadness. He eats the bread that Rā eats daily, and he drinks what Rā drinks; his provisions are those that are decreed by Geb and by the utterances of the gods. He eats what the gods eat, he drinks what they drink, he dwells as they dwell, and all the gods give him food that he may not die. He dresses as the gods dress, and his garments are made of fine, white linen ; his feet are shod with sandals. He goes with the gods to the Great Lake in Sekhet-Hetep, round which the gods seat themselves, and the great and imperishable gods give him to eat of the tree of life whereon they live, so that he likewise may live. The bread that he eats never grows stale, for it is the " Bread of Eternity " ; his beer never goes sour, for it is the " Beer of Everlastingness." He is delivered from the power of those who would steal his food. He is washed clean, and his *ka* is washed clean, and they eat bread together. He goes round about heaven, even as do the Four Sons of Horus, and he partakes of their figs and wine. He dwells without fear under the protection of the gods, from whose loins he came forth, and those who would be his foes find that they are enemies of Temu. The boatmen who row Rā row him also, and those who row Rā beneath the horizon row him also. He entered heaven in the west of the sky, and he comes forth from the east thereof.

The position of the king in the primitive Egyptian **heaven of Rā** is well described in the following address : " Now therefore, O Pepi, he that hath given unto thee life and all power and eternity and the power of speech is **Rā**. Thou hast endued thyself with the forms of the god, and thou hast become magnified thereby before the gods who dwell on the Lake. Hail, Pepi, thy soul standeth among the gods, and among the shining ones, and the fear of thee striketh into their hearts. Hail, Pepi, thou placest thyself upon the throne of Him that dwelleth among the Living Ones, and the writing which thou hast is in their hearts. Thy name shall live upon the earth, thy name shall flourish upon the earth, thou shalt neither perish nor be destroyed for ever and ever."

The king's position in the **Kingdom of Osiris** is thus described :—

" Hail, Pepi, thou hast arrived, thou art glorious, and thou hast gotten might like the god who is seated upon his throne, that is, **Osiris.** Thy soul is in thy body, thy strong form is behind thee, thy crown is upon thy head, thy head-dress is upon thy shoulders, thy face is before thee. Those who sing songs of joy are upon both sides of thee, the followers of the god are behind thee, and those who accompany him are on both sides of thee. The god cometh : Pepi hath come upon the throne of Osiris. The glorious dweller in Netat (*i.e.* Osiris), the divine dweller in Teni (This–Abydos), hath arrived. Isis speaketh to thee, Nephthys holdeth converse with thee, and the Spirits come and bow down at thy feet by reason of the writing (or, book) which thou hast, O Pepi, in the region of Saa. Thou comest to thy mother Nut, who strengtheneth thy arm and maketh a way for thee through the sky to the place where Rā is. Thou hast opened the gates of the sky and the doors of the celestial ocean. Thou didst find Rā, who protected thee, and took thee by thy hand, and brought thee into the two heavens, and set thee upon the throne of Osiris. Hail, Pepi, for the Eye of Horus hath come to hold converse with thee. As a son fighteth for his father, and as Horus defended his father, even so hath Horus defended Pepi against his enemies. And thou art defended and endowed in every

way like a god, and thou standest equipped with
all the attributes of Osiris upon the throne of
Khenti Amenti."

The heaven of Rā, though representing ancient
solar beliefs, did not appeal to the Egyptians
generally, for it was too exclusive, and its god
was too great and too remote ever to become
an object of willing and affectionate worship.
The king, being part god, would naturally find
happiness there with his fellow-gods, but it
offered no attractions to the slave, the peasant,
and the lower classes of the population in cities
and towns. The cult of Rā was essentially the
cult of the court and noblemen, and the demo-
cratic instinct of the Egyptian, which always
was and still is extremely sensitive, revolted
against all aristocratic authority in religion.
The Egyptians, as a nation, loved to worship
Osiris, the man who had been persecuted and
slain by his enemies, and had risen from the
dead, having triumphed over the power of Death
and the grave, and become the god and Judge of
the dead. They felt that Osiris the man would
understand men, and sympathize with them in
their sorrows and troubles, and the people, as
a whole, placed their hopes of immortality in
Osiris, "who made men and women to be
born again," 𓂝𓏤𓏭 𓈖 𓅿 𓃹 𓏏𓏭 𓂝 𓏤 𓅿
(Book of the Dead, Chap. clxxxii, 16). In
the heaven of Osiris they hoped to live a life
which was to all intents and purposes a glorified
duplicate of that which they led upon earth.
There they expected to find their kinsfolk and

friends and to know them and be known by them ; **reunion and recognition** with them in the Other World were necessities to them.

Their wishes in this respect are well expressed in a text written on a coffin in Cairo. The deceased Sepa prays, saying : " Hail, Rā ! Hail, Tem ! Hail, Geb ! Hail, Nut ! Grant ye to Sepa that he may travel over the heavens, and over the earth and over the waters, that he may meet his ancestors, 𓏏𓊪𓂝𓀀𓏥𓏤, may meet his father, may meet his mother, may meet his grown-up sons and daughters, and his brothers and his sisters, may meet his friends, both male and female, may meet his foster-parents, and his kinsfolk, and those who have done work for him upon earth, both male and female, and may meet the woman whom he loved and knew." Sepa goes on to say that if for any reason his father, or his mother, or his ancestors, or his children, brothers and sisters and kinsfolk and friends be prevented from having reunion with him, no more offerings shall be made to Rā ; but if they be allowed to come to him and be with him as they were upon earth, whether it be in heaven, or on the earth, or in the Tuat, or in the Nile, or in Busiris, or Abydos, or elsewhere, the usual offerings shall be made to Rā, and the circumpolar stars and the planets shall tow the Boat of Rā over the sky as usual. The text ends with an assurance from the goddess Hathor that Sepa may enter the Other World with confidence, knowing that his ancestors will come to meet him, that they will rejoice in seeing him, and that they will bear in their hands staves and mattocks and ploughs and weapons, and be ready to deliver him from the attacks of any malevolent god.

The prayer of Sepa given above was in one form or another prayed by every follower of Osiris during the whole course of dynastic history.

XI.—THE BULL

(Note to p. 115.)

The cult of the Bull Apis and of the Bull Mnevis was established officially at Memphis and Heliopolis respectively under the IInd Dynasty, but the worship of these sacred beasts in Egypt generally and in Nubia was common many centuries, perhaps even thousands of years, earlier. Another sacred Bull called Bakha was worshipped at Kakam, *i.e.* the town of the Black Bull, at a very early period. Many of the kings of Egypt delighted to call themselves " Mighty Bull," *Ka nekht*, 𓄿𓃒, and the Bull appears frequently in the Horus names of many of the kings of the XVIIIth Dynasty. Amenhetep I called himself the " conquering Bull," Thothmes I claimed to be the " Mighty Bull, whose marvels were great," 𓏏𓃒𓏏𓂝𓏤, Thothmes II proclaimed himself to be the "Mighty Bull, pre-eminent in valour," , and in remote times a king of the IInd Dynasty called himself "Bull of Bulls," 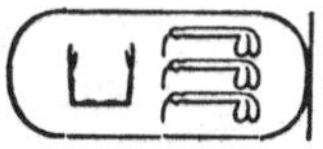. The title "Bull" was applied also to the gods, and Osiris is often addressed as "Bull of Amentt," . Many historical texts mention the "bellowings," , of the king, and the "bellowings" of Thothmes III resounded to the uttermost parts of the earth and made the people there quake. In the Kubbân Stele Rameses II, the Mighty Bull, is said to "have trampled down the Nubians under his hoofs, and to have gored them with his horns." The Mighty Bull was "ready for action," , and his "horns were always ready" to gore, ; these last words became a title of Alexander the Great, which the Arabs have prescribed in Dhu l-Karnēn. The skin of the bull played an important part in ancient Egyptian religious ceremonies, and the Masai and many other African peoples bury their dead kings wrapped up in the skins of bulls. The following hymn to the King of Timbuctoo is by His Majesty's Poet Laureate (see *New Monthly Magazine* for 1824).

Hoo ! Tamarama bow—now !
Slamarambo-pig !
Hurrah ! for the son of the Sun !
Hurrah ! for the brother of the Moon !
Throughout all the world there is none
Like Quashiboo, the only One.
    Descended from the great Baboon, Baboon,
    Descended from the Great Baboon !
Buffalo of Buffaloes, Bull of Bulls,
He sits on a throne of his enemies' skulls.
And if he wants others to play at foot-ball,
Ours are at his service—all ! all ! all !
    Hugaboo-jah ! Hugaboo-jah !
    Hail to the Royal Quashiboo,
Emperor and Lord of Timbuctoo !

BIBLIOGRAPHY

HISTORY

BREASTED, J. H. *Ancient Records*, 5 vols., Chicago, 1906.

BRUGSCH, H. *Egypt under the Pharaohs*, London, 1879.

BUDGE, E. A. WALLIS. *A History of Egypt*, 8 vols., London, 1902 ; *Short History of the Egyptian People*, London, 1914; *Egypt* (in " Home University Library," London, 1925).

HALL, H. R. H. *Ancient History of the Near East*, London, 1924 ; and Chaps. vi–viii in *Cambridge Ancient History*, Cambridge, 1923.

HERODOTUS. Translated by A. D. Godley, London, 1921.

HOMMEL, F. *Die vorsemitischen Kulturen in Aegypten und Babylonien*, Leipzig, 1882.

JÉQUIER, G. *Histoire de la Civilisation Égyptienne*, Paris, 1922.

KING, L. W., and HALL, H. R. H. *Egypt and Western Asia*, London, 1907.

KRALL, J. *Grundriss der altorientalischen Geschichte*, Vienna, 1899.

MASPERO, G. *Dawn of Civilisation*, London, 1894 ; *Struggle of the Nations*, London, 1896 ; *Passing of the Empires*, London, 1900.

MORGAN, J. J. de. *Les Premières Civilisations*, Paris, 1909.

NEWBERRY, P. E., and GARSTANG, J. *Ancient Egypt*, Boston, U.S.A., 1904.

PETRIE, W. M. F. *A History of Egypt*, 3 vols., London, 1894–1905.

WIEDEMANN, K. A. *Aegyptische Geschichte*, Gotha, 1884–1888.

CHRONOLOGY AND KING LISTS

LEPSIUS, R. *Chronologie*, Berlin, 1848.

BUDGE, E. A. WALLIS. *Book of the Kings of Egypt*, 2 vols., London, 1908.

CORY, I. P. *Ancient Fragments*, London, 1832.

HALL, H. R. H. *Cambridge Ancient History*, Vol. I, pp. 166–173.

HANNAH, H. B. *Era of Menophres*, Calcutta, 1924.

LEGGE, F. " Heliacal Risings of Sothis " (in *Recueil de Travaux*, Vol. XXXI, 1909, p. 106).

MEYER, E. *Aegyptische Chronologie*, Berlin, 1906; *die ältere Chronologie Babyloniens, Assyriens und Aegyptens*, Berlin, 1925.

NICKLIN, T. " Origin of the Egyptian Year " (in *Classical Rev.*, 1900, p. 148).

TORR, C. *Memphis and Mycenae*, Cambridge, 1896.

RELIGION

BREASTED, J. H. *Development of Religion*, New York, 1912.

BRUGSCH, H. *Religion und Mythologie*, Leipzig, 1885–1888.

BUDGE, E. A. WALLIS. *Egyptian Magic*, London, 1899.
Egyptian Ideas of the Future Life, London, 1899.
Gods of the Egyptians, 2 vols., London, 1904.
Osiris and the Egyptian Resurrection, 2 vols., London, 1911.
Legends of the Gods, London, 1912.

ERMAN, J. P. A. *Egyptian Religion*, London, 1907.

HOPFNER. *Der Tierkult der alten Aegypter*, Vienna, 1913.

MÜLLER, W. M. *Egyptian Mythology*, Boston, 1918.

NAVILLE, E. *La Religion des Anciens Égyptiens*, Paris, 1906.

PIERRET, P. *Le Panthéon Égyptien*, Paris, 1881.

Tiele, C. P. *Egyptian and Mesopotamian Religions*, London, 1882.

Wiedemann, K. A. *Religion of the Ancient Egyptians*, London, 1897.

Literature

Budge, E. A. Wallis. *The Literature of the Ancient Egyptians*, London, 1914.
The Teaching of Amen-em-apt, London, 1924.

Erman, J. P. A. *Die Literatur der Aegypter*, Leipzig, 1923.

Wiedemann, K. A. *Popular Literature in Ancient Egypt*, London, 1902.

Religious Literature

Bergmann, E. von. *Das Buch vom Durchwandeln der Ewigkeit*, Vienna, 1877.

Birch, S. *Coffin of Amamu*, London, 1886.

Budge, E. A. Wallis. *The Greenfield Papyrus*, London, 1912.
Book of Opening the Mouth, London, 1909.
Liturgy of Funerary Offerings, London, 1909.
Book of the Dead, 3 vols., London, 1910.
The Papyrus of Ani, London, 1895.
The Egyptian Heaven and Hell, reprint, three vols. in one, London, 1925.

Horrack, P. J. F. de. *Les Lamentations d'Isis*, Paris, 1907.

Jéquier, G. *Le Livre de ce qu'il y a dans l'Hadès*, Paris, 1894.

Legrain, G. *Livre des Transformations*, Paris, 1890.

MASPERO, G. *Littérature Religieuse des Anciens Égyptiens*, Paris, 1893.

MÖLLER, G. *Die beiden Totenpapyrus Rhind*, Leipzig, 1913.

SETHE, K. *Die altaegyptischen Pyramidentexte*, Leipzig, 1908.

ART

CAPART, J. *L'Art Égyptien*, Paris, 1910.
L'Architecture Égyptien, 1922.
Leçons sur l'Art Égyptien, 1920.
See also M. Capart's great work on Egyptian Art, Architecture, Sculpture, etc., now in course of publication.

HALL, H. R. H. " Art of Early Egypt and Babylonia " (in *Cambridge Ancient History*, Cambridge, 1923).

LEFÉBURE, E. *L'Art Égyptien*, Cairo, 1884.

MASPERO, G. *Égypte*, Paris, 1912.

PERROT, G., and CHIPIEZ, Ch. *History of Art in Egypt*, London, 1883.

PRISSE D'AVENNES. *Histoire de l'Art*, Paris, 1878–79.

QUIBELL, A. A. *Egyptian History and Art*, London, 1923.

GENERAL WORKS

ERMAN, J. P. A. *Aegypten und Aegyptisches Leben*, Tübingen, 1923.

MONTET, P. *Les Scênes de la vie privée dans les tombeaux Égyptiens de l'Ancien Empire*, Strasbourg, 1925.

WIEDEMANN, K. A. *Das Alte Aegypten*, Heidelberg, 1920.

ARCHAEOLOGY

BUDGE, E. A. WALLIS. *The Mummy: a Handbook to Egyptian Funerary Archaeology*, Cambridge, 1925.

MASPERO, G. *Manual of Egyptian Archaeology*, London, 1895.

WILKINSON, J. G. *Manners and Customs of the Ancient Egyptians*, 2nd Edition, edited by S. BIRCH, in 3 vols., London, 1878.

N.B.—The reader will find a great deal of useful information about Egyptian Archaeology in general, and about the unrivalled Collections of Egyptian Antiquities in the British Museum, in the following works published at low prices by the Trustees.

Guide to the Egyptian Collections, 3rd impression, 1921 ; *Guide to the Sculpture Galleries*, 1909 ; *Guide to the Egyptian Rooms*, I–III, 1924, and IV–VI, 1922 ; *Egyptian Sculptures in the British Museum*, 1913 ; *Wall Decorations of Egyptian Tombs*, 1914 ; *The Papyrus of Ani* (text volume), 1894 ; *Papyri of Hunefer, Anhai, etc.*, with large coloured plates, folio, text and translations, 1899 ; *Book of the Dead* (Monograph), 1921 ; *Rosetta Stone*, with plate, 1913 ; *Catalogue of Scarabs*, 1913, and the packets of Post Cards, coloured and uncoloured.

INDEX

Calendar, 107, 191.
Calendering, 120.
Cambyses, 11, 17, 236.
Camel, 142.
Canal in First Cataract, 7.
Canal, Nile and Red Sea, 8.
Canals, clearing of, 37.
Captives, decapitation of, 4.
Caravan-men, 43.
Caravan routes, 85.
Carians, 96.
Caricature, 240.
Carnelian, 67, 125.
Carob, 113.
Carpenter and Joiner, 121.
Cartouche, 68, 87, 184.
Caskets, jewel, 60.
Castanets, 131, 133.
Catapult, 98.
Cataract, First, 7, 8, 104; Third, 8; Fourth, 9.
Cataracts, 102; the six, 106.
Cat-goddess, 150.
Cattle, bled to death, 76; tending, 37.
Cattle, breeding of, 115; breeders of, 171; wild, 137.
Cauldrons of fire, 282.
Caution, 44.
Cavalry, 100.
Cedar, cedarwood, 122, 239.
Celibacy, 25.
Cerastes (viper), 151.
Cereals, 220.
Chabas, F., 185.
Chairs, 59; of State, 59; seats of, 59.
Chalcedon, 186.
Champollion, F., 185.
Champollion, J. F., 183 ff.
Chapters of Coming Forth, 175.
Charcoal, 49.
Chariots, 9; Hittite, 8.
Chattering, 257.

Cheating, 254, 258.
Cheeks, painting of the, 74.
Chēmē, 196.
Chenoboskia, 116.
Cheops, 14.
Chephren, 14.
Chess, 128.
Childbirth goddess, 30.
Childbirth in the Other World, 25.
Children, love of, 24; names of, 32; went naked, 37.
Chisel, 122.
Choirs, 129.
Chopper, 122.
Christians, Egyptian, 187, 208.
Christ's thorn, 113.
Chronology, 236
Cippus of Horus, 247.
Circles, the Twelve, 277.
Clappers, 131.
Clapping of hands, 128.
Classes of men, 92.
Clay as writing material, 49, 173.
Cleopatra, 183, 185, 231.
Climate, 73.
Cloaks, 64.
Clocks, 195.
Clothes, 60; chests for, 60; washing of, 65.
Clover, 112.
Club, 96, 99.
Cobra (asp), 140, 151, 198; the living, 223.
Code of Laws, 10.
Code of Osiris, 229.
Coffer-throne of Osiris, 222.
Coffin maker, 126.
Coffins, 273; how closed, 122.
Coinage, 11.
Collar, 63, 67.
Colonnade, 146.
Colossi, the, 9.
Combs, 70.

A CATALOG OF SELECTED
DOVER BOOKS
IN ALL FIELDS OF INTEREST

A CATALOG OF SELECTED
DOVER BOOKS
IN ALL FIELDS OF INTEREST

DRAWINGS OF REMBRANDT, edited by Seymour Slive. Updated Lippmann, Hofstede de Groot edition, with definitive scholarly apparatus. All portraits, biblical sketches, landscapes, nudes. Oriental figures, classical studies, together with selection of work by followers. 550 illustrations. Total of 630pp. 9⅛ × 12¼.
21485-0, 21486-9 Pa., Two-vol. set $29.90

GHOST AND HORROR STORIES OF AMBROSE BIERCE, Ambrose Bierce. 24 tales vividly imagined, strangely prophetic, and decades ahead of their time in technical skill: "The Damned Thing," "An Inhabitant of Carcosa," "The Eyes of the Panther," "Moxon's Master," and 20 more. 199pp. 5⅜ × 8½. 20767-6 Pa. $4.95

ETHICAL WRITINGS OF MAIMONIDES, Maimonides. Most significant ethical works of great medieval sage, newly translated for utmost precision, readability. Laws Concerning Character Traits, Eight Chapters, more. 192pp. 5⅜ × 8½.
24522-5 Pa. $4.50

THE EXPLORATION OF THE COLORADO RIVER AND ITS CANYONS, J. W. Powell. Full text of Powell's 1,000-mile expedition down the fabled Colorado in 1869. Superb account of terrain, geology, vegetation, Indians, famine, mutiny, treacherous rapids, mighty canyons, during exploration of last unknown part of continental U.S. 400pp. 5⅜ × 8½. 20094-9 Pa. $7.95

HISTORY OF PHILOSOPHY, Julián Marías. Clearest one-volume history on the market. Every major philosopher and dozens of others, to Existentialism and later. 505pp. 5⅜ × 8½. 21739-6 Pa. $9.95

ALL ABOUT LIGHTNING, Martin A. Uman. Highly readable nontechnical survey of nature and causes of lightning, thunderstorms, ball lightning, St. Elmo's Fire, much more. Illustrated. 192pp. 5⅜ × 8½. 25237-X Pa. $5.95

SAILING ALONE AROUND THE WORLD, Captain Joshua Slocum. First man to sail around the world, alone, in small boat. One of great feats of seamanship told in delightful manner. 67 illustrations. 294pp. 5⅜ × 8½. 20326-3 Pa. $4.95

LETTERS AND NOTES ON THE MANNERS, CUSTOMS AND CONDITIONS OF THE NORTH AMERICAN INDIANS, George Catlin. Classic account of life among Plains Indians: ceremonies, hunt, warfare, etc. 312 plates. 572pp. of text. 6⅛ × 9¼. 22118-0, 22119-9, Pa., Two-vol. set $17.90

ALASKA: The Harriman Expedition, 1899, John Burroughs, John Muir, et al. Informative, engrossing accounts of two-month, 9,000-mile expedition. Native peoples, wildlife, forests, geography, salmon industry, glaciers, more. Profusely illustrated. 240 black-and-white line drawings. 124 black-and-white photographs. 3 maps. Index. 576pp. 5⅜ × 8½. 25109-8 Pa. $11.95

THE BOOK OF BEASTS: Being a Translation from a Latin Bestiary of the Twelfth Century, T. H. White. Wonderful catalog of real and fanciful beasts: manticore, griffin, phoenix, amphivius, jaculus, many more. White's witty erudite commentary on scientific, historical aspects enhances fascinating glimpse of medieval mind. Illustrated. 296pp. 5⅜ × 8¼. (Available in U.S. only) 24609-4 Pa. $6.95

FRANK LLOYD WRIGHT: Architecture and Nature with 160 Illustrations, Donald Hoffmann. Profusely illustrated study of influence of nature—especially prairie—on Wright's designs for Fallingwater, Robie House, Guggenheim Museum, other masterpieces. 96pp. 9¼ × 10¾. 25098-9 Pa. $8.95

FRANK LLOYD WRIGHT'S FALLINGWATER, Donald Hoffmann. Wright's famous waterfall house: planning and construction of organic idea. History of site, owners, Wright's personal involvement. Photographs of various stages of building. Preface by Edgar Kaufmann, Jr. 100 illustrations. 112pp. 9¼ × 10.
23671-4 Pa. $8.95

YEARS WITH FRANK LLOYD WRIGHT: Apprentice to Genius, Edgar Tafel. Insightful memoir by a former apprentice presents a revealing portrait of Wright the man, the inspired teacher, the greatest American architect. 372 black-and-white illustrations. Preface. Index. vi + 228pp. 8¼ × 11. 24801-1 Pa. $10.95

THE STORY OF KING ARTHUR AND HIS KNIGHTS, Howard Pyle. Enchanting version of King Arthur fable has delighted generations with imaginative narratives of exciting adventures and unforgettable illustrations by the author. 41 illustrations. xviii + 313pp. 6⅛ × 9¼. 21445-1 Pa. $6.95

THE GODS OF THE EGYPTIANS, E. A. Wallis Budge. Thorough coverage of numerous gods of ancient Egypt by foremost Egyptologist. Information on evolution of cults, rites and gods; the cult of Osiris; the Book of the Dead and its rites; the sacred animals and birds; Heaven and Hell; and more. 956pp. 6⅛ × 9¼.
22055-9, 22056-7 Pa., Two-vol. set $21.90

A THEOLOGICO-POLITICAL TREATISE, Benedict Spinoza. Also contains unfinished *Political Treatise*. Great classic on religious liberty, theory of government on common consent. R. Elwes translation. Total of 421pp. 5⅜ × 8½.
20249-6 Pa. $7.95

INCIDENTS OF TRAVEL IN CENTRAL AMERICA, CHIAPAS, AND YUCATAN, John L. Stephens. Almost single-handed discovery of Maya culture; exploration of ruined cities, monuments, temples; customs of Indians. 115 drawings. 892pp. 5⅜ × 8½. 22404-X, 22405-8 Pa., Two-vol. set $17.90

LOS CAPRICHOS, Francisco Goya. 80 plates of wild, grotesque monsters and caricatures. Prado manuscript included. 183pp. 6⅝ × 9⅜. 22384-1 Pa. $5.95

AUTOBIOGRAPHY: The Story of My Experiments with Truth, Mohandas K. Gandhi. Not hagiography, but Gandhi in his own words. Boyhood, legal studies, purification, the growth of the Satyagraha (nonviolent protest) movement. Critical, inspiring work of the man who freed India. 480pp. 5⅜ × 8¼. (Available in U.S. only)
24593-4 Pa. $6.95

ILLUSTRATED DICTIONARY OF HISTORIC ARCHITECTURE, edited by Cyril M. Harris. Extraordinary compendium of clear, concise definitions for over 5,000 important architectural terms complemented by over 2,000 line drawings. Covers full spectrum of architecture from ancient ruins to 20th-century Modernism. Preface. 592pp. 7½ × 9⅝. 24444-X Pa. $15.95

THE NIGHT BEFORE CHRISTMAS, Clement C. Moore. Full text, and woodcuts from original 1848 book. Also critical, historical material. 19 illustrations. 40pp. 4⅝ × 6. 22797-9 Pa. $2.50

THE LESSON OF JAPANESE ARCHITECTURE: 165 Photographs, Jiro Harada. Memorable gallery of 165 photographs taken in the 1930s of exquisite Japanese homes of the well-to-do and historic buildings. 13 line diagrams. 192pp. 8⅜ × 11¼. 24778-3 Pa. $10.95

THE AUTOBIOGRAPHY OF CHARLES DARWIN AND SELECTED LETTERS, edited by Francis Darwin. The fascinating life of eccentric genius composed of an intimate memoir by Darwin (intended for his children); commentary by his son, Francis; hundreds of fragments from notebooks, journals, papers; and letters to and from Lyell, Hooker, Huxley, Wallace and Henslow. xi + 365pp. 5⅜ × 8.
20479-0 Pa. $6.95

WONDERS OF THE SKY: Observing Rainbows, Comets, Eclipses, the Stars and Other Phenomena, Fred Schaaf. Charming, easy-to-read poetic guide to all manner of celestial events visible to the naked eye. Mock suns, glories, Belt of Venus, more. Illustrated. 299pp. 5¼ × 8¼. 24402-4 Pa. $8.95

BURNHAM'S CELESTIAL HANDBOOK, Robert Burnham, Jr. Thorough guide to the stars beyond our solar system. Exhaustive treatment. Alphabetical by constellation: Andromeda to Cetus in Vol. 1; Chamaeleon to Orion in Vol. 2; and Pavo to Vulpecula in Vol. 3. Hundreds of illustrations. Index in Vol. 3. 2,000pp. 6⅛ × 9¼. 23567-X, 23568-8, 23673-0 Pa., Three-vol. set $41.85

STAR NAMES: Their Lore and Meaning, Richard Hinckley Allen. Fascinating history of names various cultures have given to constellations and literary and folkloristic uses that have been made of stars. Indexes to subjects. Arabic and Greek names. Biblical references. Bibliography. 563pp. 5⅜ × 8½. 21079-0 Pa. $8.95

THIRTY YEARS THAT SHOOK PHYSICS: The Story of Quantum Theory, George Gamow. Lucid, accessible introduction to influential theory of energy and matter. Careful explanations of Dirac's anti-particles, Bohr's model of the atom, much more. 12 plates. Numerous drawings. 240pp. 5⅜ × 8½. 24895-X Pa. $6.95

CHINESE DOMESTIC FURNITURE IN PHOTOGRAPHS AND MEASURED DRAWINGS, Gustav Ecke. A rare volume, now affordably priced for antique collectors, furniture buffs and art historians. Detailed review of styles ranging from early Shang to late Ming. Unabridged republication. 161 black-and-white drawings, photos. Total of 224pp. 8⅜ × 11¼. (Available in U.S. only) 25171-3 Pa. $14.95

VINCENT VAN GOGH: A Biography, Julius Meier-Graefe. Dynamic, penetrating study of artist's life, relationship with brother, Theo, painting techniques, travels, more. Readable, engrossing. 160pp. 5⅜ × 8½. (Available in U.S. only)
25253-1 Pa. $4.95

HOW TO WRITE, Gertrude Stein. Gertrude Stein claimed anyone could understand her unconventional writing—here are clues to help. Fascinating improvisations, language experiments, explanations illuminate Stein's craft and the art of writing. Total of 414pp. 4⅜ × 6⅜. 23144-5 Pa. $6.95

ADVENTURES AT SEA IN THE GREAT AGE OF SAIL: Five Firsthand Narratives, edited by Elliot Snow. Rare true accounts of exploration, whaling, shipwreck, fierce natives, trade, shipboard life, more. 33 illustrations. Introduction. 353pp. 5⅜ × 8½. 25177-2 Pa. $9.95

THE HERBAL OR GENERAL HISTORY OF PLANTS, John Gerard. Classic descriptions of about 2,850 plants—with over 2,700 illustrations—includes Latin and English names, physical descriptions, varieties, time and place of growth, more. 2,706 illustrations. xlv + 1,678pp. 8½ × 12¼. 23147-X Cloth. $75.00

DOROTHY AND THE WIZARD IN OZ, L. Frank Baum. Dorothy and the Wizard visit the center of the Earth, where people are vegetables, glass houses grow and Oz characters reappear. Classic sequel to *Wizard of Oz.* 256pp. 5⅜ × 8. 24714-7 Pa. $5.95

SONGS OF EXPERIENCE: Facsimile Reproduction with 26 Plates in Full Color, William Blake. This facsimile of Blake's original "Illuminated Book" reproduces 26 full-color plates from a rare 1826 edition. Includes "The Tyger," "London," "Holy Thursday," and other immortal poems. 26 color plates. Printed text of poems. 48pp. 5¼ × 7. 24636-1 Pa. $3.95

SONGS OF INNOCENCE, William Blake. The first and most popular of Blake's famous "Illuminated Books," in a facsimile edition reproducing all 31 brightly colored plates. Additional printed text of each poem. 64pp. 5¼ × 7. 22764-2 Pa. $3.95

PRECIOUS STONES, Max Bauer. Classic, thorough study of diamonds, rubies, emeralds, garnets, etc.: physical character, occurrence, properties, use, similar topics. 20 plates, 8 in color. 94 figures. 659pp. 6⅛ × 9¼. 21910-0, 21911-9 Pa., Two-vol. set $15.90

ENCYCLOPEDIA OF VICTORIAN NEEDLEWORK, S. F. A. Caulfeild and Blanche Saward. Full, precise descriptions of stitches, techniques for dozens of needlecrafts—most exhaustive reference of its kind. Over 800 figures. Total of 679pp. 8⅛ × 11. 22800-2, 22801-0 Pa., Two-vol. set $23.90

THE MARVELOUS LAND OF OZ, L. Frank Baum. Second Oz book, the Scarecrow and Tin Woodman are back with hero named Tip, Oz magic. 136 illustrations. 287pp. 5⅜ × 8½. 20692-0 Pa. $5.95

WILD FOWL DECOYS, Joel Barber. Basic book on the subject, by foremost authority and collector. Reveals history of decoy making and rigging, place in American culture, different kinds of decoys, how to make them, and how to use them. 140 plates. 156pp. 7⅞ × 10¾. 20011-6 Pa. $8.95

HISTORY OF LACE, Mrs. Bury Palliser. Definitive, profusely illustrated chronicle of lace from earliest times to late 19th century. Laces of Italy, Greece, England, France, Belgium, etc. Landmark of needlework scholarship. 266 illustrations. 672pp. 6⅛ × 9¼. 24742-2 Pa. $16.95

ILLUSTRATED GUIDE TO SHAKER FURNITURE, Robert Meader. All furniture and appurtenances, with much on unknown local styles. 235 photos. 146pp. 9 × 12. 22819-3 Pa. $8.95

WHALE SHIPS AND WHALING: A Pictorial Survey, George Francis Dow. Over 200 vintage engravings, drawings, photographs of barks, brigs, cutters, other vessels. Also harpoons, lances, whaling guns, many other artifacts. Comprehensive text by foremost authority. 207 black-and-white illustrations. 288pp. 6 × 9. 24808-9 Pa. $9.95

THE BERTRAMS, Anthony Trollope. Powerful portrayal of blind self-will and thwarted ambition includes one of Trollope's most heartrending love stories. 497pp. 5⅜ × 8½. 25119-5 Pa. $9.95

ADVENTURES WITH A HAND LENS, Richard Headstrom. Clearly written guide to observing and studying flowers and grasses, fish scales, moth and insect wings, egg cases, buds, feathers, seeds, leaf scars, moss, molds, ferns, common crystals, etc.—all with an ordinary, inexpensive magnifying glass. 209 exact line drawings aid in your discoveries. 220pp. 5⅜ × 8½. 23330-8 Pa. $5.95

RODIN ON ART AND ARTISTS, Auguste Rodin. Great sculptor's candid, wide-ranging comments on meaning of art; great artists; relation of sculpture to poetry, painting, music; philosophy of life, more. 76 superb black-and-white illustrations of Rodin's sculpture, drawings and prints. 119pp. 8⅜ × 11¼. 24487-3 Pa. $7.95

FIFTY CLASSIC FRENCH FILMS, 1912–1982: A Pictorial Record, Anthony Slide. Memorable stills from Grand Illusion, Beauty and the Beast, Hiroshima, Mon Amour, many more. Credits, plot synopses, reviews, etc. 160pp. 8¼ × 11. 25256-6 Pa. $11.95

THE PRINCIPLES OF PSYCHOLOGY, William James. Famous long course complete, unabridged. Stream of thought, time perception, memory, experimental methods; great work decades ahead of its time. 94 figures. 1,391pp. 5⅜ × 8½. 20381-6, 20382-4 Pa., Two-vol. set $25.90

BODIES IN A BOOKSHOP, R. T. Campbell. Challenging mystery of blackmail and murder with ingenious plot and superbly drawn characters. In the best tradition of British suspense fiction. 192pp. 5⅜ × 8½. 24720-1 Pa. $4.95

CALLAS: Portrait of a Prima Donna, George Jellinek. Renowned commentator on the musical scene chronicles incredible career and life of the most controversial, fascinating, influential operatic personality of our time. 64 black-and-white photographs. 416pp. 5⅜ × 8¼. 25047-4 Pa. $8.95

GEOMETRY, RELATIVITY AND THE FOURTH DIMENSION, Rudolph Rucker. Exposition of fourth dimension, concepts of relativity as Flatland characters continue adventures. Popular, easily followed yet accurate, profound. 141 illustrations. 133pp. 5⅜ × 8½. 23400-2 Pa. $4.95

HOUSEHOLD STORIES BY THE BROTHERS GRIMM, with pictures by Walter Crane. 53 classic stories—Rumpelstiltskin, Rapunzel, Hansel and Gretel, the Fisherman and his Wife, Snow White, Tom Thumb, Sleeping Beauty, Cinderella, and so much more—lavishly illustrated with original 19th-century drawings. 114 illustrations. x + 269pp. 5⅜ × 8½. 21080-4 Pa. $4.95

SUNDIALS, Albert Waugh. Far and away the best, most thorough coverage of ideas, mathematics concerned, types, construction, adjusting anywhere. Over 100 illustrations. 230pp. 5⅜ × 8½. 22947-5 Pa. $5.95

PICTURE HISTORY OF THE NORMANDIE: With 190 Illustrations, Frank O. Braynard. Full story of legendary French ocean liner: Art Deco interiors, design innovations, furnishings, celebrities, maiden voyage, tragic fire, much more. Extensive text. 144pp. 8⅞ × 11¾. 25257-4 Pa. $10.95

THE FIRST AMERICAN COOKBOOK: A Facsimile of "American Cookery," 1796, Amelia Simmons. Facsimile of the first American-written cookbook published in the United States contains authentic recipes for colonial favorites—pumpkin pudding, winter squash pudding, spruce beer, Indian slapjacks, and more. Introductory Essay and Glossary of colonial cooking terms. 80pp. 5⅜ × 8½. 24710-4 Pa. $3.50

101 PUZZLES IN THOUGHT AND LOGIC, C. R. Wylie, Jr. Solve murders and robberies, find out which fishermen are liars, how a blind man could possibly identify a color—purely by your own reasoning! 107pp. 5⅜ × 8½. 20367-0 Pa. $2.95

ANCIENT EGYPTIAN MYTHS AND LEGENDS, Lewis Spence. Examines animism, totemism, fetishism, creation myths, deities, alchemy, art and magic, other topics. Over 50 illustrations. 432pp. 5⅜ × 8½. 26525-0 Pa. $8.95

ANTHROPOLOGY AND MODERN LIFE, Franz Boas. Great anthropologist's classic treatise on race and culture. Introduction by Ruth Bunzel. Only inexpensive paperback edition. 255pp. 5⅜ × 8½. 25245-0 Pa. $6.95

THE TALE OF PETER RABBIT, Beatrix Potter. The inimitable Peter's terrifying adventure in Mr. McGregor's garden, with all 27 wonderful, full-color Potter illustrations. 55pp. 4¼ × 5½. (Available in U.S. only) 22827-4 Pa. $1.75

THREE PROPHETIC SCIENCE FICTION NOVELS, H. G. Wells. *When the Sleeper Wakes, A Story of the Days to Come* and *The Time Machine* (full version). 335pp. 5⅜ × 8½. (Available in U.S. only) 20605-X Pa. $8.95

APICIUS COOKERY AND DINING IN IMPERIAL ROME, edited and translated by Joseph Dommers Vehling. Oldest known cookbook in existence offers readers a clear picture of what foods Romans ate, how they prepared them, etc. 49 illustrations. 301pp. 6⅛ × 9¼. 23563-7 Pa. $7.95

SHAKESPEARE LEXICON AND QUOTATION DICTIONARY, Alexander Schmidt. Full definitions, locations, shades of meaning of every word in plays and poems. More than 50,000 exact quotations. 1,485pp. 6½ × 9¼. 22726-X, 22727-8 Pa., Two-vol. set $31.90

THE WORLD'S GREAT SPEECHES, edited by Lewis Copeland and Lawrence W. Lamm. Vast collection of 278 speeches from Greeks to 1970. Powerful and effective models; unique look at history. 842pp. 5⅜ × 8½. 20468-5 Pa. $12.95

THE BLUE FAIRY BOOK, Andrew Lang. The first, most famous collection, with many familiar tales: Little Red Riding Hood, Aladdin and the Wonderful Lamp, Puss in Boots, Sleeping Beauty, Hansel and Gretel, Rumpelstiltskin; 37 in all. 138 illustrations. 390pp. 5⅜ × 8½. 21437-0 Pa. $6.95

THE STORY OF THE CHAMPIONS OF THE ROUND TABLE, Howard Pyle. Sir Launcelot, Sir Tristram and Sir Percival in spirited adventures of love and triumph retold in Pyle's inimitable style. 50 drawings, 31 full-page. xviii + 329pp. 6½ × 9¼. 21883-X Pa. $7.95

THE MYTHS OF THE NORTH AMERICAN INDIANS, Lewis Spence. Myths and legends of the Algonquins, Iroquois, Pawnees and Sioux with comprehensive historical and ethnological commentary. 36 illustrations. 5⅜ × 8½. 25967-6 Pa. $8.95

GREAT DINOSAUR HUNTERS AND THEIR DISCOVERIES, Edwin H. Colbert. Fascinating, lavishly illustrated chronicle of dinosaur research, 1820s to 1960. Achievements of Cope, Marsh, Brown, Buckland, Mantell, Huxley, many others. 384pp. 5¼ × 8¼. 24701-5 Pa. $7.95

THE TASTEMAKERS, Russell Lynes. Informal, illustrated social history of American taste 1850s–1950s. First popularized categories Highbrow, Lowbrow, Middlebrow. 129 illustrations. New (1979) afterword. 384pp. 6 × 9. 23993-4 Pa. $8.95

DOUBLE CROSS PURPOSES, Ronald A. Knox. A treasure hunt in the Scottish Highlands, an old map, unidentified corpse, surprise discoveries keep reader guessing in this cleverly intricate tale of financial skullduggery. 2 black-and-white maps. 320pp. 5⅜ × 8½. (Available in U.S. only) 25032-6 Pa. $6.95

AUTHENTIC VICTORIAN DECORATION AND ORNAMENTATION IN FULL COLOR: 46 Plates from "Studies in Design," Christopher Dresser. Superb full-color lithographs reproduced from rare original portfolio of a major Victorian designer. 48pp. 9¼ × 12¼. 25083-0 Pa. $7.95

PRIMITIVE ART, Franz Boas. Remains the best text ever prepared on subject, thoroughly discussing Indian, African, Asian, Australian, and, especially, Northern American primitive art. Over 950 illustrations show ceramics, masks, totem poles, weapons, textiles, paintings, much more. 376pp. 5⅜ × 8. 20025-6 Pa. $7.95

SIDELIGHTS ON RELATIVITY, Albert Einstein. Unabridged republication of two lectures delivered by the great physicist in 1920–21. *Ether and Relativity* and *Geometry and Experience.* Elegant ideas in nonmathematical form, accessible to intelligent layman. vi + 56pp. 5⅜ × 8½. 24511-X Pa. $3.95

THE WIT AND HUMOR OF OSCAR WILDE, edited by Alvin Redman. More than 1,000 ripostes, paradoxes, wisecracks: Work is the curse of the drinking classes, I can resist everything except temptation, etc. 258pp. 5⅜ × 8½. 20602-5 Pa. $4.95

ADVENTURES WITH A MICROSCOPE, Richard Headstrom. 59 adventures with clothing fibers, protozoa, ferns and lichens, roots and leaves, much more. 142 illustrations. 232pp. 5⅜ × 8½. 23471-1 Pa. $3.95

PLANTS OF THE BIBLE, Harold N. Moldenke and Alma L. Moldenke. Standard reference to all 230 plants mentioned in Scriptures. Latin name, biblical reference, uses, modern identity, much more. Unsurpassed encyclopedic resource for scholars, botanists, nature lovers, students of Bible. Bibliography. Indexes. 123 black-and-white illustrations. 384pp. 6 × 9. 25069-5 Pa. $8.95

FAMOUS AMERICAN WOMEN: A Biographical Dictionary from Colonial Times to the Present, Robert McHenry, ed. From Pocahontas to Rosa Parks, 1,035 distinguished American women documented in separate biographical entries. Accurate, up-to-date data, numerous categories, spans 400 years. Indices. 493pp. 6½ × 9¼. 24523-3 Pa. $10.95

THE FABULOUS INTERIORS OF THE GREAT OCEAN LINERS IN HISTORIC PHOTOGRAPHS, William H. Miller, Jr. Some 200 superb photographs capture exquisite interiors of world's great "floating palaces"—1890s to 1980s: *Titanic, Ile de France, Queen Elizabeth, United States, Europa*, more. Approx. 200 black-and-white photographs. Captions. Text. Introduction. 160pp. 8⅞ × 11¾. 24756-2 Pa. $9.95

THE GREAT LUXURY LINERS, 1927–1954: A Photographic Record, William H. Miller, Jr. Nostalgic tribute to heyday of ocean liners. 186 photos of *Ile de France, Normandie, Leviathan, Queen Elizabeth, United States*, many others. Interior and exterior views. Introduction. Captions. 160pp. 9 × 12. 24056-8 Pa. $10.95

A NATURAL HISTORY OF THE DUCKS, John Charles Phillips. Great landmark of ornithology offers complete detailed coverage of nearly 200 species and subspecies of ducks: gadwall, sheldrake, merganser, pintail, many more. 74 full-color plates, 102 black-and-white. Bibliography. Total of 1,920pp. 8⅜ × 11¼. 25141-1, 25142-X Cloth., Two-vol. set $100.00

THE SEAWEED HANDBOOK: An Illustrated Guide to Seaweeds from North Carolina to Canada, Thomas F. Lee. Concise reference covers 78 species. Scientific and common names, habitat, distribution, more. Finding keys for easy identification. 224pp. 5⅜ × 8½. 25215-9 Pa. $6.95

THE TEN BOOKS OF ARCHITECTURE: The 1755 Leoni Edition, Leon Battista Alberti. Rare classic helped introduce the glories of ancient architecture to the Renaissance. 68 black-and-white plates. 336pp. 8⅜ × 11¼. 25239-6 Pa. $14.95

MISS MACKENZIE, Anthony Trollope. Minor masterpieces by Victorian master unmasks many truths about life in 19th-century England. First inexpensive edition in years. 392pp. 5⅜ × 8½. 25201-9 Pa. $8.95

THE RIME OF THE ANCIENT MARINER, Gustave Doré, Samuel Taylor Coleridge. Dramatic engravings considered by many to be his greatest work. The terrifying space of the open sea, the storms and whirlpools of an unknown ocean, the ice of Antarctica, more—all rendered in a powerful, chilling manner. Full text. 38 plates. 77pp. 9¼ × 12. 22305-1 Pa. $4.95

THE EXPEDITIONS OF ZEBULON MONTGOMERY PIKE, Zebulon Montgomery Pike. Fascinating firsthand accounts (1805–6) of exploration of Mississippi River, Indian wars, capture by Spanish dragoons, much more. 1,088pp. 5⅜ × 8½. 25254-X, 25255-8 Pa., Two-vol. set $25.90

A CONCISE HISTORY OF PHOTOGRAPHY: Third Revised Edition, Helmut Gernsheim. Best one-volume history—camera obscura, photochemistry, daguerreotypes, evolution of cameras, film, more. Also artistic aspects—landscape, portraits, fine art, etc. 281 black-and-white photographs. 26 in color. 176pp. 8⅜ × 11¼.
25128-4 Pa. $14.95

THE DORÉ BIBLE ILLUSTRATIONS, Gustave Doré. 241 detailed plates from the Bible: the Creation scenes, Adam and Eve, Flood, Babylon, battle sequences, life of Jesus, etc. Each plate is accompanied by the verses from the King James version of the Bible. 241pp. 9 × 12. 23004-X Pa. $9.95

WANDERINGS IN WEST AFRICA, Richard F. Burton. Great Victorian scholar/adventurer's invaluable descriptions of African tribal rituals, fetishism, culture, art, much more. Fascinating 19th-century account. 624pp. 5⅜ × 8½. 26890-X Pa. $12.95

FLATLAND, E. A. Abbott. Intriguing and enormously popular science-fiction classic explores the complexities of trying to survive as a two-dimensional being in a three-dimensional world. Amusingly illustrated by the author. 16 illustrations. 103pp. 5⅜ × 8½. 20001-9 Pa. $2.50

THE HISTORY OF THE LEWIS AND CLARK EXPEDITION, Meriwether Lewis and William Clark, edited by Elliott Coues. Classic edition of Lewis and Clark's day-by-day journals that later became the basis for U.S. claims to Oregon and the West. Accurate and invaluable geographical, botanical, biological, meteorological and anthropological material. Total of 1,508pp. 5⅜ × 8½.
21268-8, 21269-6, 21270-X Pa., Three-vol. set $29.85

LANGUAGE, TRUTH AND LOGIC, Alfred J. Ayer. Famous, clear introduction to Vienna, Cambridge schools of Logical Positivism. Role of philosophy, elimination of metaphysics, nature of analysis, etc. 160pp. 5⅜ × 8½. (Available in U.S. and Canada only) 20010-8 Pa. $3.95

MATHEMATICS FOR THE NONMATHEMATICIAN, Morris Kline. Detailed, college-level treatment of mathematics in cultural and historical context, with numerous exercises. For liberal arts students. Preface. Recommended Reading Lists. Tables. Index. Numerous black-and-white figures. xvi + 641pp. 5⅜ × 8½.
24823-2 Pa. $11.95

HANDBOOK OF PICTORIAL SYMBOLS, Rudolph Modley. 3,250 signs and symbols, many systems in full; official or heavy commercial use. Arranged by subject. Most in Pictorial Archive series. 143pp. 8⅛ × 11. 23357-X Pa. $7.95

INCIDENTS OF TRAVEL IN YUCATAN, John L. Stephens. Classic (1843) exploration of jungles of Yucatan, looking for evidences of Maya civilization. Travel adventures, Mexican and Indian culture, etc. Total of 669pp. 5⅜ × 8½.
20926-1, 20927-X Pa., Two-vol. set $11.90

DEGAS: An Intimate Portrait, Ambroise Vollard. Charming, anecdotal memoir by famous art dealer of one of the greatest 19th-century French painters. 14 black-and-white illustrations. Introduction by Harold L. Van Doren. 96pp. 5⅜ × 8½.
25131-4 Pa. $4.95

PERSONAL NARRATIVE OF A PILGRIMAGE TO AL-MADINAII AND MECCAH, Richard F. Burton. Great travel classic by remarkably colorful personality. Burton, disguised as a Moroccan, visited sacred shrines of Islam, narrowly escaping death. 47 illustrations. 959pp. 5⅜ × 8½.
21217-3, 21218-1 Pa., Two-vol. set $19.90

PHRASE AND WORD ORIGINS, A. H. Holt. Entertaining, reliable, modern study of more than 1,200 colorful words, phrases, origins and histories. Much unexpected information. 254pp. 5⅜ × 8½.
20758-7 Pa. $5.95

THE RED THUMB MARK, R. Austin Freeman. In this first Dr. Thorndyke case, the great scientific detective draws fascinating conclusions from the nature of a single fingerprint. Exciting story, authentic science. 320pp. 5⅜ × 8½. (Available in U.S. only)
25210-8 Pa. $6.95

AN EGYPTIAN HIEROGLYPHIC DICTIONARY, E. A. Wallis Budge. Monumental work containing about 25,000 words or terms that occur in texts ranging from 3000 B.C. to 600 A.D. Each entry consists of a transliteration of the word, the word in hieroglyphs, and the meaning in English. 1,314pp. 6⅝ × 10.
23615-3, 23616-1 Pa., Two-vol. set $35.90

THE COMPLEAT STRATEGYST: Being a Primer on the Theory of Games of Strategy, J. D. Williams. Highly entertaining classic describes, with many illustrated examples, how to select best strategies in conflict situations. Prefaces. Appendices. xvi + 268pp. 5⅜ × 8½.
25101-2 Pa. $6.95

THE ROAD TO OZ, L. Frank Baum. Dorothy meets the Shaggy Man, little Button-Bright and the Rainbow's beautiful daughter in this delightful trip to the magical Land of Oz. 272pp. 5⅜ × 8.
25208-6 Pa. $5.95

POINT AND LINE TO PLANE, Wassily Kandinsky. Seminal exposition of role of point, line, other elements in nonobjective painting. Essential to understanding 20th-century art. 127 illustrations. 192pp. 6½ × 9¼.
23808-3 Pa. $5.95

LADY ANNA, Anthony Trollope. Moving chronicle of Countess Lovel's bitter struggle to win for herself and daughter Anna their rightful rank and fortune—perhaps at cost of sanity itself. 384pp. 5⅜ × 8½.
24669-8 Pa. $8.95

EGYPTIAN MAGIC, E. A. Wallis Budge. Sums up all that is known about magic in Ancient Egypt: the role of magic in controlling the gods, powerful amulets that warded off evil spirits, scarabs of immortality, use of wax images, formulas and spells, the secret name, much more. 253pp. 5⅜ × 8½.
22681-6 Pa. $4.50

THE DANCE OF SIVA, Ananda Coomaraswamy. Preeminent authority unfolds the vast metaphysic of India: the revelation of her art, conception of the universe, social organization, etc. 27 reproductions of art masterpieces. 192pp. 5⅜ × 8½.
24817-8 Pa. $6.95

CHRISTMAS CUSTOMS AND TRADITIONS, Clement A. Miles. Origin, evolution, significance of religious, secular practices. Caroling, gifts, yule logs, much more. Full, scholarly yet fascinating; non-sectarian. 400pp. 5⅜ × 8½.
23354-5 Pa. $6.95

THE HUMAN FIGURE IN MOTION, Eadweard Muybridge. More than 4,500 stopped-action photos, in action series, showing undraped men, women, children jumping, lying down, throwing, sitting, wrestling, carrying, etc. 390pp. 7⅞ × 10⅝.
20204-6 Cloth. $24.95

THE MAN WHO WAS THURSDAY, Gilbert Keith Chesterton. Witty, fast-paced novel about a club of anarchists in turn-of-the-century London. Brilliant social, religious, philosophical speculations. 128pp. 5⅜ × 8½.
25121-7 Pa. $3.95

A CÉZANNE SKETCHBOOK: Figures, Portraits, Landscapes and Still Lifes, Paul Cézanne. Great artist experiments with tonal effects, light, mass, other qualities in over 100 drawings. A revealing view of developing master painter, precursor of Cubism. 102 black-and-white illustrations. 144pp. 8¾ × 6⅝.
24790-2 Pa. $6.95

AN ENCYCLOPEDIA OF BATTLES: Accounts of Over 1,560 Battles from 1479 B.C. to the Present, David Eggenberger. Presents essential details of every major battle in recorded history, from the first battle of Megiddo in 1479 B.C. to Grenada in 1984. List of Battle Maps. New Appendix covering the years 1967–1984. Index. 99 illustrations. 544pp. 6½ × 9¼.
24913-1 Pa. $14.95

AN ETYMOLOGICAL DICTIONARY OF MODERN ENGLISH, Ernest Weekley. Richest, fullest work, by foremost British lexicographer. Detailed word histories. Inexhaustible. Total of 856pp. 6½ × 9¼.
21873-2, 21874-0 Pa., Two-vol. set $19.90

WEBSTER'S AMERICAN MILITARY BIOGRAPHIES, edited by Robert McHenry. Over 1,000 figures who shaped 3 centuries of American military history. Detailed biographies of Nathan Hale, Douglas MacArthur, Mary Hallaren, others. Chronologies of engagements, more. Introduction. Addenda. 1,033 entries in alphabetical order. xi + 548pp. 6½ × 9¼. (Available in U.S. only)
24758-9 Pa. $13.95

LIFE IN ANCIENT EGYPT, Adolf Erman. Detailed older account, with much not in more recent books: domestic life, religion, magic, medicine, commerce, and whatever else needed for complete picture. Many illustrations. 597pp. 5⅜ × 8½.
22632-8 Pa. $8.95

HISTORIC COSTUME IN PICTURES, Braun & Schneider. Over 1,450 costumed figures shown, covering a wide variety of peoples: kings, emperors, nobles, priests, servants, soldiers, scholars, townsfolk, peasants, merchants, courtiers, cavaliers, and more. 256pp. 8⅜ × 11¼.
23150-X Pa. $9.95

THE NOTEBOOKS OF LEONARDO DA VINCI, edited by J. P. Richter. Extracts from manuscripts reveal great genius; on painting, sculpture, anatomy, sciences, geography, etc. Both Italian and English. 186 ms. pages reproduced, plus 500 additional drawings, including studies for *Last Supper, Sforza* monument, etc. 860pp. 7⅞ × 10¾. (Available in U.S. only) 22572-0, 22573-9 Pa., Two-vol. set $31.90

THE ART NOUVEAU STYLE BOOK OF ALPHONSE MUCHA: All 72 Plates from "Documents Decoratifs" in Original Color, Alphonse Mucha. Rare copyright-free design portfolio by high priest of Art Nouveau. Jewelry, wallpaper, stained glass, furniture, figure studies, plant and animal motifs, etc. Only complete one-volume edition. 80pp. 9⅜ × 12¼. 24044-4 Pa. $10.95

ANIMALS: 1,419 Copyright-Free Illustrations of Mammals, Birds, Fish, Insects, Etc., edited by Jim Harter. Clear wood engravings present, in extremely lifelike poses, over 1,000 species of animals. One of the most extensive pictorial sourcebooks of its kind. Captions. Index. 284pp. 9 × 12. 23766-4 Pa. $10.95

OBELISTS FLY HIGH, C. Daly King. Masterpiece of American detective fiction, long out of print, involves murder on a 1935 transcontinental flight—"a very thrilling story"—*NY Times*. Unabridged and unaltered republication of the edition published by William Collins Sons & Co. Ltd., London, 1935. 288pp. 5⅜ × 8½. (Available in U.S. only) 25036-9 Pa. $5.95

VICTORIAN AND EDWARDIAN FASHION: A Photographic Survey, Alison Gernsheim. First fashion history completely illustrated by contemporary photographs. Full text plus 235 photos, 1840–1914, in which many celebrities appear. 240pp. 6½ × 9¼. 24205-6 Pa. $8.95

THE ART OF THE FRENCH ILLUSTRATED BOOK, 1700–1914, Gordon N. Ray. Over 630 superb book illustrations by Fragonard, Delacroix, Daumier, Doré, Grandville, Manet, Mucha, Steinlen, Toulouse-Lautrec and many others. Preface. Introduction. 633 halftones. Indices of artists, authors & titles, binders and provenances. Appendices. Bibliography. 608pp. 8⅜ × 11¼. 25086-5 Pa. $24.95

THE WONDERFUL WIZARD OF OZ, L. Frank Baum. Facsimile in full color of America's finest children's classic. 143 illustrations by W. W. Denslow. 267pp. 5⅜ × 8½. 20691-2 Pa. $7.95

FOLLOWING THE EQUATOR: A Journey Around the World, Mark Twain. Great writer's 1897 account of circumnavigating the globe by steamship. Ironic humor, keen observations, vivid and fascinating descriptions of exotic places. 197 illustrations. 720pp. 5⅜ × 8½. 26113-1 Pa. $15.95

THE FRIENDLY STARS, Martha Evans Martin & Donald Howard Menzel. Classic text marshalls the stars together in an engaging, nontechnical survey, presenting them as sources of beauty in night sky. 23 illustrations. Foreword. 2 star charts. Index. 147pp. 5⅜ × 8½. 21099-5 Pa. $3.95

FADS AND FALLACIES IN THE NAME OF SCIENCE, Martin Gardner. Fair, witty appraisal of cranks, quacks, and quackeries of science and pseudoscience: hollow earth, Velikovsky, orgone energy, Dianetics, flying saucers, Bridey Murphy, food and medical fads, etc. Revised, expanded In the Name of Science. "A very able and even-tempered presentation."—*The New Yorker*. 363pp. 5⅜ × 8. 20394-8 Pa. $6.95

ANCIENT EGYPT: Its Culture and History, J. E. Manchip White. From predynastics through Ptolemies: society, history, political structure, religion, daily life, literature, cultural heritage. 48 plates. 217pp. 5⅜ × 8½. 22548-8 Pa. $5.95

SIR HARRY HOTSPUR OF HUMBLETHWAITE, Anthony Trollope. Incisive, unconventional psychological study of a conflict between a wealthy baronet, his idealistic daughter, and their scapegrace cousin. The 1870 novel in its first inexpensive edition in years. 250pp. 5⅜ × 8½. 24953-0 Pa. $6.95

LASERS AND HOLOGRAPHY, Winston E. Kock. Sound introduction to burgeoning field, expanded (1981) for second edition. Wave patterns, coherence, lasers, diffraction, zone plates, properties of holograms, recent advances. 84 illustrations. 160pp. 5⅜ × 8¼. (Except in United Kingdom) 24041-X Pa. $3.95

INTRODUCTION TO ARTIFICIAL INTELLIGENCE: Second, Enlarged Edition, Philip C. Jackson, Jr. Comprehensive survey of artificial intelligence—the study of how machines (computers) can be made to act intelligently. Includes introductory and advanced material. Extensive notes updating the main text. 132 black-and-white illustrations. 512pp. 5⅜ × 8½. 24864-X Pa. $10.95

HISTORY OF INDIAN AND INDONESIAN ART, Ananda K. Coomaraswamy. Over 400 illustrations illuminate classic study of Indian art from earliest Harappa finds to early 20th century. Provides philosophical, religious and social insights. 304pp. 6⅜ × 9⅜. 25005-9 Pa. $11.95

THE GOLEM, Gustav Meyrink. Most famous supernatural novel in modern European literature, set in Ghetto of Old Prague around 1890. Compelling story of mystical experiences, strange transformations, profound terror. 13 black-and-white illustrations. 224pp. 5⅜ × 8½. (Available in U.S. only) 25025-3 Pa. $6.95

PICTORIAL ENCYCLOPEDIA OF HISTORIC ARCHITECTURAL PLANS, DETAILS AND ELEMENTS: With 1,880 Line Drawings of Arches, Domes, Doorways, Facades, Gables, Windows, etc., John Theodore Haneman. Sourcebook of inspiration for architects, designers, others. Bibliography. Captions. 141pp. 9×12. 24605-1 Pa. $7.95

BENCHLEY LOST AND FOUND, Robert Benchley. Finest humor from early 30s, about pet peeves, child psychologists, post office and others. Mostly unavailable elsewhere. 73 illustrations by Peter Arno and others. 183pp. 5⅜ × 8½. 22410-4 Pa. $4.95

ERTÉ GRAPHICS, Erté. Collection of striking color graphics: *Seasons, Alphabet, Numerals, Aces* and *Precious Stones*. 50 plates, including 4 on covers. 48pp. 9⅜×12¼. 23580-7 Pa. $7.95

THE JOURNAL OF HENRY D. THOREAU, edited by Bradford Torrey, F. H. Allen. Complete reprinting of 14 volumes, 1837–61, over two million words; the sourcebooks for *Walden*, etc. Definitive. All original sketches, plus 75 photographs. 1,804pp. 8½ × 12¼. 20312-3, 20313-1 Cloth., Two-vol. set $130.00

CASTLES: Their Construction and History, Sidney Toy. Traces castle development from ancient roots. Nearly 200 photographs and drawings illustrate moats, keeps, baileys, many other features. Caernarvon, Dover Castles, Hadrian's Wall, Tower of London, dozens more. 256pp. 5⅜ × 8¼. 24898-4 Pa. $6.95

AMERICAN CLIPPER SHIPS: 1833–1858, Octavius T. Howe & Frederick C. Matthews. Fully-illustrated, encyclopedic review of 352 clipper ships from the period of America's greatest maritime supremacy. Introduction. 109 halftones. 5 black-and-white line illustrations. Index. Total of 928pp. 5⅜ × 8½.
25115-2, 25116-0 Pa., Two-vol. set $17.90

TOWARDS A NEW ARCHITECTURE, Le Corbusier. Pioneering manifesto by great architect, near legendary founder of "International School." Technical and aesthetic theories, views on industry, economics, relation of form to function, "mass-production spirit," much more. Profusely illustrated. Unabridged translation of 13th French edition. Introduction by Frederick Etchells. 320pp. 6⅛ × 9¼. (Available in U.S. only)
25023-7 Pa. $8.95

THE BOOK OF KELLS, edited by Blanche Cirker. Inexpensive collection of 32 full-color, full-page plates from the greatest illuminated manuscript of the Middle Ages, painstakingly reproduced from rare facsimile edition. Publisher's Note. Captions. 32pp. 9⅜ × 12¼.
24345-1 Pa. $5.95

BEST SCIENCE FICTION STORIES OF H. G. WELLS, H. G. Wells. Full novel *The Invisible Man*, plus 17 short stories: "The Crystal Egg," "Aepyornis Island," "The Strange Orchid," etc. 303pp. 5⅜ × 8½. (Available in U.S. only)
21531-8 Pa. $6.95

AMERICAN SAILING SHIPS: Their Plans and History, Charles G. Davis. Photos, construction details of schooners, frigates, clippers, other sailcraft of 18th to early 20th centuries—plus entertaining discourse on design, rigging, nautical lore, much more. 137 black-and-white illustrations. 240pp. 6⅛ × 9¼.
24658-2 Pa. $6.95

ENTERTAINING MATHEMATICAL PUZZLES, Martin Gardner. Selection of author's favorite conundrums involving arithmetic, money, speed, etc., with lively commentary. Complete solutions. 112pp. 5⅜ × 8½.
25211-6 Pa. $3.50

THE WILL TO BELIEVE, HUMAN IMMORTALITY, William James. Two books bound together. Effect of irrational on logical, and arguments for human immortality. 402pp. 5⅜ × 8½.
20291-7 Pa. $8.95

THE HAUNTED MONASTERY and THE CHINESE MAZE MURDERS, Robert Van Gulik. 2 full novels by Van Gulik continue adventures of Judge Dee and his companions. An evil Taoist monastery, seemingly supernatural events; overgrown topiary maze that hides strange crimes. Set in 7th-century China. 27 illustrations. 328pp. 5⅜ × 8½.
23502-5 Pa. $6.95

CELEBRATED CASES OF JUDGE DEE (DEE GOONG AN), translated by Robert Van Gulik. Authentic 18th-century Chinese detective novel; Dee and associates solve three interlocked cases. Led to Van Gulik's own stories with same characters. Extensive introduction. 9 illustrations. 237pp. 5⅜ × 8½.
23337-5 Pa. $5.95

Prices subject to change without notice.

Available at your book dealer or write for free catalog to Dept. GI, Dover Publications, Inc., 31 East 2nd St., Mineola, N.Y. 11501. Dover publishes more than 175 books each year on science, elementary and advanced mathematics, biology, music, art, literary history, social sciences and other areas.